Piet
2020

TOM EATON

IS IT ME OR IS IT GETTING HOT IN HERE?

TAFELBERG

For Tanya,
who has shown me how to take in the journey,
and who makes every step a delight.

Tafelberg, an imprint of NB Publishers,
a division of Media24 Books Pty (Ltd),
40 Heerengracht, Cape Town, South Africa
www.tafelberg.com

Set in Palatino
Cover by Fuel Design
Book design by Nazli Jacobs
Edited by Alison Lowry
Proof read by Kathleen Sutton
Commissioning editor: Gill Moodie

Printed by ***novus print***, a division of Novus Holdings

First edition, first impression 2020

ISBN: 978-0-624-08890-5
Epub: 978-0-624-08891-2
Mobi: 978-0-624-08892-9

Contents

Preface 7

Introduction 11

Chapter 1: Great Expectations 21

Chapter 2: Laughing While Rome Burns 39

Chapter 3: If Only They Didn't Wear Suits 51

Chapter 4: How to Cook a Nightmare Apocalypse Information Quagmire 63

Chapter 5: HALTO! 91

Chapter 6: A Better (After)Life for All 101

Chapter 7: SOE What? A Parable in Two Parts 122

Chapter 8: Love and Marriage, Politics and Sport 147

Chapter 9: How the Other Half Lives 164

Chapter 10: The Penalty of Death 179

Chapter 11: On Immigration 194

Chapter 12: La Dolce Vita 196

Chapter 13: Robbing Us Blind 220

Chapter 14: Back in The RSA 240

Chapter 15: The Frank-N-Furter Theory of Everything 262

Acknowledgements 269

About the Author 271

Preface

In April of this year, Nobel Prize-winning economist Paul Krugman explained in *The New York Times* that the locked-down US economy – and by extension every other economy that had shut itself down during the Covid-19 pandemic – had been put in 'the equivalent of a medically induced coma'.

This book was written before we all slipped into that coma. My publisher brought me the proofs the day before South Africa's lock-down began in March 2020, and the pages she handed me – the ones you are about to read – describe a country and a world that seemed to have fairly different priorities.

Now, we are all waking up to a subtly changed reality. Many of the opinions and beliefs we held in February feel like something from another life. A cigarette and a glass of wine, once a casual pleasure, are being savoured by many South Africans as if they were the last cigar and cognac on the planet.

Many of us are still seeing our neighbours in a different light, whether they are the shy introvert next door who revealed herself as a generous sharer of baked goods, or the polite couple up the road who outed themselves as renegades, their dog walks in March and April distinguishing them, depending on your politics, as freedom fighters, iconoclasts or entitled wankers.

Our relationship with public figures, too, has shifted in unexpected directions. Cyril Ramaphosa's decisiveness in the early weeks of the crisis, when he gambled that a wrecked economy was a safer bet than an overwhelmed healthcare system, was unrecognisable from the cautious, eternally 'shocked' president of 2018 and 2019. Bheki Cele, on the other hand, went into the lockdown regarded as a somewhat comical figure but quickly revealed a very unfunny penchant for authoritarianism, confirming that he has no place in leadership in a democracy that claims to prize human rights.

It is possible those reputations have swung back the other way by the time you read this. The lockdown gave me time to make some small updates to this book before it went to print, but I don't know what you know. However, if I was forced to guess what has happened in the weeks and months since I wrote this preface, I would suggest the following.

I would suggest that some of the state's strategies and interventions have been pragmatic and sensible, that others have been eye-wateringly stupid or deeply disconcerting, and that, in at least one or two key areas, the state has failed to do anything whatsoever. I would suggest that Ramaphosa's supporters have seen him act in ways that have repaid their faith in him, and that his detractors have had their worst fears confirmed. I would suggest that the opposition parties, having faded into almost complete obscurity during the lockdown, are now making hay with the mistakes, whether inevitable or unnecessary, made by the state in the past few months.

Beyond the realm of politics, I would suggest that millions of South Africans believe the government did the right thing by locking down for as long as it did, while millions more believe it was a form of national suicide. I would suggest that we have pulled together in some ways, and split off into acrimony and mutual distrust in others. I would suggest that the rich have come through more or less intact, and that the poor haven't.

In other words, pretty much like before.

South Africa may have been battered – perhaps even shattered – by the economic and social upheaval of Covid-19, but this is still the same country it was before the pandemic and, in many fundamental ways, it will continue to be the same country after the last trace of the virus is gone.

The systems that were broken are still broken. Many of the politicians and parasites who helped break them, or who don't know how to mend them, are still in the same offices. We are still vexed by the same outrages, and still determined to have the same arguments with the same people as before. This is still South Africa, and we are still South Africans.

But because this is still South Africa, and because we are still South Africans, the same hopes still beckon us into the future. The same resilience still steels us. The same energy still animates us. And the same questions we asked ourselves before still demand answers.

This is still South Africa, and we are still South Africans.

Introduction

On a stove there sits a pot of water, and inside the pot, floating in the water, there is a frog.

Small bubbles are forming on the bottom of the pot below the frog's outstretched feet. The water is getting warmer. And yet the frog isn't moving. It's just hanging there, its serene little face poking out above the surface.

One of the small bubbles frees itself from the floor of the pot and rises up past the frog. It doesn't react. Another bubble. Again, nothing.

Two more bubbles. Then five. But still the frog doesn't move. It doesn't know that it's in danger because it is adapting to the warmer water. It can't remember what the cooler water felt like. This doesn't feel great, but, well, it's normal. And it's the same water in the same pot. Maybe this is just the way things work.

Steam begins blowing across the surface. The frog paddles feebly, starting to sense that something might be wrong.

And then the water is roiling, and it's too late: the frog rolls onto its back, dead.

We've all heard about this experiment: throw a frog into boiling water and it jumps right out (presumably with severe injuries); but slowly turn the heat up in tiny increments, and the frog won't react until it can't.

It's a dramatic, compelling metaphor. For South Africans, it seems a perfect parable for the experience of living in this anxious, angry, unjust country where every day the dial is cranked up by another degree with the latest corruption scandal, the latest monstrous crime, the latest depressing, numbing statistic about how our country and economy are fading.

Right now always feels normal, more or less, no matter how hot it gets.

One of the best examples of our frog-in-a-pot experience of South Africa is our response to corruption. In 1996, the then minister of Health, Nkosazana Dlamini-Zuma, oversaw the payment of R14 million (about R50 million in today's money) to playwright Mbongeni Ngema for a play about HIV/AIDS. The amount was 20 per cent of the entire national budget dedicated to tackling the pandemic.

The *Sarafina 2* scandal made international headlines and had the Mandela government scrambling for answers and alibis. 'The ANC is pained immensely by stories of corruption,' Cyril Ramaphosa, then widely seen as Mandela's anointed successor, told *The New York Times*. 'We are highly conscious of the damage that corruption does to a party and a country.'

Twenty-three years later, we were told that state capture looted between R100 billion and R1.4 trillion from South Africa over the course of about 10 years. In October 2019, Ramaphosa himself told investors at the *Financial Times* Africa Summit in London that state capture had cost R500 billion. If we accept his estimate, then that R50 million (in today's money) spent on *Sarafina 2*, an amount middle-class South Africa considered morally outrageous and politically shocking in 1996, is about nine hours' worth of state capture looting.

In short, we have experienced a *Sarafina 2* every nine hours – almost three times a day – for the last ten years.

As was the case in 1996, the response to state capture by the media-consuming middle class has been anger, surprise at some of the details, and contempt for its leading figures. But while many South Africans were genuinely shocked in 1996, I don't believe any of us are truly shocked any more. Indeed, the only person in South Africa who keeps claiming to be shocked by corruption is Ramaphosa, suggesting that he is either a liar or has the memory of a goldfish. Or perhaps he's just a politician.

That steady ebbing away of shock, that relentless numbing of our response to wholesale corruption (or violence, or economic malaise, or anything else that once might have kept you awake at night but now just makes you a bit depressed a few times a week) is how habituation works. It's why the boiling frog metaphor seems perfect.

It's also why it's so frightening. Because, in the end, the frog dies. The metaphor seems to present not only a perfect description of the present, but also a science-based, and therefore terrifyingly accurate prediction of our future.

Yes, it's a great metaphor. Except for one small thing.

It's not true.

Granted, it is true is that, in 1869, a German scientist named Friedrich Leopold Goltz published his research on the nervous systems of frogs. Thanks to this volume, we know that it is also true that Goltz put frogs into water which he slowly made hotter. And it is most definitely true that he observed frogs sitting absolutely still as the water became lethally hot around them.

But here's the bit history has slowly erased from that otherwise true story about verified research: the frogs that boiled to death *didn't have brains*. Goltz had removed them. I'm picturing *Silence of the Lambs* as written by Beatrix Potter.

According to a 2009 piece in *The Atlantic* by Michael Jones, Goltz's research was picked up by an English philosopher, literary critic and amateur physiologist named George Henry Lewes. Lewes took it upon himself to 'extend the slowly-boiled brainless frog oeuvre by slowly-boiling frogs with partial brains or with their spinal cords severed at various locations'. In his own writings, published 'four years and many frogs later', Lewes reiterated that frogs *with brains* become agitated in heated water and either flee or, if they can't, thrash about until the end, while frogs *with no brains* sit passively.

I don't know how the original observations became so crucially blurred, or how they took on a new life as folklore, but I can guess. Lewes was a literary figure – he lived with his great love, Marian Evans, better known as the novelist George Eliot, and personally knew Charles Dickens – and while I'm sure that he and they had a scientist's love of precision, I can imagine some lesser literary lushes listening wide-eyed to accounts of his experiments and then rushing off to tell a garbled account to their friends. It would only have been a matter of time before this new version was heard by someone who understood its tremendous power as a metaphor, and ran with it.

Today, the story is everywhere. It is a staple of priests and journalists, politicians and activists. It has been quoted, without correction or explanation, by the likes of Barack Obama and Paul Krugman. In 1960 the *Chicago Tribune* used it to warn Americans that they were slowly being overwhelmed by the subtle rise of communism in their midst. Half a century later it was still going strong, used by Al Gore in *An Inconvenient Truth* to describe our response to climate change. And of course, it has been cited, often with great anxiety, by many South Africans.

But its popularity, and the prestige of its most famous supporters, shouldn't distract us from a second inconvenient truth: when you boil frogs that still have their brains, the only thing that rolls over and dies is that metaphor and its usefulness in describing anything at all.

And yet it survives. The writings of Goltz, Lewes and many others are easily available to researchers. The myth has been debunked many times, and not just by academics or critics in journals and niche publications. In March 2019, the *Daily Mail*, one of the biggest tabloids in the world, reported that scientists from the University of California were worried that people were 'normalising' extreme weather events and thereby clouding their perception of climate change. The analogy the scientists used? You guessed it. Frogs in a warming pot. But the *Mail* was having none of it: in a bizarre upending of the traditional roles of academia and the press, the tabloid added a sidebar to its story, titled 'What is the fable of the boiling frog?', explaining the origin of the myth and stating, very clearly, that 'real-life experiments show that the frog-in-boiling-water story is wrong'.

It is a myth that should be fading from public life, so why does it persist?

That it still has such a grip on our imaginations and emotions suggests a sobering truth about ourselves: we continue to believe that it is true because we *want* it to be true.

For a metaphor which is usually invoked as a pragmatic warning – an exhortation to stay alert, to be prepared, to plan for the worst – it is, in fact, a bizarrely masochistic plunge into fatalism.

After all, if you choose to believe the myth, faulty science and all, and you feel that a frog passively boiling to death is an accurate representation of life in South Africa, then you have to believe in the existence of some kind of sadistic god-scientist, plucking us out of our natural, organic lives and plunging us into a nightmare scenario that has nothing to do with our real lives. You have to believe that some huge, malevolent Watcher is slowly and deliberately torturing this country to death just to prove or disprove a point.

Now, you are fully entitled to believe that. But I would urge you, in that case, to stop appealing to science and simply walk around wearing a sandwich board that says 'WE'RE F*CKED'.

This would be helpful for two reasons.

Firstly, it's more honest than nonsense about frogs. But secondly, and much more importantly, it will allow the rest of us to recognise that you are broadcasting your personal, subjective emotional state and not an objectively true fact about the rest of us. And that would allow us to pay more attention to people broadcasting actual knowledge.

That, for me, is the destructive power of the boiling frog metaphor. It's not just that it is a pronouncement of supreme helplessness, even going out of its way to deny the existence of solutions (it literally denies that frogs do, in fact, try to save themselves from bad situations). It's that, by weaselling into our accepted beliefs by pretending to be a scientific truth and claiming to present an intelligent, pragmatic analysis of our current state, it crowds out ways of interpreting this county that are actually based on science and research and expertise. It places fatalism, based on a fiction, on a par with the thousands of South Africans who are, in very real ways, working and fighting and striving to invest in this country and make it better. It claims truth in a loud, plaintive voice, and in so doing makes it that much harder to hear the people who actually know what they're talking about, or to recognise and celebrate those South Africans who work tirelessly to keep pulling us back from the brink.

I'm not dismantling the boiling frog metaphor to mock those South Africans who feel desperately despondent or scared about the future. They have their reasons for believing what they believe. I am also not suggesting that this country isn't a frightening, violent, confusing, divided place. Just because the frog metaphor is wrong doesn't mean that a good outcome is guaranteed for South Africa.

But I think it is a glaring and current example of the kind of thinking that can take hold of our imaginations and our fears in the absence of a clearer, more informed national conversation.

I understand its appeal and its power. I feel its magnetic pull. Pessimism is an old friend of mine. I use it as a coping strategy, a suit of armour I strap on to pre-emptively protect me from the inevitable stupidity and arrogance in the news every day.

But I have to admit that I have also found myself handicapped by pessimism. This has usually happened when I've held a simplistic, dogmatically gloomy view of an issue or a situation and then been presented with complex, informed, dispassionate facts.

That process is best illustrated by one particular video on YouTube, in which a racoon is trying to eat small blocks of candyfloss. Being a well-brought-up racoon, it washes its treat first; but water has a magical effect on candyfloss: it makes it dissolve to nothing. The racoon is astonished to find its matchbox-sized meal disappearing between its groping paws.

This is the effect facts tend to have on the sweet, fluffy, ultimately sickening treats I know as my preconceptions. It makes them shrivel into their component parts, and makes me peer more closely at what's left. It forces me to admit that my position on current events – felt so keenly that they can affect my mood for days on end – is simply a fluffy cloud of assumptions and emotional triggers.

More annoyingly, facts often demand that I change my attitude away from pessimism towards, if not optimism, at least a more balanced, complex position of being open to various outcomes.

And that is the moment I feel entirely locked in by pessimism. It is an almost physical sensation of being stuck, as if my self-protective carapace has calcified into a shell in which I can no longer move. When I am locked into that state, good news cannot reach me: I either dismiss it or disbelieve it.

In other words, I know all too well what it feels like to hold onto beliefs or ways of thinking that don't allow more complex, adult or better-informed attitudes to penetrate my mind.

Which brings me to why I wrote this book.

Perhaps I should tell you first what this book isn't.

Firstly, I make no claims to universality. As a white, middle-aged, middle-class man, I understand that I am speaking from inside the tiniest niche of our society. I am also aware that I am speaking to a very specific, and very small group of people: a subset (people who read books) containing a subset (people who buy books) containing a subset (people who buy books about South Africa) containing the tiniest subset of all (people who buy books about South Africa written by me). To you and the 73 other people like you, I say welcome and thank you.

Secondly, this book is not an attempt to downplay the alarming realities facing this country. I am not going to try to persuade you to stay in South Africa if you think you need to leave it. If you genuinely believe that we are seconds from destruction, or that the boiling frog analogy describes your reality, then I won't try to dissuade you. (I might wonder why you spent money on this book rather than sending it offshore, but I won't complain. As they say, never look a gift nihilist in the mouth.)

So what is this book? Well, I suppose it is, simply, an attempt on my part to think more clearly about certain South African preconceptions and misconceptions; to try, for myself, to quiet down the noise and the unthinking, pessimistic overreactions and preconceptions that dominate our society. It is an exercise in practising how to lower my defences so that I might be more open to things as they are, rather than how I think they are.

We are not about to boil to death, but it *is* hot in here and it is most definitely getting hotter, as our economy, already on its knees after decades of mismanagement and graft, reels from the impact of junk status and the Covid-19 pandemic. We are going to keep having the same conversations and reading the same headlines, for many years to come. But perhaps there is a way to have those conversations and to read those headlines without letting anger and anxiety parade as objective truths, so that the noise doesn't drown out the voices of experts, and fictions don't masquerade as scientific facts.

It is my sincere hope that in these pages you will also find a different view of our country; a perspective which reminds you that we are not brainless frogs in a pot, but complex, tired, hopeful, petty, generous, tight-fisted, pig-headed, free-thinking, bitter, forgiving human beings trying to make sense of ourselves in a country endlessly pulled in different directions and often straining the limits of credulity.

Chapter 1

Great Expectations

Every so often, it is claimed, a young Japanese woman has a nervous breakdown in Paris.

The story is almost always the same.

She is bursting with joy and anticipation when she arrives, relishing the first few steps of a lifelong dream fulfilled. Within days, however, she is an anxious wreck, comforted by medical experts or worried friends, waiting for the first available flight back to Tokyo.

What could cause such a dramatic and precipitous decline?

The answer is a mysterious psychological malady called Paris Syndrome.

Before I continue I should explain that Paris Syndrome might not be a real thing. It is not widely accepted by the psychiatric mainstream, and evidence seems to be more anecdotal than empirical.

Indeed, when I googled Paris Syndrome, I found a number of general interest pieces, each claiming that the syndrome is real. Each piece, however, seemed to cite an earlier one, which in turn echoed an even earlier one. It is possible that once, decades ago, a Japanese tourist had a wobble in Paris and it has now become a media trope to be trotted out once every five years at the start of the European tourist season. Indeed, the name 'Paris Syndrome' seems to be a creation of the media rather than the medical fraternity. It was coined by the French weekly *Journal du Dimanche* in 2004.

I should also point out that French doctors have been known to diagnose maladies which only exist in France. French people, for example, seem to be the only people in the world who suffer from *jambes lourdes*, or heavy legs, a general ache and sense of lethargy in the lower extremities, which can become so severe that victims have to miss work, presumably because their legs are too heavy to lug them to the office.

To be fair, the French are not the only Europeans who have national maladies. According to a gently sardonic account by BBC journalist Dany Mitzman, who lived in Italy for some time, hundreds of thousand of Italians are reportedly afflicted by *la cervicale*, a vague crisis of the general neck area, requiring warm scarves. Mitzman also reveals the much feared *colpo d'aria*, or 'hit of air', which seems to be what happens when earth's atmosphere makes unexpected contact with an unprotected Italian head.

My own experience of French medicine has left me very open to the possibility that their doctors are less reliable than one might assume.

Years ago I found myself in Strasbourg, my suddenly and alarmingly untrustworthy orifices convincing me that I had contracted swine flu. The hotel concierge told me about a marvellous service: a nation-wide house-call. I dialled a number, talked the operator through my symptoms, and they duly dispatched a GP to my hotel. She was brisk, professional and sorted me right out. (It was a stomach bug, not swine flu.) But as she rummaged in her bag she made polite smalltalk, and the conversation went like this:

'So you are from Sous Africa?'

'Yes.' *Horp* 'Yes.'

'*Bon*. And tell me . . . do you have ziss in Sous Africa?' She gestured at herself and her bag in a cool Gallic sort of way. I didn't understand.

'This?'

'Doctors who . . . how you say . . . ?'

'Oh, you mean this service? No, this is amazing, we don't have this.'

'No no,' she laughed charmingly. 'No, I mean . . . do you have . . . like me . . . doctors?'

It is possible there was a communication problem and that we were on two linguistic Eurostars passing each other in a tunnel, but I'm pretty damned sure she was asking me if we had Western medicine in South Africa and people who knew how to administer it.

Y-yes, I said. We had doctors in South Africa. In fact – ah, this would win her over! – South Africans had performed the world's first heart transplant!

She looked at me with an expression of extreme surprise and delight, and then burst out laughing. 'No,' she giggled, 'they did not.' It was the best joke she'd heard in years.

So please believe me when I say I am open to the possibility of French doctors getting it very wrong.

Still, a number of medical practitioners seem to have staked their reputations on the existence of Paris Syndrome. In 2007, *Journal du Dimanche* quoted Yousef Mahmoudia, a psychologist at the Hôtel-Dieu hospital in Paris, who revealed that 'a third of patients get better immediately, a third suffer relapses and the rest have psychoses'. Psychologist Herve Menhamou agreed. 'Fragile travellers can lose their bearings,' he told the newspaper, before cutting to the heart of Paris Syndrome: 'When the idea they have of the country meets the reality of what they discover it can provoke a crisis.'

What this means, in practice, is that some particularly naïve travellers arrive in Paris expecting *Amelie* and what they get is a French remake of *Trainspotting*.

Raised on Hollywood clichés and marinated in their own fantasies, they step out of Gare du Nord expecting a flock of pigeons to clatter into a sky full of accordion music. They raise their eyes to the skyline, expecting to see the Moulin Rouge nestled against the feet of the Eiffel Tower, with nuns hurrying to Montmartre or Notre-Dame across the street, while beautiful women, smelling of perfume, rattle past on bicycles, freshly baked baguettes tucked into a wicker basket on the handlebars.

What they get is a modern European capital: impersonal, entirely focused on its own private busyness, sparing only the most cursory glances at the newcomer to make sure they're not in the way; the roar of cars and money and private conversations punctuated by the wail of sirens.

If they are lucky, the first human they meet will be an ancient Romanian wearing plastic bags, muttering unintelligible requests for alms. If they are less lucky, it will be someone in the French service industry. ('*Bonjour*,' I stammered to the man in the tourist information kiosk in one French town, knowing how much they dislike anglophone tourists. '*Puis . . . je . . . anglais* . . . Er, may I speak English?' '*Non*!' he shouted, and slammed the shutters closed.)

For those travellers who have drunk particularly deep of the *Amelie* Kool-Aid, it can be a terrible shock, great enough to leave its victims profoundly unstrung: that report in 2007 claimed that Japan's embassy in Paris had repatriated sufferers who had believed their rooms were bugged, that they were being attacked by microwaves, and that they were Louis XIV . . .

Again, I have no doubt that embassies around the world are always having to deal with these sorts of things. Holidays are stressful at the best of times, and, to be honest, which of us hasn't felt, from time to time, that they are a French king being attacked by microwaves?

But the fact remains that most of us have, from time to time, experienced a mild version of Paris Syndrome. Perhaps that's why journalists seem to return to it every few years: it feels true.

Certainly, culture shock is a very real phenomenon, and this might be where the idea of Paris Syndrome first took hold.

According to Deborah Swallow, an intercultural communication specialist interviewed by news.com.au, it might have started almost 50 years ago among the wives of Japanese diplomats.

'The wives were typically not well-educated at the time,' said Swallow, 'and they'd come to Paris knowing what they'd seen in movies. Back then [the 1970s], at least, Paris was one of the rudest places on earth, and they experienced this huge culture shock.'

So what went wrong? What was the fundamental psychological problem that led to this very real suffering?

The simple answer seems to be a kind of psychological and emotional allergic reaction: two incompatible realities bumping up against each other; realities that are so different that there is no space in which they can happily co-habit.

And yet, why was the reaction so severe? Humans can cope very well with extreme contrasts. Some of those diplomats' wives in the 1970s might have been old enough to have survived World War 2. Some might even have lived through the firebombing of Japan, the extreme hunger and fear of 1945, and the mind-bending social changes that happened in the subsequent years. How could someone who had survived firebombing by B-29s, or at the very least who had parents blown up or burned, be so profoundly alarmed by rude café waiters? And how could modern Japanese women, growing up neck deep in rampant materialism and commodified, alienated humanity, suffer a nervous breakdown when they don't see quaint nuns and mimes in striped shirts?

I believe the answer to that question is central to a great deal of the stress and confusion many South Africans are feeling right now. And what that answer is, quite simply, is the crisis of misaligned expectations.

Paris didn't hurt those travellers. The thing that hurt them was inside their own heads: their expectations of what they would find in Paris.

If they'd expected to arrive in a city plastered in graffiti and haunted by pickpockets, where people either ignored them or rebuffed them, they would have felt none of that shock. Indeed, they might, instead, have been struck by the beauty and grandeur which manages to rise above those more grotty traits.

Same city; radically different experience.

I believe this same phenomenon lies beneath a great deal of the noise, outrage and anger in our country right now. Anyone who reads the news can tell you the problems facing South Africa. But along with these familiar crises, I think we need to start considering another problem: the extent to which our expectations are warping our perception of reality, and plunging us into a deeply stressful experience as we try to inhabit a country that doesn't really exist.

Let me give you a practical example, which doesn't have anything to do with abstract politics or the Japanese tourism industry. Let me give you the example of my Facebook page.

Now, my Facebook page is a cesspool.

It is this way for two reasons. Firstly, because I have made a career out of writing critical things about the government, and the government has made a lot of people angry, a lot of angry people tend to gravitate towards my online persona like rage-moths around a sputtering Bunsen burner. Secondly – and this is my own fault entirely – I am completely undiscriminating when it comes to accepting 'friend' requests. If you're not obviously a Russian bot, you're in.

The benefit of this is that I am exposed to people and opinions outside my white, English-speaking, middle-aged bourgeois silo. The downside is that I frequently have to bathe first my computer and then myself in Jik and Dettol.

This, of course, will not surprise you if you're on social media, or have ever ventured into the comments below any article on the internet: with few exceptions, the comments are a peep-show of humanity's most grotesque instincts.

Now, while I am slightly chagrined that my Facebook page is a cesspool, I don't feel that I am particularly guilty in this regard. Social media can be an awful, awful place. Everybody who pays any attention at all really should know this.

And yet last year, as things degenerated yet again on my page, a couple of besieged commenters appealed to me to intervene. Since it was my page, they told me, I needed to police the comments and put a stop to some of the abuse that they were copping. I had, they insisted, failed to create a 'safe space' for them. Those aren't sarcastic quotation marks, by the way: they actually wrote that.

This was a perfect example of misaligned expectations. Despite the lived experience of almost every person who uses social media, those commenters believe that Facebook is a place for rational and polite debate. Furthermore, they believed that *my* Facebook page should be similarly calm. And when the seething, steaming rage addicts arrived to yell at them, they were genuinely shocked and upset.

They felt those unpleasant feelings because, for their own reasons, their expectations had become dramatically unhooked from reality. Going onto social media and expecting a 'safe space' is like descending into a basement, hearing the distant sounds of barking and shrieking, seeing a sign that reads 'DOG FIGHTING AHEAD', being passed on the stairs by blood-stained thugs with lots of muscles – and then being genuinely confused and upset when you see dogs fighting rather than, say, a performance of *Waiting For Godot*.

I know this sounds a bit dismissive, and maybe it's unfair because until recently I felt something very similar. Every week, as Twitter or the Sunday papers splashed some new outrage into my eyeballs, I felt that same ragged indignation and that despairing disbelief; that desire to appeal to Someone to Do Something.

Now, however, I feel it less. Because I have started to believe that I am afflicted with a South African form of Paris Syndrome.

And that has changed everything.

This particular syndrome doesn't have very much to do with a tourist's perception of South Africa, although it is possible, I suppose, that on every flight into OR Tambo there is at least one passenger straining at a window, desperately peering down in the hope of seeing a crag where an ordained baboon is holding up a baby lion cub as the sun rises over James Earl Jones' vocal cords. Perhaps this unfortunate expects to be ushered into their hotel by a chorus line of bowing giraffes, and, when this does not happen, has a complete breakdown.

Very few South Africans, however, think this way about their country. I suspect that a handful do cling to certain fairy tales about it, remembering a kind of Disney-fied version of How Things Once Were, a place eternally bathed in sunshine, with all the smoke and Casspirs airbrushed out. More of us have vague, half-formed notions of how this country might still become better, without being able to pin down exactly what 'better' looks like.

For the rest – we know the score. We know what this country is and what it isn't. We know what to expect of our politicians. We know how to live with disappointment and sometimes despair. We're hard. Yes, we know the score.

But what if we don't? What if so much of the outrage and anger experienced by middle-class people reading the news is the result of a kind of lurking Paris Syndrome that afflicts South African citizens – a condition called, let's say, Parys Poepstring?

What if many of our emotional reactions are not based on reality but misaligned expectations? And what if we could feel a lot better – or at least stop experiencing the same outrage and disappointment again and again – if we tried to align our expectations with reality a little bit more? This is what happened to me when I realised I was suffering from Parys Poepstring, and how I am starting to overcome it. Here's how it happened.

For years, the ANC made me angry.

For years, it felt as if, when presented with a good choice, a middle choice and a bad choice, the ANC would set fire to all three, blame the middle class for its own pyrotechnic tendencies, and then steal the insurance payout. For years, I was infuriated by the ANC's contempt for our intelligence and our aspirations. I was outraged by its incompetence and the vast, legalised campaign of sabotage it called 'cadre deployment'. I was soul-sickened by its self-righteous pomposity and piousness as it gorged on our money while children drowned in sewage.

For years, I was incensed by its unconditional surrender to the enemies of this country: to the criminals who keep South Africans in a constant state of agitation and depression; to the predatory monopolies and corporations which milk us every day; to entropy, bringing basic education and Eskom and God knows what else to a slow, silent halt; whereby we are all used to national blackouts and are getting used to the fact that most nine year olds in this country can't read or do arithmetic.

I felt these things, and perhaps you do, too, for a very obvious and logical reason: the ANC is the ruling party and has almost complete control of the government and bureaucracy of this country. It is the ANC, therefore, that should run South Africa. Its leaders should lead. Its politicians must establish the conditions in which the country progresses. Its bureaucrats must pull the right levers to make things happen.

And yet they didn't, and – barring the efforts of a few during the Covid-19 crisis – still don't. If anything, they did and continue to do the opposite.

By the end of Jacob Zuma's presidency, I felt I understood the situation very well: the ANC was a terrible government, employing hopelessly clueless or wicked people, all of whom were fantastically bad at their jobs.

I was absolutely sure of one immutable truth: the ANC was the problem.

Except I was wrong. And at some point in the last year or so, I finally realised how wrong I had been.

The problem wasn't the ANC.

It was me.

I had become completely deluded. I had drifted away from reality. Worse, I had done it to myself: I had twisted myself into a mess of outrage and anger, shock and disbelief, because I had been entirely focused on my expectations rather than on what was actually happening. And to be fair, the ANC had tried to tell me the truth, more times than I could count.

It had told me during the arms deal, outlining in detail how it would rather spend billions on weapons to fight non-existent enemies than build toilets and schools and police stations. It had told me when it had appointed, and then defended, a close friend of organised crime as police commissioner.

It had told me when it paid tenderpreneurs billions to dump school textbooks in the veld. It had told me when it voted en masse in support of Zuma keeping his Nkandla loot, and then had its puppet, Blade Nzimande, describe the allegations as 'white people's lies'. It told me when it refused to arrest a genocidal war criminal.

It told me when it killed 143 mentally ill patients and then elected the person responsible to high office. It told me when it had its police murder 34 miners at Marikana. It told me when it sold this country to the Guptas, and used my taxes to hire Bell Pottinger to pretend that 'white monopoly capital' and a hollowed-out African liberation movement were somehow separate things.

It had tried everything, short of hiring a Silver Falcons aerobatics team to write huge letters in the sky:

> WE ARE NOT GOVERNING BECAUSE WE ARE NOT HERE TO GOVERN.
> PLEASE UNDERSTAND.
> WE DO NOT WORK FOR YOU.
> WE DO NOT GIVE A SHIT ABOUT YOU.
> YOU ARE ON YOUR OWN.
> NOW PAY YOUR TAXES AND SHUT UP, OR FUCK OFF.

The ANC told me this, month after month, scandal after scandal, but I refused to hear it.

Instead, I brandished my expectations ever more angrily, waving them at the ANC as I yelled, 'Why can't you be like *this*? Why aren't you governing, or apologising for your endless waste or your contempt? Why aren't you trying to be more like I expect you to be?'

It was like being shocked that Paris isn't a scene from *Amelie*. It was like expecting art in a dog-fighting pit. It was mad.

There is never any accounting for when the penny finally drops. We can be told something for 10 years by family, friends, colleagues, therapists and coaches, and it never makes it past the front gate of our awareness. Then a bus drives past with the same thing written on the side and the message penetrates straight to our core. So I can't tell you why I finally heard the ANC, or when, exactly. But one day I understood what the ANC had been saying for all those years, and in that moment everything made so much more sense.

The ANC, I realised, is not a government doing a very bad job. It is a money-making scheme doing a very good job.

Its senior politicians are not bad leaders. They are excellent entrepreneurs. All those taxes written off as 'wasteful or irregular expenditure' aren't loot or loss. They are a return on an investment of loyalty and time.

And the most skillful and consistent liars? They weren't the snake-oil salesmen promising 'A Better Life For All'. They were the voices in my own head, convincing me that these ambitious, venal, dishonest, cynical, wasteful hustlers are, in fact, public servants.

I understand if this shift in perspective sounds like defeatism or a general surrender to cynicism and disinterest. We're encouraged to believe that outrage is a measure of how much we care, and that how much we care is a measure of how virtuous we are. In this worldview, to step back from outrage or to disconnect from its triggers is to abandon your responsibility to be angry on behalf of others, or in solidarity with right-thinking people; and to abandon that responsibility is to reveal yourself as a bad person.

Whether you subscribe to that worldview is up to you, but I would suggest that it is not your responsibility to self-harm by staying locked inside a delusion. It is not your responsibility, for example, to stand at the seashore and to scream at the sharks in the ocean, accusing them of being rubbish public servants and not representing you properly in parliament. Because that's what we're doing by accusing the ANC of the same thing.

I've been accused of being cynical. I don't think I am. I still believe that many people are motived by sincere goodness, and that most want justice and fairness, not because they are compelled to but because they believe it is right. I seldom despair, preferring to range between fragile hope and a more robust optimism that our country can rid itself of those compulsions which keep dragging it back towards the brink. I am certainly not suggesting that, by detaching from our expectations, we should stop expecting good people to be good, or intelligent people to be intelligent, or our friends to care about us.

But I will no longer waste emotional energy on getting upset that corrupt people are corrupt or that sharks are sharks and not public servants.

Life – and my nerves – are much too short for that.

Paris Syndrome and Parys Poepstring are, fundamentally, a problem of misapprehension. They are conditions whereby we are unable to see the truth in front of our eyes.

To move clear of them, therefore, is the opposite of giving up or surrendering or ceasing to care. Instead, it is a move towards clarity and focus; towards an honest diagnosis that will allow effective treatment.

Since I started hearing the ANC – and all the other powerful, wealthy, untouchable Big Men who endlessly tell us who and what they are – my experience of the news is no longer an endless series of shocks. Instead, it has become a sobering stroll through an exhibition of snapshots of people being people. Instead of being battered this way and that by disbelief and disappointment, I find myself pausing in front of certain snapshots and saying, sometimes ruefully, 'Ah yes, well, that probably makes sense.'

Let me give you a fairly extreme example.

In April of 2018, King Mswati III of eSwatini turned 50. This was quite an achievement, and not just because life expectancy in his personal fiefdom is around 58, which meant he was almost home and dry.

It was also a moment in which to step back and savour how sweet it is to be alive rather than guillotined or shot in a forest along with your family or strangled by your bodyguards or burned at the stake or sealed into a barrel stuck full of nails and rolled down a hill, or, indeed, any of the other surprises meted out to absolute rulers over the millennia by the people they had squatted upon until that fateful bang on the door.

But it wasn't just a personal milestone. In the same month, eSwatini was celebrating its own 50th birthday, a golden jubilee. Clearly, this double triumph needed to be marked with a gesture of supreme generosity by the king.

Which is why Mswati bought himself an Airbus A340, and a large high-tech hangar to keep it in, for R2.7 billion. What do you give the man who has everything except a grasp of reality? Other than a subscription to *Up Yours Monthly*, the answer seems to be an Airbus catalogue.[1]

Now, Mswati is no fool. He's been around. Granted, it's usually in a Maybach driven by a team of maidens, crunching slowly across a red carpet made of the felted remains of subsistence farmers.

But he wasn't born yesterday, and he has a 50th birthday present to prove it. Clearly he understood how it would look, spending R2.7 billion on himself in a country in which 40 per cent of adults

---

1 His mother, the Queen Mother, Ntombi Twala, reportedly gave Mswati a dining room suite 'made of gold and decorated with precious stones sourced from the sea'. I don't doubt that the suite was made of gold – now that the Italian Mafia is in decline, the royal families of the world are the only people keeping manufacturers of high-grade kitsch in business – but the vagueness of that last bit intrigues me . . .

'And what are these interesting little things embedded in the table, mother?'

'Ah, they are precious stones sourced from the sea.'

'Interesting. Precious stones, you say?'

'Sourced from the sea.'

'Interesting.'

'W-why?'

'Well, no, it's just . . . they look a bit like . . . well, like bottle tops.'

'No, they are precious stones sourced from the sea.'

'This one says "Lion Lager" on it . . . '

'No. As I have explained, that one is a precious stone sourced from the sea.'

'Which sea, mother?'

'More fois gras, birthday boy?'

'Mother, which sea?'

'This crouton is delicious.'

'Which s – '

'Durban harbour, okay? It's a fucking precious stone from the bottom of Durban harbour, and yes, it looks like a bottle top, but I paid a million fucking dollars for this suite and they said it would take another week to source actual stones and I didn't want to miss your birthday and I'm not having this conversation, okay?'

are stunted by malnutrition, and in which 60 per cent live below the poverty line. He knew he'd look like the most decadent and reviled emperors of antiquity, wretched and venal little men who emptied their treasuries on a whim. And he wasn't going to let that happen.

Which is why, during a soirée to celebrate the jubilee, he told a grateful nation that they could look forward to giving him R100 million to prove that the country was booming.

'I am very happy that emaSwati have proved that their businesses are thriving,' he told guests at the Lozitha Royal Palace, 'and I look forward to more presents to the tune of 100 million lilangeni [R100 million] so that the world can see that the country's economy is on the crest of a wave.'

See? eSwatini isn't the personal playground of one megalomaniac! It's royal *ubuntu*: I am rich because you are not quite poor enough to stop making me more rich!

When news of these revels reached South Africa, the response was predictably noisy, rancorous shock and outrage. *City Press* marvelled at the excess of a 'king who pays his old age pensioners R400 per month'.

Clearly, this was an act of supreme vanity and contempt for the people of eSwatini. But the only way you could be shocked by Mswati's shopping spree is if you believe that Swazis are citizens of a modern state rather than subjects in a monarchy, and that Mswati is a modern public servant and not someone straight out of the Old Testament or the Middle Ages.

If you put aside your expectations of how a leader *should* behave – rather than how unaccountable strongmen really *do* behave – then what comes into sharp focus is a fairly unexceptional medieval king, gorging on medieval privileges. The problem, it becomes clear, isn't Mswati's royal appetite, but rather the continued stronghold of the monarchy on eSwatini, and how its backers, both domestic and abroad, prevent the formation of a democratic government.

When he bought himself that plane, Mswati was being obscene and arrogant, but in the end he was just doing what unaccountable kings do. Likewise, when he told the kingdom to cough up those 'presents' to the tune of R100 million, he was just enjoying the divine right of kings to help himself to other people's money.

Why a South African corporation, on the other hand, would crawl up Mswati's bum is another matter entirely. MTN is based in a constitutional democracy. It purports to support democracy and to be opposed to exploitation and poverty. And yet, when Mswati made his outrageous call for 'presents', MTN Swaziland squealed, 'Ooh! Me! Pick me!' and wrote him a cheque for R1 million. Why? It's not like he needs the money: his wristwatch alone is worth R20 million.

Luckily, the South African press was all over the story. You probably remember some of these headlines from the time:

> LET THEM EAT DATA! CELL GIANT BENDS KNEE TO MAD KING
>
> WE ALWAYS KNEW MTN WAS YELLOW BUT THIS IS A BIT RICH
>
> MTN PUTS ON SEXY DRESS, SINGS BREATHLESS VERSION OF 'HAPPY BIRTHDAY, MR PRESIDENT', OR IT WOULD IF ESWATINI HAD AN ELECTED PRESIDENT INSTEAD OF UNELECTED FRAT BOY WITH MAGICAL BLOOD WHICH FOR SOME REASON MAKES HIM THE BOSS OF EVERYONE

Not really. None of those headlines got written, because MTN's descent into abject toadying and fart-catching went largely unnoticed in South Africa.

To be fair, there were sensible explanations for this. It is hard to get agitated about R1 million when R2.7 billion has just been dropped down an immense golden toilet. Also, it's possible that South Africans are just tired of complaining about MTN.

But I would also suggest that MTN escaped public condemnation because most of us were too busy being shocked by a decadent king behaving like a decadent king. Expectations got in the way of reality, and other villains – or, in MTN's case, enablers of undemocratic excess straight out of eighteenth century Versailles – were ignored.

This, for me, is the most essential reason to go clear of expectations. Part of it is self-care, to be sure. Shock is a recoil, endlessly pushing us backwards and preparing us only for the next shock. It contributes nothing. Anger, likewise, is largely useless as a tool for social change. Mostly it is, as the old cliché says, like taking poison and expecting your enemy to die.

But the real point of keeping an even keel is to be able to see who is worth worrying about and who isn't; about being able to tell friend from foe from waste of time. It is about stepping off this endless carousel of outrage, where we bounce between the high of anger and the low of despair, to see our home and our times more clearly. It is to arrive in Paris expecting a real city; to seek a safe space somewhere other than Facebook.

South Africa is complicated enough without blundering through it blindfolded by projection and expectation. It's time to see where we live, so that we can figure out how to live here.

Chapter 2

Laughing While Rome Burns

As a scholar, I lived by one golden rule: adequacy.

I blame my formative years, spent at a Waldorf school, where I failed to develop a fetish for marks or learn that they are the currency of academic achievement. Our tests, when they cropped up, were gentler, less transactional things, involving lamb's wool and varnish and perhaps some Rescue Remedy afterwards. To me, failure wasn't a number somewhere below 50 per cent. Rather it was working for five weeks on a hand-stitched, carefully stuffed tiger and then, at the very last, discovering that one leg was slightly too short and that the beast could not stand without being propped up against the wall.

When I left the pagan bosom of that school, exchanging fading corduroys and North Stars for the 1930s conformist chic of the state school system, I discovered that I really wasn't very interested in getting an A. Obviously I didn't want an F, because failing, I learned, required you to do the work all over again. An E was perilously close to an F and should also be avoided. But above those scandals, B, C and D felt like my intellectual Goldilocks spot, neither too hot nor too cool. (Fortunately for me, I was neither hot nor cool in high school, so it all worked out quite nicely.)

I wasn't a lazy child. I worked hard enough on the things that mattered to me, or on the things that made my mother worry about my future, which was mostly my profound inability to do maths. The trouble was, I just didn't *feel* those marks. I was like someone raised on a commune being introduced to money on their 21st birthday: I wasn't going to say no if some cash came my way quite easily, but I was unlikely to go into mergers and acquisitions.

This lack of an emotional connection to marks was why I never, ever prepared for my English orals. I was quite proud of this fact at the time. I think it made me seem blasé and sophisticated, or as blasé and sophisticated as someone with a breaking voice wearing an oversized blazer and with pie pastry stuck in their braces can seem.

In retrospect, it wasn't a successful attitude. Relying on self-deprecating, off-the-cuff humour allowed me to avoid developing a work ethic or any real beliefs. In short, I was in serious danger of becoming Boris Johnson.

Still, it's what happened, and it was why, one particular morning, I was standing in front of the class, weaselling my way out of any kind of academic rigour with a droll anecdote about my trip to school that morning or the quality of school lunches or why it was, exactly, that Steri Stumpies never seemed to go off. I was just hitting my stride, my teacher having settled on a cadaverous half-smile that was somewhere between faint amusement and deep pity, when the classroom door was flung open and in rushed a girl from a different class. She was out of breath and she was crying. She was sorry to interrupt, she said, but she had important news: a boy, a pupil at another school but known and loved by many of my classmates through a local church, had died of an illness.

I don't want to make this all about me, but that was the moment I lost the room. Girls put their arms around each other and began to sob. Boys whispered 'Oh my God' and clutched their heads and stared at the wall, trying not to cry.

I looked at my teacher. Obviously, I muttered, it would be better if I didn't finish my funny story, right?

No, she said. I should carry on. Just, you know, finish up.

So I did. I offered a few more damp zingers to a room full of weeping children, and then sat down in that moist silence, hating my teacher and myself in equal parts.

At the time I thought she had been quite cruel, but in retrospect it was my first taste of my current career.

That's because every week, I sit down and try to get anxious, *gatvol*, even sad people to laugh at the hypocrisy, cynicism, strategic neglect and downright sociopathy of our politics. I crack wise in front of a room of people sighing, growling, staring blankly ahead of themselves or massaging the pulsating veins that are bulging out of their temples. It's a strange impulse. And yet, thanks to the rise of commercial satire, currently exemplified by lucrative machines like *The Daily Show* and *The John Oliver Show*, it has become normalised. I never get asked why I do what I do, or who it's for, or, most importantly, what it's for.

On the contrary, a kind of unconscious belief has sprung up, helped in part by writers of comedy, satire or snark, that mocking the powerful is a form of activism.

Now, as much as I'd like to claim a few revolutionary credentials, I'm afraid this simply isn't true.

For starters, activism is a process of creating lines of communication between opposing groups – of reconnecting human connections severed by injustice or inequality – whereas comedy is, almost by definition, balkanised. Anyone can be reached by the right intellectual or emotional argument, but we only laugh at things we find funny. Humour is entirely subjective: we all prefer our own brand and can't understand why anyone would want the other stuff. I enjoy political satire for its wit and playfulness, but I would bet Trevor Noah's salary that not one Trump-voting Midwesterner has ever had his or her mind changed by a funny bit on *The Daily Show*. Activism changes minds. Satire, in my experience, often reinforces them.

Which is why the people who are going to turn this country – or indeed this world – away from self-destructive patterns will not be comedians or satirists but serious, soft-spoken experts.

Of course, I want to believe differently. Because this is my career, I sometimes tell myself that I am the modern equivalent of the medieval court jester, an analogy that seems very popular among satirists and comedians, who, in their more introspective moments, will tell you that they are outsiders given special dispensation by our society to say things nobody else is allowed to say. Well, okay. Fair enough. But do you know what medieval court jesters accomplished?

Fokkol.

Year after year they put on their silly outfits and their pointy hats with bells on the end, and punned and prodded and provoked, belittling and teasing the hypocrisy and squalid excess of absolute, totalitarian monarchy; and the royal family of the day roared with laughter and wiped the duck fat from their chins and rolled on for another century. In the end, the power of god-kings and emperors wasn't defeated by jokes. It wasn't wit or truth that shifted power. It was war, disease, revolution or economic collapse. It's why British satirist Peter Cook, when founding The Establishment club in 1961, said he hoped it would be a satirical venue like 'those wonderful Berlin cabarets which did so much to stop the rise of Hitler and prevent the outbreak of the Second World War'.

Indeed, if you put a couple of drinks into most writers, whether of satire, fiction, academic research, punditry, analysis, commentary or opinion, I suspect most would gloomily admit that the global hierarchy of influence – that is, the people or organisations or organisms whose thoughts and words influence the greatest number of human beings and therefore exert the greatest influence on the fate of this planet – looks a bit like this:

1. Beyoncé's gut bacteria
2. Everyone else's gut bacteria
3. Bad parents
4. Footballers
5. Good parents
6. YouTubers catering to children younger than eight
7. Khloe Kardashian
8. Mark Zuckerberg
9. The other Kardashians
10. Prosperity gospel preachers
11. Businesspeople owed favours by politicians
12. Politicians
13. Peppa Pig
14. Reruns of Oprah
15. The religious beliefs of your ancestors, arbitrarily assigned depending on where they were born, which constellate once a week to convince you that you are failing to live according to guidelines laid out by:
16. Priests, imams, rabbis and gurus
17. The person who writes the free medical diagnosis on the internet which suggests that you're probably fine but that you should probably get that thing checked out because you're probably dying

18. The cocaine dealers of creative directors at advertising agencies
19. Astrologers
20. Porn stars
21. The mothers of rappers
22. Taylor Swift
23. Whoever Taylor Swift is fighting with
24. Dominatrices blackmailing the accountants of Hollywood producers
25. Accountants of Hollywood producers
26. Hollywood producers suddenly being told with weird urgency by their accountants that they need to make another blockbuster
27. Divorce lawyers of Hollywood stars, looking at bank statements and advising their clients that they really need to audition for that new blockbuster
28. Hollywood stars, somewhat inexplicably acting in that new blockbuster
29. Other animated characters on TV shows
30. Academics in the hard sciences
31. Animated characters in advertisements, such as talking bowls of breakfast
32. Pet psychics
33. Logos on T-shirts
34. Instagram pictures of logos on T-shirts
35. Bestselling horror and crime novelists
36. Animal behaviourists
37. Conceptual dance troupes
38. Instagram influencers
39. Re-enactors of historical battles
40. Makers of dream-catchers
41. The person in China who embroiders misspelt, fictitious Mark Twain quotes onto pencil cases

42. Joke writers working for famous American comedians, satirists and talk show hosts
43. Umpires and referees
44. Famous American comedians, satirists and talk show hosts
45. People spinning signs saying 'CASH FOR GOLD!' or pointing at car-washes with large yellow styrofoam hands
46. Investigative journalists
47. Pamphlets offering cures for bad luck, low salary and weak erection
48. Academics in the humanities and social sciences
49. The pilot who flies over Cape Town every day dragging a banner advertising strip club Mavericks
50. Satirists and opinion columnists

So, no, laughing while Rome burns isn't going to put out the fire. Indeed, I have sometimes felt quite embarrassed by my trade when I've met activists or academics whose work constantly changes lives or helps build policy on fundamental issues like health or land reform. When my friend Chris, a surgeon, asks me how work is going, and I've wanted to have a moan about the difficulties of thinking up a suitable metaphor for the week's biggest news story, I've had to remind myself that he spent last night sewing a child's face back together. This is partly why, when people refer to me as a journalist, I stress that I am a *columnist*: while I'm constructing puns, journalists are sifting through bank statements and getting phone calls in the middle of the night from people who hang up when they answer.

Having said all of that, however, I think comedy and satire do have two crucial functions.

The first is to inoculate ourselves against the disease of obedience.

Authority always takes itself entirely seriously. This is normal.

Kings, religious zealots, politicians and billionaires are, by definition, sure of their rightness. You could even argue that they reached those positions in society precisely because they were so confident of their rightness. After all, nobody ever became a Supreme Leader by putting up a hand from the back row and saying, 'Guys, I just think we need a second opinion on this one.' This is how authority rolls. A certain kind of bossy arsehole wants the world to be a certain way and sets about finding a team of unscrupulous lieutenants and useful idiots to help him make it happen. Which would be fine if nobody paid any attention to them. But things go pear-shaped when everybody else starts taking them seriously, too. That, after all, is the moment when a commune of megalomaniac sociology graduates becomes a government, or when a huddle of hallucinating goat-herders becomes a council of infallible prophets.

Now, laughter has no effect on those people. It bounces right off them, along with humility, insight, compassion and acceptance. This is why laughing at authority can never be a form of direct activism: it's like blowing soap bubbles at a tank.

The followers of authority, however, are a different story; because laughter can save them before the disease of obedience becomes terminal.

People want to prostrate themselves before authority for many reasons, which is why followers take on a wide variety of forms. Some are skinhead neo-Nazis bellowing about racial purity and Jewish conspiracies. Some are grandmothers, figuring out how much of their small pension they can afford to give to a church worth billions. Some are academics or Twitter sin-sniffers, policing thoughts they feel are sacrilegious to the prevailing pieties of the day. Some are middle managers, tolerating illegal or inhumane or simply inefficient practices to keep the boat from rocking. All, however, have one thing in common: they feel vulnerable, and seek the protection of a Big Daddy who will save them from their secret, private terrors.

For some, that protection takes the form of all-encompassing, ever-present paternal love, such as you might get from God or a cult leader called Chad who sometimes gets divine instructions through the Toaster of Anointment. Others seek out a Big Daddy who will not just protect them from their enemies but rain down righteous vengeance on them, the sort of violence they could never – or would never – commit personally. For a few, Big Daddy represents the blessed relief of being told what to do, sparing them the terrible burden of independence.

Of course, hard-core followers can't be vaccinated against obedience because it's the thing they desire most. Just as athletes want to win and artists want to make, hard-core followers want to obey the strong and be obeyed by the weak, spending their lives in blissful suspension between the desire to be a god and a doormat. Infatuated with authority, they are, like their idols, immune to laughter.

But beyond this inner circle of disciples there are millions and millions of 'undecideds', people who are attracted to some aspects of authority but unsettled or even repelled by others; who want to be told what to do but who do not want to be told to do unpleasant things, or be told in a way that they find bullying; who want to feel part of a group but have the freedom to leave it when they want to; who want the security and reassurance of a parental figure but who don't necessarily want a Big Daddy. It is these people, hovering in the doorway of obedience, pausing in front of the snake-oil salesman's soapbox, who can be kept safe by laughter. And that's because of what happens when we laugh at Big Daddy.

Nothing.

Nothing happens. Nobody gets struck by lightning. Nobody's spouse turns into a pillar of salt. Nobody shrivels into a desiccated husk, or is dragged down into a crack in the earth by a horde of demons. The crops don't wither. The wells don't fizz with poison. Armies don't rampage across our borders.

I suspect that this immense anticlimax can have a powerful, unconscious effect on undecided followers. The point of following a Big Daddy is not only that he is Big, but that he is a Daddy: he comes down hard on people who step out of line. And yet here is someone laughing at him – challenging his authority, denying his dignity – and there seem to be no consequences at all. And so the would-be follower begins to wonder: if this potential protector can't even stop something as small as a laugh, how can he protect me from Them From Over There? Of course, that question will cause even greater anxiety for some people and they will go in search of a bigger, louder authority figure. But for many, I think that moment of doubt is enough: the door is opened, and they wander away into confusing, vexing freedom. To laugh at authority is to sneak up onto the mountain of the gods and to reveal that their thunderbolts are made of painted cardboard and that the thunder is a metal sheet being wobbled by a tired lackey hiding in the wings.

But I think there's another, even better reason to keep laughing in stressful or difficult times, and that is self-care.

The great humorist and cartoonist James Thurber wrote: 'Humour is emotional chaos remembered in tranquility.' I think that gets to the heart of the process better than anything else I've read, because it draws such a clear link between laughter and extreme stress. It suggests that laughing isn't just an involuntary response to an amusing stimulus. It is also a way of picking up the fragments of recent anxieties, the shards of stressful, upsetting experiences or discoveries, and re-assembling them in a way that feels soothing and clear-eyed. Indeed, I believe that Thurber's equation can be reverse-engineered to artificially generate a better mental state; that emotional chaos, filtered through the lens of humour, can induce a kind of tranquillity.

Consider the sort of praise directed at our most popular political cartoonists and satirists. I don't often hear people like Zapiro described as funny. Rather, I hear words like 'insight' and 'perspective'. John Oliver has some good punch-lines, but most of his viewers, I would argue, watch him for the clarity he brings to complex current affairs. Both, in short, are taking emotional chaos, forcing it through a humorous filter, and producing a temporary sort of tranquillity. God knows it doesn't always feel like tranquillity. Often my laughter is bitter and tight, somewhere between a derisive snort and an exasperated sigh. But perhaps that is the sound humans make when they let off steam. Maybe that's the sound of pressure being released. If that is the case, then laughing while Rome burns isn't callous or facile or a sign that we have checked out. It is a form of self-care. It is a way of looking after ourselves until the flames die down.

All of which is why we should keep laughing – or at least letting that little spurt of steam out of our noses – as the powerful and the pompous, the sanctimonious and the dishonest, wag their fingers from behind podiums and altars and boardroom tables, telling us to behave and be respectful.

We should laugh at them because they are laughable. We should laugh at their appeals to power and infallibility because, under all that finery, they are also naked and soft, with silly little wobbly buttocks and jolly little knock-knees, just like the rest of us. They might stand and thunder about the unstoppable march of their particular cause, but every so often they have to stop marching and hurry off to go and make a poo, and worry that the next person in the loo after them will think it was them who left that pong.

When they demand our obedience, laugh at them in the knowledge that they haven't phoned their mother in two weeks. And when they have been revealed as thieves, laugh because it's all so fabulously sordid and low grade, all that money spent on gigantic, terribly painted portraits of themselves, and on porcelain whippets they once saw on *Top Billing* and thought might make people respect them more, and on booze to help them forget the exact moment they sold out and that emptiness inside them started growing.

But most of all, we should laugh at them because it's good for us. They're not going anywhere, but neither are we.

Chapter 3

If Only They Didn't Wear Suits

I'm going to assume that you haven't heard of Rick Wiles.

I'm going to assume this because you are reading this book, and if you're a follower of Mr Wiles it means you've only read two books: a well-thumbed copy of the Bible in which you've urgently underlined your favourite passages about smiting Sodomites; and a diary, written in your own blood, in which you scribble treatises on the importance of snaring a fecund mother-wife and always being on the lookout for Jewish shape-shifters trying to poison your well.

Zoologists would probably classify Mr Wiles as an evangelical Christian, that unfortunate group of Americans that has confused the teachings of Jesus Christ with the late-night yell-slurring of a backwoods windbag courting his sister; a toxic cult that has translated 'love they neighbour' into 'hate the poor, fear the foreign and the unconventional, and show disdain for the rest' and which clearly believes it is easier for a rich man to enter the kingdom of heaven if he's napalmed a few hundred camels first.

As you'd expect, Wiles does a roaring trade in paranoid racist fantasy. He has, for example, stated that the 2017 Las Vegas massacre was ordered by a secret 'gay/lesbian Nazi regime' which controls America. I'm not sure if he sees this regime as good or bad because, while he is fanatically homophobic, he is also extremely simpatico with Nazis when it comes to anti-Semitism. In November 2019, for example, he took to his TruNews online soapbox to present a rant titled 'Jew Coup: Seditious Jews Orchestrating Trump Impeachment Lynching', in which he proclaimed that 'that's the way the Jews work, they are deceivers, they plot, they lie . . . They kill babies. They promote homosexuality. They promote sorcery and witchcraft. They're evil. They're wicked. Their wickedness is beyond our comprehension.'[2]

It will therefore probably surprise you to learn that Rick Wiles has standards.

In 2013 Alex Jones, a frenzied instigator of right-wing conspiracy theories, began to insist to his audience of misanthropic idiots that the murder of 20 children at the Sandy Hook Elementary School the previous year had never happened. Instead, he ranted into his spittle-flecked microphone, it had been a 'false flag' operation, staged using child actors and special effects, to give the government an excuse to confiscate guns.

Five years later, as Jones reached the climax of his vile apoplexy, Rick Wiles took a stand. After showing his TruNews flock a segment in which a literally panting, grunting Jones begs God to save him from CNN fact-checkers (whom Jones describes in the segment as 'the literal demon spawn of the pit of hell' who are 'drunk on our children's blood') a sorrowfully shocked Wiles urged Christians to 'disavow' Jones, explaining that 'if I were in a room with somebody acting like that, I would be casting out devils. I would be binding

---

2 TruNews has White House media accreditation. I'm not making this up.

the devil, using the name of Jesus and the blood of Christ to bind those devils that are coming out of that man's mouth'.

So what had caused this Damascene conversion?

Had it happened because Jones had led a mob of thugs to the front doors of grieving parents whose children had just been murdered to yell abuse at them? Was it because he'd sent images of child sexual abuse to the small group of parents who sued him for insisting that the massacre was a hoax? Or was it because Wiles purports to be a Christian while Jones is clearly a cheerleader for undiluted evil?

Nope. Wiles wanted Christians to reject Jones because he feared his own show might get taken off air.

The name of that TruNews segment, the one in which Jones frothed and raved and the one that Wiles used to denounce him, said it all: 'Does the fate of the 1st Amendment rest with Alex Jones?' In the segment, Wiles fretted that Jones might spew so much poison that the government would be handed a reason to 'ban freedom of speech'. The subtext was clear. Wiles was scrambling to disavow his fellow bigot not because that bigot was a monster, but because Jones had broken the first rule of Hate Club: sell hate, but not so much, or so luridly, that civilised society is forced to take notice and shut you down.

It was an act of supreme cowardice, but it worked. Wiles remains on air, free to proclaim, as he did during the Covid-19 pandemic, that God was spreading the virus through synagogues in Israel because Jews were 'under judgement because [they] oppose his son, Jesus Christ'. But Wiles doesn't just preach hate. He also preaches insanity. And, in 2019, he took a brief break from anti-semitism to warn his flock about one of the greatest threats humanity has ever faced: meat grown in laboratories.

You find this amusing, do you? Well, laugh it up while you can, you heathen vegan seaweed-steaming demon feeder. Because when you die you're going straight to hell!

I'll let Rick explain.

'When you go to your favourite fast food restaurant, you're going to be eating a fake hamburger,' he warns. So why is this a problem? Well, says Rick, 'God is an environmentalist. He takes this very seriously. He created this planet, he created the universe and he's watching these Luciferians destroy this planet, destroy the animal kingdom, destroy the plant kingdom . . . '

I know that I sometimes struggle to keep up with very stupid prose so let me just confirm that you did, in fact, read that correctly: God wants us to keep eating real meat, which means we need to stop destroying the animal and plant kingdoms so that we can keep slaughtering hundreds of billions of animals a year and replacing forests and wetlands with monoculture, the way Baby Jeebus intended.

But I'm getting in the way of Rick's big reveal, so let's return to the Luciferians and their diabolical plan. Look! There they are, now, a coven of witches and warlocks in lab coats, hunched over their petri dishes, their familiars gambolling around their ankles on tiny cloven hoofs, the whole orgiastic mob flaunting their 'science' and other fake ideas invented by the gay/lesbian Nazi regime.

So why are they doing it? Reader, I hope you're sitting down . . .

'They want to change human DNA so that you can't be born again,' says Rick. 'They want to create ***a race of soulless creatures on this planet***.'

You hear that, you eaters of faux meats? Your doom is at hand! Behold, the riders of the culinary apocalypse! Sham ham! Phony polony! Fake steak! Look upon the works of these peddlers of unholy flesh and despair!

For lo, when the day comes, as it must, that you wish to be born again and become an American Evangelical, and you raise your eyes up to the Lord, sitting in splendour in His whites-only golf estate, flanked by His wife, Stepfanie, and His son, Chad, and Stepfanie's pilates instructor, Miguel (who wouldn't normally get to sit up on the main throne area except Stepfanie has been feeling particularly tight in her glutes so he's there just to, you know, keep an eye) your words shall fail you as you choke on the bogus pork banger of sin, and your eyes shall be dimmed by cataracts made from tiny slivers of bacon-flavoured tofu.

And one day, when you die, probably at the ungodly age of 125 because you're a Luciferian who doesn't even have a favourite 'fast food restaurant', you will hover above your dead body and look around you. And over yonder, lit up in the heavenly glow of a celestial McDonald's drive-through, you will see Rick and all his friends and followers, singing hallelujahs and playing harps, and all of them will look surprisingly young, mainly because most of them died at 55 of a stroke. You will drift over to this gathering of the recently infarcted and ask them where they are going. 'To heaven!' they will sing. 'We are going to heaven because *we ate real hamburgers*!'

You will find this all very strange, mainly because until moments ago you were an atheist or an agnostic, and the existence of an afterlife, or at least a sort of limbo, is raising very alarming questions for you about where it is, exactly, you're about to go.

But before you can ask Rick and the Cholesterol Choir for more details, they will all be whisked up to American Evangelical heaven, to do nothing all day long but complain on Facebook about how immigrant angels are taking the jobs of law-abiding angels and how millennial angels are lazy and entitled and over sensitive about dying young.

And then the ground will open up beneath your feet, and you will tumble straight down into hell; and there you will find everybody who didn't get into Rick Wiles' heaven. You will find yourself in a great multitude of people who have read widely, and who can understand subtext and hold two conflicting ideas in their heads; people who can admit their limitations and apologise when they're wrong; who feel, but do not succumb to, the urge to argue about things they know nothing about.

And as one they will smile and raise a glass to you, and cry, 'Welcome to hell!' and then they will invite you to dinner at the local Moroccan restaurant, after which you will go back to theirs and have a lot of very good sex.

I know that all sounds a bit silly, but you must agree it's not nearly as silly as Rick Wiles.

So why mention him at all?

Because he wears a suit.

Let me explain.

In 2018, Jon Sopel, the BBC's North American Editor, wrote a book about his experience covering the politics and the people of Donald Trump's America. It was called *If Only They Didn't Speak English.*

'You see,' wrote Sopel, 'if only they didn't speak English in America, then we'd treat it as a foreign country – and probably understand it a lot better.'

What Sopel was talking about, of course, is, something I write a lot about in this book: expectations and projections.

For well over two centuries there has existed a belief in the English-speaking world that Americans are more or less the same people as English speakers in the rest of the former British Empire; that there is a kind of kinship between them; that, to put it simply, Americans are their cousins.

It was a threadbare fiction – I'm not sure many of the British politicians who waxed lyrical about their strong connection to the New World in the 1940s felt particularly connected to Latino Los

Angelinos or black or Jewish New Yorkers – but it established a powerful grip on the imagination of the English-speaking world, thanks in no small part to Hollywood: when films become a familiar part of your world, you inevitably imagine that the world that made those films must be just as familiar. The result was a powerful sense of kinship. But this expectation of sameness is a projection, not a fact.

That projection – those misaligned expectations – were on full view in 2016. When Donald Trump was elected president, millions of English-speaking people around the globe, many living in former British colonies, expressed dismay. How could our kin, they protested, elect someone so obviously, well, not kin? There was a sense of betrayal, as if the cousins across the pond had sold the family silver to a passing conman. But they were blaming the wrong thing. They hadn't been betrayed by family. They'd been betrayed by their projections. Because, of course, many millions of the Americans who voted for Donald Trump have nothing in common with liberal, left-leaning Londoners or Melbournians except for a shared language.

To understand Americans, Sopel was suggesting, we need to understand what they are but also what they're not. For the British English speakers he was writing for, this meant getting past the camouflage of language, and seeing what lies beneath that superficial similarity.

Perhaps the easiest way to see this process of assumption and projection in action is to look at the Anglo response – by which I mean the general media and social media reaction – to the election of right-wing governments in the rest of the world. When some slick bigot wins an election there is alarm, there is concern, there is condemnation, but there isn't the same visceral response – the appalled 'What were you *thinking*?' – that Trump elicited. Part of that might be a kind of unconscious racism – revealing a belief that

Americans should know better whereas when Brazilians elect a creature like Jair Bolsonaro, well, they're emotional South Americans so what do you expect? But I think the main reason is that *Guardian* readers in London and *Daily Maverick* readers in Johannesburg do not feel culturally 'related' – connected by manufactured, projected kinship – to Brazilians or Hungarians.

Which brings me back to Rick Wiles and his suit.

When I watch Rick Wiles, I get confused, the way English-speaking Londoners got confused when English-speaking Nebraskans voted for Donald Trump. I get confused because my eyes are contradicting my ears.

What I'm hearing coming out of Rick Wiles' mouth is the sound of ancient, frightened, ignorant, superstitious humanity. I'm hearing the primitive, stumbling, god-addled murmurings of a prophet who lives in a cave two days' walk from Babylon; a wide-eyed, wild-haired, buck-naked man who eats frogs and scorpions and longs for the apocalypse to end his ghastly life. I'm hearing the dark, vengeful, urgent babbling of a hermit who lives in a forest in medieval France, living off scraps tossed to him by travelling friars and cursing the children who throw rocks at him. I'm hearing the ancient sound of raw, unfiltered, undiluted human ignorance; the primordial fizzing and popping and spluttering that happens when fear, creativity and a desperate search for meaning mix together inside an otherwise empty head.

What I'm seeing, however, is a suit.

Rick Wiles isn't covered in flies. He isn't wearing a desiccated squirrel as a hat, or a necklace of holy camel penises. He isn't licking a snake, or nursing the black eye he got when those French children pelted him with rocks for making the crops fail.

He's wearing a suit, like an academic at a conference, or a school principal, or a retired aeronautical engineer. He looks entirely like someone who has lived his life in contact with most of the thoughts of the Enlightenment and much of the science of the last 200 years.

He looks like a newsreader. In his brightly lit studio, he looks like someone who is informed; someone I should listen to; someone I should trust.

I know he's a hateful bigot. I know that he is a greater coward than Alex Jones, and that's saying something. I know that he preaches a brand of Christianity that is almost entirely barbarous. I know these things.

But there's that suit.

And because of the suit, and the fact that it has knocked me ever so slightly off balance, a small, credulous, childlike part of my brain asks me: Are you sure? Are you sure he's a primitive, barbarous man? Aren't you maybe being unfair? Are you sure you're not just misunderstanding him? Because look! He's wearing a suit! He's on a screen, in your house, like Riaan Cruywagen or Christiane Amanpour or Stephen Colbert. Are you sure the fault doesn't lie with you? Are you sure he's wrong? What if he's, well, not right, exactly, but less wrong than you think?

If only Americans didn't speak English. If only, like in the Bronze Age, messianic cult leaders like Rick Wiles wore rat pelt loincloths and necklaces made of desiccated goat penises. If only they didn't wear suits. If only modern Nazis wore black uniforms and caps with silver skulls on them, and not football jerseys or floral Hawaiian shirts. If only sin-sniffing thought-police wore trench-coats emblazoned with party insignia, or the robes of an inquisitor, rather than hoodies embroidered with the name of their university. If only capitalist hypocrites wore monocles and top hats, not red overalls with 'EFF' embroidered on them. If only pirates brandished bloody hooks instead of business cards saying 'CEO' and 'Chartered Accountant' and 'Solicitor'.

But everybody wears a disguise these days, and no matter how wary you are, disguises work, and before you know it the cult leader and the Nazi and the hypocrite and the pirate are through the door.

I don't know the strange sequence of events that carried Rick Wiles out of his cultural cave on the other side of the world and onto my computer. But I do know that he got there, with astonishing ease, to warn me about soul-sucking hamburgers.

Just as global trade carried the plague everywhere, so the internet has destroyed the protection that privacy, anonymity and distance have always provided. Bad, irrational, ignorant, hateful people can demand as much of our attention as more benign ones.

And because we haven't yet developed an immunity to the most basic disguise of all – how people look – they will continue to catch us off guard, and make us wonder, just for a second, if they're right.

I don't know how we safeguard ourselves against this terrible hole in our defences. I don't know how we stop equating cloth hanging off our bodies in certain configurations to success or failure as human beings, believing that someone in a cassock and white collar is automatically good and someone in low-hanging trousers is almost certainly wicked.

Nervous public speakers are urged to picture their audience naked. There is a certain logic to this: strip people of their lying clothes – those ensembles of stitched or glued rags which claim, so loudly and powerfully, that the wearer is powerful or intelligent or rich or intimidating – and you are less likely to be overwhelmed by projections and assumptions. Personally I've always found this very hard work: one is so busy configuring the specifics (a pot-belly there, a left breast slightly larger than the right, a single varicose vein on an angle over in the second row) that it's easy to lose one's thread and become even more nervous.

Mainly, though, I cannot in good conscience urge you to imagine Rick Wiles naked. It would definitely strip away a lot of pretence, but at what cost?

It seems crazy that we should need to develop psychological strategies to keep the likes of Rick Wiles out of our heads. It should be obvious that certain people or ideas are toxic. And, to be fair, sometimes it is.

The trouble is, mostly it's not. It's not because we're stupid or gullible. It's just what we are: a social animal, easily agitated by noises in its head, still trying to make sense of the recent, startling changes of the agricultural revolution 4 000 years ago, and now suddenly asked to incorporate quantum physics and Kim Kardashian into its worldview. We are the excitable, gregarious, violent, self-deluding, brain-fart-having simian that has decided that footballers should earn thousands of times more than nurses and police officers; that what we urgently need are self-driving cars rather than mass public transport systems; that the politicians who tell the best lies are the ones we should vote for.

It has become fashionable to bemoan our resistance to facts and closed-mindedness. But I don't think that's the problem. I think we're far too open to each other. This was probably a good thing when it came to our evolution. Being eager to share and believe information, whether it was hard data or supernatural hallucinations, kept us informed of the whereabouts of tar-pits and murder-cats and made sure we didn't anger the gods by engaging in too much incest or eating of rotten food.

Now, however, one of the traits that made us the dominant species on the planet – this openness to new ideas, whether based in reality or cooked up in a fevered brain – comes with a downside. That downside is Rick Wiles and *The Real Housewives of Orange County* and Flat Earthers being interviewed by reputable news sources.

Some people are more resistant to bad information, but I don't believe anyone is entirely immune, especially not those people who confidently insist that they have a foolproof bullshit detector. (Whenever I meet someone loudly denouncing conspiracy theory and declaring all humans to be gullible idiots, I know they are seconds away from insisting I read the collected works of some howling backwoods snake-oil salesman who, they insist, really knows his stuff.)

So what's the solution?

We can't switch off the internet or stop reading, but what we can do is ask ourselves a simple, reasonable question: are they kin?

After all, that's how they've presented themselves. That's what they're asking us to accept: that we and they are simpatico; that they have something of value to tell us, because they are like us, and we are like them, and our fates are intertwined.

But is it true? Are they family? Are they friends? Are they the sorts of people who might become family or friends? No? Then what do they really want, and why aren't they getting to the part about money more quickly and honestly?

Perhaps, when confronted by Bronze Age prophets, a Bronze Age response is required. We can't keep them from walking up to our city gates and announcing that they have a beautiful, enormous statue of a wooden horse for us, but we can keep the gates firmly shut, stand up on the walls, and wonder why they're not giving their lovely horse to their real friends and family somewhere else.

And if we're still not sure, well, we can always call down to them and ask if they like their meat done rare, medium or in a test tube. We'll know the truth soon enough.

Still. If only they didn't wear suits.

Chapter 4

How to Cook a Nightmare Apocalypse Information Quagmire

'Have you read *The Da Vinci Code*?'

In 2005, when people asked you that question it was usually pulsating with the sort of breathless, delicious shame of someone at an orgy asking you if you want to play Nancy Pelosi to their Donald Trump. Two years after its publication, Dan Brown's breakout thriller had transcended pop culture and was a full-blown religious crisis, with its own cardinal, a certain Tarcisio Bertone, appointed by the Vatican to run a one-man inquisition against the book.[3]

On that particular morning, however, the person asking me if I'd read the novel was asking for much more practical reasons: Jeremy Boraine, a charming and shrewd publisher then with Penguin SA, wanted me to bang out a spoof of *The Da Vinci Code* for the Christmas market that year. I obliged, and *The De Villiers Code* – a silly book that was enormous fun to write – sold very well.

---

3 I don't believe in miracles, but just before Bertone started telling Catholics that the book was 'rotten food' and a 'sack full of lies', it had sold 18 million copies. Four years later, it had sold 80 million. Truly, God works in mysterious ways.

Before I go on, it is important for me to tell you how silly it was.

In this version of the chase towards an earth-shattering secret, symbologist and savant Christmas Cobra Langa and his assistant, the beautiful Stienie Labuschagne, follow a series of clues across a minefield of South African clichés. Pitted against them are the assassin Victor Verster (a very pale white bloke who suffers from debilitating sunburn), the shadowy Bishop Aringarosi, and someone called The Teacher, who is a teacher. The big secret turns out to be a wax replica of Cecil John Rhodes' penis. The De Villiers of the title refers to almost nothing: I thought 'De Villiers' was a good local version of 'Da Vinci' and then promptly forgot to include it in the book, eventually shoe-horning it into one paragraph near the end when our heroes find a clue leading them to a Dutch Reformed church in a fictitious De Villiers Street.

I cannot stress enough that it was a silly, silly book.

For some, it was too silly. A lawyer from Mpumalanga wrote to my publisher to explain that buying my book was the worst mistake he had ever made. I would argue that this was a case of literary Parys Poepstring: I mean, what was the guy expecting from a book whose back cover describes the author as 'the most important literary figure to emerge from Kenilworth in the last four hundred years'?

But then things got properly weird.

It started with another letter to my publisher. This letter also expressed shock and disappointment. But where Mpumalanga's pre-eminent literary critic and non-reader of blurbs had been horrified by the contents, this person was objecting to the book's very existence. How, she asked, had a reputable company like Penguin failed to recognise such an obvious copy of *The Da Vinci Code*? What disastrous series of events had led to Penguin actually publishing such a shameful piece of plagiarism?

Now, I would have understood if this letter was written by someone who lived in America and had therefore never encountered irony. But this was a South African and, apparently, someone who had read books before. She knew what plagiarism was and that it was wrong, which in itself put her ahead of many of the students I lectured in the English department at UCT. She knew that publishers are supposed to be arbiters of taste and quality. At the very least, she knew how to look up the postal address of Penguin SA.

I wasn't so much much offended as fascinated. How, I wondered, did her planet look, and just how alarming must this one seem to her? I imagined her outrage every time she picked up a dictionary and discovered anew that thousands and thousands of words had been stolen from the books of hard-working novelists, lumped together in one long list and re-sold by those mercenary monsters at Oxford and Cambridge.

This strangeness, however, was soon forgotten as I received some wonderful news: *The De Villiers Code* was going to be translated and published in Romania. Penguin SA had even been sent a mocked-up cover of the new edition, they told me, and were emailing it over right away. I clicked on the attachment with shaking fingers, and there it was: my name, in gothic lettering, over an extremely muscular male arm, hairless and glistening with oil, flexing a very large bicep on which was tattooed the Mona Lisa.

I had to admit that it was a fantastically good cover for my book, if my book had been about piping hot sex in the gay clubs of Bucharest. But my book wasn't about piping hot sex in the gay clubs of Bucharest, and if anyone in Romania had actually read it before they expressed interest to Penguin SA, they might have saved both of us a great deal of disappointment. Because, of course, someone eventually got past page two and plans for a Romanian edition suddenly evaporated.

So now I knew: just because someone buys books, or, indeed, publishes them, you can't assume they actually read them.[4]

And then, in 2012, that aliterate trajectory reached its logical conclusion.

Now, at the risk of repeating myself, I need to tell you again that *The De Villiers Code* is a silly book. If you haven't read it, just imagine the Ron Howard film of *The Da Vinci Code* but instead of Tom Hanks, Audrey Tatou and Ian McKellen racing around Europe, it's the cast of *Poena is Koning* poking at the Salad Valley in the Thunder Eagle Spur in Brakpan. Proust it is not.

Which is why, while googling myself one day, I was intrigued to read the following:

'Tom Eaton's The De Villiers Code . . . is a satire directed against the TRC's epidemic search for the truth: Susan de Villiers is the name of the editor of the five volumes of the "findings" of the TRC.'

This was a genuine surprise for me. Until that moment I had honestly had no idea that my novel was a satire directed against the TRC's epidemic search for the truth, or that I had been thinking of Susan de Villiers when I named it. Naturally I had to know more, but this would have required me to buy a very long anthology of academic essays called *Trauma, Memory and Narrative in the Contemporary South African Novel*, which sounds like pretty much the worst possible weekend one could buy oneself, and so I chose to

---

4 This was confirmed to me somewhat spectacularly a few years ago when I found myself at a book launch in Cape Town. The publisher was talking to her newest author about the book being launched that evening, and gushily revealed that she *hadn't read more than a fragment of the manuscript before she'd agreed to publish the book*. She was, however, very enthusiastic about the final product, which she soon made clear she still hadn't read by saying: 'You managed to write so *much* about your topic!' And you thought it was only naughty schoolchildren doing book reports on books they haven't read who say 'Well, it's got lots of words.'

know less. All I can tell you is that this revelation was produced by one Ewald Mengel of the English department at the University of Vienna, and that he did, in fact, read the book: he provides an oddly specific plot summary in the paragraph after the one I've quoted above.

Which is why I still can't explain how he arrived at his revelation or why he didn't bother emailing me to check if he was somewhere in the ballpark with his whole 'epidemic search' hypotheses. Perhaps he had already moved on to his next projects: an exploration of Thomas the Tank Engine as a critique of the class violence inherent in the industrialisation of Britain in the first half of the twentieth century, and an analysis of the Famous Five as a meta-narrative for celebrity culture.[5]

It was funny, but it did raise a fairly sobering question: if even professional scholars, trained for years in the arts of comprehending words on a page, can misread a text so spectacularly, or just make stuff up and hope nobody notices, then what hope is there for the billions of ordinary, amateur readers? As we all try to tread water in an ever-rising tide of information surging up around our chins, will we sink or swim?

The short answer is that we're rapidly going down for the third time, weighed down by technology, political trends and deep human vulnerabilities, dragged under into this flood of word manipulation and confusion.

Then again, perhaps that's the wrong metaphor. Floods are natural phenomena, and what we've been tipped into is more like a cauldron of poisonous soup, cooked up by a particularly malicious chef. It is a broth made according to a very specific recipe, the sort of thing you might find on page 666 of *Satan's Cookbook* . . .

---

5 These are jokes but they are also really good topics for a PhD, so if you're an English postgrad please call me to arrange payment.

Nightmare Apocalypse Information Quagmire

Ideal for a light supper with a few friends, or a more formal dinner in which you hope to roll back the gains of the Enlightenment and plunge us all into a hellscape of superstition, paranoid credulity, self-righteous ignorance and sectarian violence.

Ingredients: politicians, sociopathic tech bros, media moguls, money, 7 billion human brains

Cooking time: ± one generation

Serves: the 0.1 per cent

METHOD:

1. Democratise publishing!

Invent a technology called 'the internet' that takes publishing out of the hands of priests, kings, academics, captains of industry and news editors and places it in the eager hands of billions of people. Watch the gatekeepers of knowledge in their ivory towers tremble and flee before the awesome power of a true publishing democracy, as the citizens of the earth are given the power to read, write and broadcast the ideas that matter to them most: cats, pornography, photographs of food, and blog posts proving the moon landings were faked, the earth is flat and that lizard people run global finance.

2. Make it free!

They say the best things in life are free, but you're not elitist: it's time to make the worst things in life free, too.

If you made your 'internet' properly in Step 1, it should already be fermenting and starting to fizz with millions upon millions of tiny, spore-like forums, chat groups, sex tapes, blog posts and cat pictures. This fungus is a free-for-all that is also, coincidentally, free for all. (Be careful not to add too much heat just yet: you don't want a Dot Com Bubble to form in your mixture.)

Encourage the fermentation to expand so that people start associating the 'internet' with free stuff.

To speed up this process, start stirring in advertising that pays for content so that users don't have to. Keep stirring until access to free content stops feeling too good to be true, as if someone has accidentally left the bank vault open, and starts feeling like the natural order of things. The more advertising you add, and the less intrusive it is, the faster you will break the connection between product and payment and the sooner you can start making people feel entitled to free information or entertainment. You'll know you're succeeding when it becomes socially acceptable for people to talk about how many films or books they have recently stolen, even if conversations involve self-absolving euphemisms like 'downloading', 'sharing' and 'PDF version', as if the PDF version of a book is one that somehow exists independently of copyright law and commerce.

First prize, however, is when people reach a stage of entitlement in which they become disgruntled or feel offended if you ask them to pay for content.

To know if you're reaching that stage, check your mixture for little blobs like Hugh. Hugh used to shout at me on Facebook every week. Every week, whenever I posted the link to one of my columns, there was Hugh, shouting. And what Hugh shouted was always the same thing.

'Paywall!' Just that. 'Paywall!'

It was, I think, part reproach to me, part warning to other readers, and it made me wonder if Hugh's life was an endless series of outrages and disappointments. I pictured him, puce with rage, holding aloft a small bag of treats at a supermarket till, yelling his warning to other shoppers: 'Paywall! These muffins are behind a paywall!' I imagined him storming into his doctor's office, banging down an account from his medical aid and roaring, 'Why didn't you tell me you were behind a paywall? A *paywall*, doctor!'

But of course those were absurd imaginings, because people only expect free things if those things can be downloaded via the internet. If you told your spouse you were going to steal a product from Woolworths that cost R50 to produce, they would be alarmed. If you told them you were planning to steal a film that cost $100 million to produce, they would make popcorn.

Right. On with the stew.

If you've completed this step correctly, you should start seeing certain publishers rise to the top and others sink down and boil away into nothing. This all depends on how much advertising you've stirred into the mix: publishers with more advertising can offer more free content, which attracts more people, which attracts more advertising. The more advertising that goes to the biggest publishers, the less goes to smaller ones.

And there they are! Facebook and Google, rising up like two beautiful dumplings made of free stuff and pure evil, growing bigger and bigger as they suck in all the advertising money in the pot! And there go all those other publishers, including your city's last reputable newspaper, sinking away into oblivion! Well done!

In Step 1 you democratised publishing, taking it out of the hands of a few hundred unelected, unaccountable, secretive millionaires. In Step 2, you have now put it in the hands of a few dozen unelected, unaccountable, secretive billionaires. Thanks to our embrace of democracy and the choices offered by a free market, just over a quarter of all humans have their news-reading and content-consuming habits dictated by Mark Zuckerberg.

Viva la zombie revolucion!

3. Shrink attention spans!

You're still reading? Well, we'll soon change that!

It's time to render the human attention span right down into a delicious little nothing; just a froth of distraction sitting delicately on a *jus* of dissatisfaction.

Fortunately, if you've made your internet properly, this should be happening by itself. Thanks to the medium of a computer screen, the human brain should already be physically altering: new studies suggest that babies exposed to too much screen time fail to develop the parts of the brain that deal with learning and language.

If, however, you can't wait for a new generation of screen-addled, dead-eyed thumb-twitchers to mature, try more traditional brain-shrinking methods like five-second soundbites taken out of context, clickbait headlines, frantic editing of all visual media, thumping soundtracks over all moving images, and social media platforms that encourage people to fight with each other but give them only 120 characters to do it in, just to really pump that rage up into the red zone. To top it all off, throw in generous helpings of 'persuasive design', a dirty little spice recently admitted to by Silicon Valley supervillains who have, it turns out, been using our own brain chemistry to keep us clicking away.[6]

Don't be discouraged if people still insist on reading a whole tweet before reacting. Persevere, and you, too, will experience the majesty of Zero Per Cent Mental Effort as I often do when I post a column on Facebook and then watch the comments unfolding below.

Consider, for example, the responses to a column I wrote about Woolworths apparently helping itself to someone else's design for

---

6 Swiping on your smartphone, whether to check for emails, refresh Twitter or to reject a Tinder date, fires up exactly the same part of your brain that gets excited by slot machines in a casino.

a baby carrier. In this column, I mentioned that Woolworths had already been accused of nicking a sunbird motif for a cushion cover and had been sued by Frankie's Soft Drinks for an alarmingly similar range of sodas. I also wondered which Woolworths executives, specifically, had signed off on the idea of stealing other people's ideas.

Someone kicked off the comments on Facebook with a general objection to Woolworths, and then it was business as usual:

> Commenter #2: 'They've been caught out before, with the Sunbird saga . . .'
>
> Me: 'Yep, I mention this in the column.'
>
> Commenter #4: 'What I want is the names of the people who keep making the decisions to steal designs . . .'
>
> Me: 'Indeed. As I write in the column.'
>
> Commenter #5: 'Don't forget the Frankie's Soft Drinks that Woolworth's copied.'
>
> Me: 'Nope, I didn't forget them. It's in the column.'
>
> Commenter #2 again: 'I'm not subscribed so I could only read half of it, sorry! Did you mention Frankie's Old Fashioned cooldrinks too? Similar scenario.'
>
> Me: 'I did indeed mention Frankie's in the column. And in the comment directly above this one.'

This is what you're aiming for.

If you can make people so disoriented, anxious and frantic to blurt out their feelings that they don't read past the headline before commenting, that's good. If you can make them unashamed of admitting it, because it's become perfectly normal for people to engage in debates about texts they haven't read, then you're doing very well. But if they're not even bothering to read the previous comment, if they're unwilling to roll their eyes upwards by one degree to see if anyone else has already offered the same two cents, then you have essentially arrived at a point where everyone is jamming celery stalks in their ears and screaming 'Me! Me! Me!', and you are well on the way to making the perfect Nightmare Apocalypse Information Quagmire.

4. Discredit experts and dissolve facts!

While you're doing the first two steps, heat a pan, and, using a generous amount of snake-oil, make the public suspicious and eventually dismissive of expertise.

If you're on the political right, condemn the findings of experts as a snobbish insult to the common-sense beliefs of good, honest, traditional, God-fearing people who tell it like it is. Endlessly remind the public that expertise is a toxic by-product of the knowledge industry – the Sodom of Academe – which, as everyone knows, has been hijacked by rabid social justice warriors, virtue signallers and snowflakes.

The Republican Party in the United States is an especially fine chef to emulate in this regard. Consider, for example, adding a pinch of Donald Trump's Prime Handmaiden, Kellyanne Conway, or a soupçon of Republican congressman from Texas, Louie Gohmert. In 2019, when three law professors testified before the House that Trump had committed impeachable offences, Conway decided to focus her rage on Professor Pamela Karlan, who had apparently broken the first rule of Stepford Wives Club by going and getting three degrees from Yale. Addressing the White House press corps the next day, Conway scolded: 'If you went to work today to manicure nails, to manicure lawns, if you went to work with a jackhammer or a welding machine or mechanic's tools or a carpentry belt, and not three degrees from Yale, that woman yesterday looks her nose down at you (sic). She thinks that you are less than her, and I have had it.'

If, however, you want a simpler, more basic condiment – the salt of the earth, its fans would insist – Gohmert offers you plenty of bang for your idiocy-inducing buck. Surrounded by a posse of good old-fashioned commonsensical folks, Gohmert cut right to the chase as he tried to vaccinate American motherhood against producing a plague of experts 20 years hence, telling CSPAN: 'All I got to say is, if you love America, mommas, don't let your babies grow up to go to Harvard or Stanford law school.'

Of course, it's not only the political right that wants to obliterate expertise. Hitler might have killed a good number of intellectuals but when it comes to discrediting, framing, jailing, banishing, torturing or flat-out murdering experts, nobody has come close to leftist godfathers Josef Stalin and Mao Zhedong. But times have changed. The modern leftist can't just murder experts. You'll have to use your words. Which is a problem since the left's penchant for pompous verbiage doesn't translate well into easily digestible soundbytes. Still, you should find fertile soil in which to plant the idea that expertise should be treated with extreme suspicion since it might be a Trojan horse stuffed full of old white men, and that therefore any knowledge not produced in the last 24 hours by a collective of empaths must be assumed to be an elitist, oppressive lie. Question the legitimacy of expertise in general, perhaps suggesting that it is a product of structural privilege rather than a reflection of an individual's actual ability. Make it clear that many so-called experts are, in fact, quasi-intellectual cuckoos who got to where they are by keeping much more talented and worthy people out of those positions, and that expertise is therefore a commodity that can be bought, like Saudi oil or blood diamonds. Also, you want to be creating a subtle, unconscious idea that expertise is a violation of our basic human right not to be an expert, and that it is therefore a form of violence.

Whichever way you go, let this simmer for about 10 years, and watch in delight as left and right merge and unite around a new populist principle best described by science fiction maestro Isaac Asimov, whereby democracy comes to mean that 'my ignorance is just as good as your knowledge', or, as Carl Sagan put it, we are 'unable to distinguish between what feels good and what's true'.

If you've completed this step correctly, you should be able to see trust evaporating and blowing away like steam. This is excellent: it means that people are not only becoming suspicious of expertise but are starting to doubt the existence of facts in general. The presidents of powerful countries will talk about 'alternative facts', as if those are actual things. The presidents of more insignificant countries will gaslight on a smaller scale, saying that they never met anyone who died of AIDS.

Once everyone is rushing away from the library and towards the nursery, you're ready to . . .

5. Hit them right in the childhood!

About ten years ago I was head writer of a website called Hayibo, or, as it proudly claimed, South Africa's second-best source of made-up news after the SABC.

We called it satire but a lot of the time it wasn't. Sometimes it was snark. Sometimes it was vaudeville. Sometimes it was just a mess. Some stories were playful and kind, a few were snide and bitter. But all, almost without exception, were very obviously not true. We broke the news that Liewe Heksie was emigrating to Perth and that excavations for the new Gautrain were wreaking havoc with Johannesburg's communities of Gummi Bears. We quoted spokespeople with names like Poepies McFartface.

And yet, every few weeks one of our obviously impossible, eminently silly stories would be believed. When we wrote, for example, that Jeannie D had been arrested after trying to do a *Top Billing* insert at Nkandla, some of her fans were so alarmed that she had to tweet that it was just a silly fabrication. During the London riots of 2011, we wrote that the African Union was going to send peacekeeping troops, food aid and basic oral hygiene to the desperate people of Britain. A few days later, I found the story being discussed – and worried about – on a forum used by commodities traders: how, one of them wondered, would a sudden influx of AU millet affect prices in the UK?

Fake news had not yet been weaponised. We didn't know the appalling damage it would do in the decade to come. There was no reason to be alarmed by these credulous responses to our obviously silly stories. And yet I started feeling increasingly unsettled by them. People sometimes asked me if I enjoyed 'tricking' readers. I absolutely did not, and the more it happened, the less I enjoyed it.

But it was only in Hayibo's final months that I understood why my unease had turned into a kind of morbid despair.

I had started suspecting a horrible truth: that your website can be festooned with stories about a beached pod of SABC executives being euthanised or Schabir Shaik being rushed to the spa for an emergency massage, but if the website looks a bit like the BBC or CNN, has no-nonsense headlines and little rectangular photographs of people or places, and has quotation marks around words allegedly spoken by spokespeople, *you can write literally anything and a stunning number of people will believe it.*

I'm not even talking about the fake news that people believe because they want it to be true. That's a different story. I'm talking about a much more instinctive response, which happens before the words even reach the brain and the brain starts imposing its prejudices on them.

My time with Hayibo.com showed me that the power of fake news isn't about what the words say. It's about how the words look.

Long before we can read, we have started figuring out what words look like, forming a visual relationship with them. For example, we know that large pages with a few words on them and lots of pictures are stories for children. Small pages with endless rectangles of small words on them, and no pictures, are stories for adults. Words of different sizes, printed on thin, crinkly paper, with photographs of smiling people, are magazines, which seem to be somewhere between stories for children and stories for adults. Tiny, endless words with numbers scattered between them, that get read by a man in a robe once a week, are special words, appearing in a holy book, which is a very long story but is also not a story because stories aren't true except . . . well, we'll figure it out later. And words that are printed on large sheets of very papery paper, in long columns, well, those words are news.

And news isn't a story.

Because news is true.

I mean, it's wearing a suit, right?

Unless we have been raised by a wild-eyed, gun-hoarding, tin-foil-hat-wearing, beard-scratching prepper in a homemade bunker, or a professor of media studies, which is pretty much the same thing, we begin our experience of reading steadfast in the knowledge that words that look like news – with a headline about current events, a picture depicting said events, and quotation marks around certain banal statements – are as true as everything Mom and the President says, as real as Santa Claus, and as trustworthy as the policeman and banker on the corner.

It's why fake news has been a form of entertainment for well over a century.

The newspaper business was still relatively young when Mark Twain started sending it up. Newsreels, likewise, had only been around for 20 years when MGM produced its Wataphony Newsreel, pioneering the trope of deadpan, absurd commentary read over real footage. Thirty years later, the British 'satire boom' saw the likes of Peter Cook, Alan Bennett and David Frost turn fake news into an art form, while the Monty Python lads took it to its illogical conclusion, parodying the earnestness and comedic arbitrariness of journalistic tropes by having interviewers go off the rails, vox pops inserts in which idiots admired Hitler's legs, and finally dragging a German newsreader into an Alpine lake as she continued, professionally but vainly, to read the day's headlines.

It was funny, but only now, in our post-truth world, are we realising why.

It was funny because it was iconoclastic, and it was iconoclastic because an absolute truth was being teased and played with. We laughed because our deadly serious, entirely credulous inner five year old was being shocked and scandalised; and the wider its little eyes got, the more we laughed. Someone dressed as a newsreader, saying silly falsehoods to camera in an earnest, BBC voice? You might as well send up the New Testament. Which is, of course, what Monty Python did next.

In other words, I don't believe that our relationship with news has anything to do with logic, reason, critical insight or even literacy. Instead, I believe it is an entirely emotional relationship, formed in early childhood. This makes it extremely volatile, and very easy to explode. In short, a perfect ingredient in your recipe.

All it takes is a few fake news stories, and one or two genuine screw-ups by legitimate news sources, and people will start reacting like hurt five year olds whose trust has been destroyed. Instead of saying, 'These stories aren't true,' they'll blurt out, 'No stories are true!' Instead of saying, 'It is possible to curate a selection of generally trustworthy news sources', they'll cry, 'You can't believe anything you read!'

Which means they are now primed and ready as you . . .

6. Separate them into thought-camps!

For this step you'll need a well-greased muffin tray, but if you don't have one of those you can always just use humanity's ancient love of rigid, ultimately murderous us-and-them binaries.

In fact, most people will separate themselves for you, climbing into various ideological muffin tins of their own accord with very little encouragement required. This is because we enjoy gathering in like-minded groups, whether it is to pray, have orgies, watch people kicking a ball (which is how most people have orgies), or commit genocide.

The tricky part of this stage, therefore, is not separating people but making sure they stay separated: to remove any possibility of them finding consensus, common ground, or even just learning how to have a civil debate.

If you're on the right, you can help this segregation by talking about respecting tradition or giving people the freedom to mix with their own kind. If you're on the left, tell people to stay in their lane. Both work wonders at removing the potential for confusing or upsetting conversations and thoughts, or, indeed any conversations or thoughts at all.

Helpful hint: if for whatever reason your mix is still disappointingly unified and keeps trying to find common ground and shared humanity, sprinkle in some spicy false dichotomies or divisive binaries. Explain to people that there is no middle ground when it comes to your particular ideology: they are either with you or against you, and being in the middle is an especially cowardly way of being against you.

For example: if you see people starting to find some point of agreement as they grope towards an idea of a more workable and just economic system than the current one, explain to them that they either have to support unregulated capitalism, in which unions are smashed and wealth is a reflection of human worth, or a socialist apocalypse like in Venezuela.

If that doesn't get them going, the Generational War definitely will. To assassinate that particular archduke, simply repeat, as often and loudly as you can, that Millennials are entitled snowflakes who spend all their money on avocado toast and then whine about being poor, while Baby Boomers deliberately set fire to the planet and are selfishly squatting on jobs, housing and inheritances by cynically refusing to commit mass suicide.

Note: it is very important, if you go this route, not to mention capitalism or human nature. If you're going to back the Millennials and slag off Boomers, you should endlessly imply that all humans were living in perfect harmony with nature and each other until 1945, at which point a diabolical generation was conceived which, even as it gestated evilly in the womb, invented both industrialisation and the concept, hitherto unknown, of self-interest.

On the other hand, if you're going to slag off Millennials and support the Boomers, explain that Boomers' views on the youth are extremely accurate and are definitely nothing like the views of the previous 6 000 generations of elderly humans who have despaired about the fragility and entitlement of the young. Those guys were all wrong, but the Boomers are right.

If you're going to slag off both, because you're one of the media companies that invented this intergenerational feud to provide you with an almost infinite supply of clicks, well, you already know what you're doing so just keep on keeping on.

But whichever approach you've taken, it's time to . . .

7. Get Medieval!

Remember, your goal here is to undo the gains of the Enlightenment and to drag humanity back to a time before reason, informed debate, evidence and the scientific method. Which means you're ready to add another vital ingredient: white-hot self-righteousness.

Convince people that every conversation about ideas is actually about their own moral virtue – that their thoughts and beliefs are a reflection of their own personal goodness or wickedness rather than a reflection of which country and class they were born into, how they were parented and educated, and how they've tried to make sense of those random variables – and watch in awe as society begins to judge information not as true or false, or essential or peripheral, but as righteous or wicked.

In this new medieval world, people who disagree with you are not just ignorant or mistaken: since you are righteous and worthy, basic logic dictates that anyone who disagrees with you is literally evil and probably wants to eat your baby. Monsters!

The distinction between facts, claims, beliefs, fantasies and lies should now be evaporating in a hissing, spitting ball of self-righteous subjectivity.

And thanks to this shift, all written or spoken words can now be one of only two things: gospel, or the devil's lies.

Where once people agreed to disagree, or argued and debated and then stayed friends, all are now prophets in the wilderness, thundering 'Blasphemer!' at each other as they implore their One True God – Donald Trump, Julius Malema, Helen Zille, E! Entertainment News, it doesn't matter – to smite down the heathen and hasten the apocalypse. 'Behold! She has been seen reading *The Daily Vox* in a glade on midsummer's eve! Burn her!' 'See! He consorts with familiars who subscribe to *Rapport*! Shun him!'

What you want is a state in which overreaction is the only

reaction. The only response to anything should be anger. Not transformative anger, mind you. You don't want that. You don't want a revolution. You want the opposite. You want anaesthetising anger. Counterbalanced anger.

And that's the beauty of this medieval variety of anger. Because when the reaction to everything is an overreaction, all reactions become the same, and that means they cancel themselves out. Someone can say, 'Climate change requires a radical change in how we consume resources' and someone else can say, 'Slavery should be brought back', and both will be howled down at roughly the same volume (11, the default setting on social media), which will make them sound equally important, equally untrue and therefore equally true; and because there is no clear winner or loser, our exhausted, deafened society will unconsciously call it a draw.

At this point, you've followed each step perfectly. Even if a few people still want to debate the veracity of claims, facts no longer matter. Experts have been silenced or sidelined. Which means that Russia Today, Fox News or the EFF Twitter feed can claim to be as trustworthy as Reuters or the AmaBhungane, and that claim cannot be debunked because nobody trusts the debunking process. Evidence no longer exists. All that remains is belief. And who cares what the critics of your One True Gospel believe when the only thing that matters is what *you* believe?[7]

If you're doing this right, you will see people start using their

7 A handy hint: if you see someone whose Twitter biography includes the phrase 'Opinions are my own', do not point out to them that their opinions, like the opinions of almost every human on the planet, are not their own but are instead a huge amalgamation of the opinions of other people. If you're going to make people properly medieval, it is vital that you nurture this idea that people thought up their terrible ideas all by themselves so that they feel extra passionate about them.

made-up facts as a kind of supernatural protection against the forces of evil crowding around them, a bit like hanging garlic around your neck to protect you from vampires. It won't matter to them if the facts are true or not. In fact, they might even know that the facts are lies. After all, garlic stinks like hell. But it's better than being attacked by imaginary shape-shifters who want to suck your blood.

I've seen this digital garlic waved around on Facebook surprisingly often. Some convert will post a piece of clearly fake news, proclaiming that a politician they loathe has said or done something impossibly outrageous. Without exception, these fake news reports are the stuff of medieval rumour, only a few degrees removed from accusations of witchcraft and Jews poisoning wells.

Soon, someone will post a comment under the article, pointing out that it is fake and asking the original poster to delete it. And that's when the garlic really starts being swung.

If the original poster is in a philosophical mood, he or she will respond by saying that the politician in question *could* have said something like this, and, indeed, probably *would* say it at some stage, and that the story is therefore true in its basic, general gist. Even though the story is entirely fictional, it is used as empirical evidence, much as a medieval monk might hold up a fragment of a dog's femur and claim that it is St Paul's toe and therefore irrefutable proof of the monk's holiness.

A great many people who post fake news, however, are not in philosophical mood. They have not posted their particular fake story in order to share information or discuss ideas. They have posted it to test the faith of assembled congregants. To this kind of person, a request to delete patently fake news is proof of sin. It is like stepping forward at a witch trial and asking to see evidence: it is proof that you are not only an enemy of the original poster, but probably in league with the accused. To such people – and there are millions and millions of them on Facebook – fake news is not information. It is a weapon of the inquisition. Facts do not matter. All that matters is that the post angers their enemies and encourages their fellow believers. It can contain every bigoted lie and dangerous scientific untruth known to humanity, but if it is landing emotional blows on people the poster fears or dislikes, then it is an instrument of righteousness, and therefore truer than the most fundamental laws of physics.

You're almost there. Your Nightmare Apocalypse Information Quagmire is just about ready. But before you can serve it to the applause of your oligarch friends, and watch in delight as humanity runs screaming back towards the cave, you need to add the final, magic ingredient . . .

8. Money!

The beauty of this recipe is that anyone can make it in its most basic form. Whether you're the CEO of a toxic and dysfunctional corporation, the despotic chairperson of a tuckshop committee or just a passionate amateur in your mom's basement, waging a war against the experts and society who haven't recognised you as the living reincarnation of Thor and Nietsche, you can make a respectable information quagmire in the privacy of your own Facebook page.

A full-blown Nightmare Apocalypse Information Quagmire, however, demands a scale well beyond most amateurs. Anyone can cook up a dish of half-truth, outright lies, distorted knowledge, unabashed ignorance, good intentions and cynical manipulation, all bubbling along in a merry broth of rancour, confusion and psychic fatigue. But to really make this recipe pop, to let it swell into every aspect of human life and balloon like a vast, pus-filled bubo, you need cash. Enormous amounts of cash.

Yes, this might cost you hundreds of millions of dollars, but trust me, it will be worth it in the end when you're all sitting in your luxurious End Times bunker in New Zealand raising a glass to the complete and final subjugation of human thought.

Whether you're going with bot farms in Eastern Europe targeting individual politicians, journalists and activists, or hiring high-profile PR firms to pump out propaganda about entire countries, money makes everything better and much, much stupider. And it works! Are you an anti-democratic strongman whose political opponents keep being forced into exile or simply disappearing? Have you banned civil society groups from criticising your policies? Have you refused to co-operate with the United Nations Subcommittee on Prevention of Torture? No problem! Just hire a firm like Racepoint, a London PR agency noted for what the *Guardian* called 'reputation-laundering', to tell the world that you're a brilliant modernising statesman and that your country is Wakanda, and soon commentators will be writing about Paul Kagame and Rwanda like starry-eyed tweens journaling about pop stars.

Best of all, thanks to steps 1 to 7, anyone who tries to point out Kagame's *kragdadige* tendencies will be branded an Afro-pessimist, or, better yet, ignored entirely because everyone is too busy watching Khloe Kardashian do a video tutorial on how to look perpetually glum about being young and rich.

Remember, when it comes to digital lobotomy, bigger is always better, especially when it comes to stamping out the last shreds of resistance. Even the best cook will find little clusters of people still trying to think for themselves. But thanks to big money, you can perform the final act of intellectual obliteration: if they can't be moved by your one or two official narratives, stun them with a thousand. Power brokers of the past had to hook people with a lure and bait. Now you can just pump a million volts through the water and watch everyone float to the top, the credulous and the critical alike, stunned into resignation.

And that's it.

Season your Nightmare Apocalypse Information Quagmire to taste, serve, and celebrate as the sun sets on modernity and the Twitter mob's torches flicker into life down in the darkness of the valley below.

• • •

I know. It's a lot, and it's depressing. But we can still politely decline to eat the shit sandwich being offered to us by the post-truth, post-literate world. More importantly, we can refuse to offer it around.

That, however, requires conscious action on our part. Whenever people worry about the Nightmare Apocalypse Information Quagmire, there are appeals for other people to do something. Governments must regulate Facebook. Media organisations must work harder to restore damaged or broken trust. These are true, but individuals need to work just as hard if they are to become readers rather than consumers.

For me, there are certain basic strategies that I try to stick to.

Firstly, I pay for some information. Subscribing or donating to a news source is not just a financial decision. It is an ideological and political statement which says that you understand that good information requires money. Money to buy experienced and skilful editors, journalists and sub-editors; to hire good lawyers to fight the endless attempts by the state and private corporations to gag them; to stay human as information is increasingly marshalled against us by armies of bots and algorithms.

Secondly, I read the nutritional information on the box, or at least the journalistic version of it. If we spent half as much time researching what we put into our eyeballs as we put in our stomachs, we'd be a lot healthier and happier. Ten minutes on Google will reveal a surprising amount of consensus about the ideological slant of the world's major news organisations. I don't care if you prefer your opinion and analysis a little right or a little left of centre. But if your favourite hard news website is Telling It Like It Is With Honest Vlad: Putin' It In Perspective and nobody has told you that it is far beyond the fringes of media respectability, it's time you found out.[8]

On current form, the most reliable (or least prone to bias or editorialising disguised as news) are Reuters, AP, NPR and, as long as it's not about Brexit or the property portfolios of Conservative MPs, the BBC. Barring the odd startling lack of judgement, the *New York Times* is also fairly solid. Al Jazeera produces superb reports on under-reported conflicts and crises, and Deutsche Welle's documentaries are magnificently thorough. At the other extreme, Fox News is what happens when blonde hair dye and weaponised Wasp entitlement seep into the human nervous system. Russia Today is an almost perfect propaganda organisation and is great to watch for entertainment value, but otherwise it's pure poison. (I continue to see people insisting that RT is a good antidote to American imperialist propaganda, which is rather like lemmings throwing themselves under a truck to debunk the myth that lemmings only ever throw themselves off cliffs.)

---

8 I concede that one's ability to research the trustworthiness of news sources is, by definition, limited by one's biases. In the same TruNews segment in which Rick Wiles explained that Alex Jones was going to have free speech banned, he also urged his followers to check the veracity of articles, presumably by using the Old Testament and the entrails of a prize hog. When you believe that Reuters is the mouthpiece of Satan and TruNews is gospel, no amount of checking is going to help.

In South Africa, I tend to gravitate towards individual journalists and commentators rather than news titles. When it comes to hard news, I trust the likes of Sam Sole, Sipho Masondo, Qaanitah Hunter, Pauli van Wyk, Karyn Maughan and Marianne Thamm. For analysis and commentary, I regularly enjoy people like Carol Paton, Max du Preez, Ferial Haffajee, Ralph Mathekga, Claire Bisseker and Peter Bruce.

Which brings me to my third strategy: being clear about the difference between news, analysis and comment. I want the first to be accurate, the second to be informed and fair, and the third to be generally informative but also elegantly and compellingly written. I understand that when it comes to comment, objectivity is a fantasy. Opinion columnists are not soothsayers: they are performers. Some are comedians. Some stand on street corners and whoop at the moon. All, however, are fundamentally entertainment, so when I choose them, I am deciding which performance I want to attend.

Fourth, I assume the absolute worst of Facebook. Even if it's just showing me pictures of kittens and updates about a rainstorm in Edenvale, I hold firm to the fact that it is the antichrist of thought. When I log on, I do it in the knowledge that I am taking a mind-altering drug specifically and deliberately cooked up to make me compulsive, compliant and credulous. There is a glimmer of hope here: Zuckerberg seems to be tiring of being a news mogul and having to deal with endless complaints from his harem of publishers. But Facebook will remain toxic for years. If you want to go and thrash around in the shark tank, feel free, but don't ever believe that Facebook is your friend or showing you anything but a wildly – and deliberately – distorted picture of the world.

Finally, I try to remember a piece of essential advice which seems to be gaining traction, but was put to me first and most succinctly by UCT academic and philosopher Jacques Rousseau. It is, simply, to be intellectually humble.

In essence, this is about admitting to myself, as often as I can manage it, that I can't always tell truth from lies or meaning from manipulation. It is about remembering that, because I am human, I have deep biases and vulnerabilities, and that what I read, and how much I believe or reject, is influenced by psychological and emotional tendencies I can't always recognise.

An example that would be familiar to most of us is confirmation bias, the deeply seductive tendency to read or believe things that confirm our view of the world while we ignore or condemn as 'stupid' or 'fake' the things that challenge or contradict that view. Indeed, in my experience when someone insists to us that So-And-So is an excellent writer, what they're often saying is that that writer regularly articulates their own beliefs in a very satisfying way. I've experienced this personally from the other side of the screen: I can write five columns criticising the ANC and a certain reader will tell me that I am a brilliant lone voice of truth, but when I criticise the DA in my next column, the same reader will tell me that I'm losing my touch and that my editor needs a word with me.

I admit that these strategies are not bulletproof. Once lost, trust – in journalists, in facts themselves – is hard to regain. Unconscious biases will always tug us this way or that: I know that I enjoy certain writers or news outlets more than others because they cover the sort of news I want covered in a way that appeals to me. But it's a start; and it's a damn sight better than lolling back in the online high chair, mouth open, eyes shut, letting Uncle Mark or Grandaddy Rupert Murdoch spoon pulp down our gullets.

I can't fix fake news. I can't put the genie back in the bottle, or restore your faith in the written or broadcast word. But before I go, I can offer you something that is increasingly rare, and therefore increasingly valuable: a piece of absolute truth. Simply, it is this: if you ever find yourself stuck in a lift with an Austrian academic who is insisting that *The De Villiers Code* is a satire directed against the TRC's epidemic search for truth, you can tell him that it just isn't. Not even a little bit.

I promise.

Chapter 5

HALTO!

This book is one of opinions rather than prescriptions. I would not presume to tell you how to live your life. I wrote it as an attempt to figure out for myself different ways of reacting to our national narratives, and in the hope that you will find in these pages some new perspectives. Perhaps even solace.

When it comes to keeping a more even keel, however, there is one strategy which has been so helpful and so surprisingly potent that I feel I would be remiss not to include it.

Known as the HALT principle, this strategy has its origins in the field of addiction and mental health treatment. Its basic idea is that certain feelings, ordinary but powerful things we all feel every day, can tip us over into states of emotional and psychological vulnerability. For addicts in recovery this might mean finding themselves exposed to thoughts or feelings that make them want to use a substance or engage in behaviour for which they've sought treatment. For people struggling with mental illness, it may manifest as an urge to avoid or derail treatment.

Given its association with the recovery process, you might assume that HALT is an acronym for some unpronounceable medical definition, but it's much simpler than that. In fact, it is its simplicity that makes the strategy so powerful. Because what HALT stands for is Hungry, Angry, Lonely and Tired.

Feeling any one of those feelings is enough to shift my mood. Should two or more coincide, I can easily lose perspective and start slouching down the rabbit hole of gloom, grumpiness, and even despair. If, however, I have the presence of mind to recognise that I am heading for said hole, then I have found it enormously helpful to HALT and to ask myself: Am I hungry? Am I angry? Lonely? Tired? Startlingly often, I answer yes to at least one of those. And once I know what the problem is, the remedy is often simple, and the result is a climb out of the hole and a return to relative equilibrium.

Of course, the challenge is that presence of mind I mentioned earlier. Anger, outrage, pessimism and despair all have the magical ability to convince me that they are not feelings but logical, reasonable, objective truths; that they are not reactions or beliefs but concrete realities. It can be difficult, especially for an opinionated person like me, to step back and say, 'Hold on, Hemingway: is the world going to hell or do you just need to have lunch?'

I should be very clear at this point: I am not suggesting that recovering addicts or people battling mental illness just need to buck up and have a snack or phone a friend and all will be well. This kind of thinking leads to the harmful and ignorant 'advice' that clinically depressed people should just cheer up or get a hobby or more exercise. HALT makes no claims as a cure or even a treatment. But it is a useful strategy for avoiding a state of vulnerability where self-destructive reactions can lie.

When I first heard about it, it seemed so simple that I think I dismissed it as patronising and somewhat infantilising, as if someone had cooked up a whole theory of self-care which focused on not running blindfolded through traffic. Well, duh, I thought. Hunger, anger, loneliness and tiredness all seemed like obvious problems that would be simple to identify. Now that I'm paying attention to them, however, I see how often that is not the case. Which is why I think it's worth lingering for a moment on each, to remember just how un-obvious these obvious triggers can be.

Hungry: For a clear, physiological state, this one can be surprisingly difficult to identify. When my blood sugar has plunged so far that I've become hangry – that short-fused sense of supreme persecution that comes when you've left hunger too long – my anger seems pure, righteous, objective and completely unconnected from something as banal as the contents of my stomach. Not recognising my basic need to eat can also spiral, as ennui slides into nihilism: the hungrier I get, the more moody I get and the less I feel like eating, because how could a banana possibly drag me back from these great, vexing questions of our time? The answer is: It can, and often does.

Angry: We South Africans are often complimented by international visitors on our sunny demeanour. We're so open! So honest! Such real, salt-of-the-earth folks who are quick to laughter and reluctant to complain.

So much for the wisdom of tourists.

To be South African is to carry anger. For many, the anger is the result of trauma. For others, anger is the inevitable result of layers and layers of stress, each one laid down by another day of pressure, fear or hardship. For some, that stress comes from the syndrome I described at the start of this book: the debilitating shock that comes from slowly realising that the place you find yourself is nothing like the place you imagined you were. I also believe that millions of South Africans carry the burden of shame with them, whether it is about their socio-economic circumstances, their sexuality, their culpability in society's ills or their role in a dysfunctional family; and shame often manifests as anger, a phenomenon perfectly described in Afrikaans as *skaam-kwaad*. (A superficial but common example: the South African driver who runs the red light, and who, when you hoot or express disapproval, explodes with rage as if you're the one endangering lives.)

South Africa carries anger the way someone might carry an enormous cyst. It's become part of us, but it's not killing us (yet), and since we're not sure how to get rid of it, we try to ignore it: a 20-kilogram ball of rage that feels almost normal.

Anger, however, doesn't even need to be the big, seething, existential kind to derail us and trip us into a vulnerable state. Sometimes it can be the fallout from a toxic boss, or the injustice of a decision going against you, or simply an argument with a friend or an unkind word from a stranger.

I have had the luxury of talking to a therapist, but sometimes the best way to alleviate anger is simply to acknowledge it; to tell a loved one, 'Yes, I'm angry. I'm fucking *furious*,' and then to talk and talk until the ember cools and becomes ash. Just don't go on Facebook. For the love of God, don't go on Facebook.

Lonely: In Steve Martin's masterful romantic/existential comedy, *LA Story*, TV weatherman Harris K Telemacher lives an apparently idyllic life in Los Angeles, a dream of manicured lawns and exclusive restaurants, a life he introduces thus: 'Let's just say I was deeply unhappy, but I didn't know it because I was so happy all the time.' Loneliness can work the same way. In a society in which we are always surrounded by people – at work, in the traffic, buying groceries, even at home with family – it can be difficult even to realise that we are lonely. But if you do feel isolated and disconnected from people, it can help to acknowledge it and try to connect with somebody, even if it's just a text message.

Tired: If acknowledging loneliness is hard, admitting to being tired can be almost impossible. The unholy union of capitalism and Calvinism has produced some particularly hideous children, but few are as pervasive and pernicious as the belief that to be tired is to be weak, and that weakness is a mortal sin that must be punished with penury and humiliation. In the movie of our lives we're all supposed to be young interns striding down Fifth Avenue, heads erect, eyes sparkling, high-fiving newspaper sellers who gaze at us admiringly. If we have a moment to relax, the myth insists, we must spend it in age-appropriate ways. This means that if we are younger than 35, we must sit on a park bench in an expensive suburb, like Hugh Grant and Julia Roberts at the end of *Notting Hill,* reading an important novel or stroking a pregnant belly. Alternatively, it is acceptable for the under-35s to sit around a bonfire on a beach, making Treasured Memories (TM). If we are older than 35, we are required to spend our quiet moments in a leather armchair, swirling a glass of cognac, listening to the crackle of the fireplace and the snore of the golden retriever. If we are older than 55, it is just – just – acceptable to spend leisure time walking hand in hand near ponds at early evening, the general fading of the light providing a touching visual metaphor for our impending death. But we are never, ever, ever allowed to feel that we want to do nothing but take off our pants, stretch out on the couch, complain loudly for ten minutes, and then fall asleep with the TV remote on our chests and a half-chewed potato chip slipping gently down our chins.

Oh, we can be burned out, or sick in bed. Those are professionally and socially permissible conditions, with their own appropriate responses. Your boss explains to a colleague in sympathetic tones that you're going through a rough patch; everyone sends a card. But if you aren't lying sobbing on your office floor, having reached your absolute, ragged limit, or aren't waving bravely out from inside an inflatable quarantine chamber, you are simply not allowed to be tired.

This is pure poison for the soul. We are all allowed to be tired, and telling your friends or family that work has disintegrated your sleep hygiene or that life is simply feeling too relentless, can bring instant relief. Fortunately, our exhausted society seems to be showing the first glimmers – or yawns – of questioning the capitalist dogma that 16-hour days are the only path to success and that you can sleep when you're dead. In 2016, A-type A-lister Arianna Huffington stepped off the hamster wheel with her bestselling *The Sleep Revolution: Transforming Your Life, One Night At A Time*, a book that will have given hundreds of thousands of red-eyed, hollow-cheeked corporate wrecks the permission they desperately needed to get some sleep. Still, the Calvinist prejudice runs deep, even in well-rested freelancers like me: in the first draft of this essay, this paragraph began: 'We are allowed to be tired, and admitting it to your friends . . .' Admitting. As if being tired is a crime!

No, the sooner we reject the pernicious belief that sleep is for the lazy and that success requires chronic sleep deficiency, the happier we'll all be. So let's shout it out together:

What are we?

Tired!

What do we want?

Sleep!

When do we want it?

Zzzzz . . .

Remembering to remember HALT – finding the objective distance to ask yourself if you feel hungry, angry, lonely or tired, and then acting on your answers – can be essential in helping us deal with a country and a world which seem to be getting hotter all the time. But if I may be so bold as to suggest an addition to those four riders of the emotional apocalypse, I believe that HALT needs to be updated with the addition of a new letter: O.

Hunger, anger, loneliness and tiredness are ancient states, as old as humanity itself; but as we evolve, so do the ways we hurt ourselves. Which is why I feel that HALT needs to become HALTO to include a new, and particularly awful state of being which has afflicted us in the last 20 years: that of being Online.

In some ways, the O in HALTO has the power to agitate and aggravate all the other states. Being online for more than an hour or two a day makes me angry. It makes me lonely. It makes me tired. It can even make me hungry: if you've ever been sucked into the internet, you will know that you can miss meals in a blur of endless scrolling and clicking. The basic premise of HALT is to look after yourself so that you don't end up in a vulnerable frame of mind that might lead to worse thoughts, actions or responses. For me, the internet – and especially social media – is a high-speed, one-way train ticket straight to the heart of that vulnerable, emotionally ragged place, working much faster and more viciously than hunger, anger, loneliness or tiredness ever could.

I know this sounds fairly luddite. In *The Salmon of Doubt*, Douglas Adams suggests that people tend to believe that any technology invented after they are 35 is 'against the natural order of things', and even though Facebook and Twitter were invented while I was in my 20s, I know I sound like someone about to smash a loom. But honestly, the longer I spend online, and the more I watch the internet spread superstition and self-righteousness, normalise bullying and break down our ability to have relationships with people we know while encouraging us to have ones with people we don't, the more I'm convinced that, barring a few obvious exceptions, the online world is a profoundly destructive place.

When I'm feeling very optimistic, I like to imagine that the people of the twenty-second century will look back at us the way we look back at smokers in the 1950s. 'Those poor wretches,' our descendants will murmur, looking at tragic scenes from the 2020s of people sucking digital poison out of their phones in search of a fleeting hit of validation or companionship. 'To think that Facebook wasn't just legal but completely unregulated! You could spend hours on it, getting picked clean by the data-scrapers and the election-buyers in return for an illusion of community and a cruel parody of conversation. And it was on their phones. Their *phones*! Can you imagine carrying a tumour like Twitter *in your pocket all the time*? Jesus wept. The poor bastards never stood a chance.'

I like to imagine that in this future, nobody will be able to access the internet without a licence, which they will only be granted after proving that they can read at the level of a 10 year old and believe that the world is a sphere and that genocide is bad. I imagine that, once a licence is awarded, going online will require the user to put on an array of sensors which monitor the buildup of toxins in the brain and body. I imagine that, once dangerous levels have been reached, the internet connection will be severed for the next 72 hours and the user legally required to go outside and take a walk and talk to actual people.

And then I wake up, and I realise that these are naïve fantasies. We will continue to slip into our internet dream, perhaps sooner than we know. In 2019, Elon Musk announced that he was months away from testing his Neuralink system, a plan to implant a chip into the human brain that would, in effect, connect it permanently to the internet. Obviously it's far too early to charge Musk for planning a crime against humanity. So far, his scheme is probably more about publicity for Tesla than digitally lobotomising human beings by replacing what remains of their minds with Buzzfeed listicles and Pewdie Pie's YouTube channel. But at some point, some billionaire with a very damaged soul will get it right, at which point we'll be done.

I am genuinely grateful that I am in middle age now and probably won't be alive when neural implants are commonplace (or compulsory) because that world will make the opium dens of the nineteenth century look as athletic and collegial as an Amish barn-raising. Films like *The Matrix* and *Cloud Atlas* show us future dystopias in which humans are farmed like battery chickens, naked and oblivious, sleeping in tanks of nutrient goop as their life force is sucked out of them. In these films, this farming process is portrayed as monstrous: the people in their goop puddles are victims, and the people doing the milking are diabolical villains. But I think this is a fairly naïve view. Because once we can plug the digital world directly into our minds and experience literally anything a computer can conjure, we'll be doing it to ourselves and paying for the privilege. We'll sign the indemnity forms, hand over all our money, and disappear into a digital dream, living extraordinary lives and accomplishing great deeds until we run out of credit and they unplug us and throw us out into the shattering reality of our actual lives. Of course, many will be able to go straight back inside thanks to the banks that will mushroom outside the dream palaces, offering loans specifically tailored to the disoriented, grief-stricken dreamers desperate to get back to a love affair or an interstellar adventure or simply the ordinary, deeply fulfilling little family they think they've lived with for the last 10 years . . .

Mercifully, this is not yet our everyday reality. It is still physically possible, and legal, to disconnect from the online world. But being able to disconnect and being able to remember to disconnect are two very different things. Which is why the O of HALTO has been so useful for me; reminding me that when the old, ratty, dissatisfied, over-stimulated, under-socialised feeling comes over me, or when I start grumbling about digital dream palaces with loan sharks outside on the pavement, it's probably time to log off, stand up, and return to the real world.

Hungry. Angry. Lonely. Tired. Online. What a minefield they can be.

May HALTO help you to tread lightly, and help you as it has helped me.

Chapter 6

A Better (After)Life for All

It happened on a Monday.

Monday, 15 March 2004, to be precise. That was when it was formally announced. *Business Day* carried the story, clearly laid out in black and white, like an edict nailed onto a great oaken door.

I'm sure many people read it but I don't think anybody took it to heart or understood what had just happened. Not when there was so much else going on on that particular Monday.

Two weeks earlier Charlize Theron had won an Oscar, and we were slowly making peace with the fact that she was now a Therrin forever and would never again be a T'rawn. A week earlier, a number of former apartheid-era special forces soldiers, now rumoured to be mercenaries, had been arrested in Equatorial Guinea and accused of planning a coup, allegedly funded by Mark Thatcher, son of Margaret, to install a president who would grant lucrative energy rights to the coup's backers. Four days earlier the world had been sickened by terror attacks in Madrid, where suicide bombers killed 193 commuters. And finally, on the Sunday morning before this particular Monday, one final controversy, albeit mercifully minor compared to the Madrid horror: something called the South African Sports Commission had told South African rugby that it would have to drop the springbok from its official emblem in favour of the king protea.

Then again, it could have been the quietest news week in a century and we still wouldn't have heard what the ANC was telling us on Monday, 15 March 2004. That's how Parys Poepstring works.

The statement was fairly succinct by the longwinded standards of the ANC. There was a bit of waffle on either end of it, but ultimately it came down to a single, luminously transparent sentence, spoken by Jacob Zuma:

> *'The ANC will rule South Africa until Jesus comes back.'*

Over the next 14 years, this article of faith was repeated many times. Sometimes it was recited straight, like the Lord's Prayer or the Hail Mary. Sometimes it came with embellishments, like illuminations in the borders of a Medieval Bible.

In 2006, for example, Zuma told *The Sowetan* that he was 'like Christ', claiming that elements in the media wanted to 'crucify' him. In 2007, he opted for the simpler version, saying that the ANC 'will be in power forever until the son of man comes back'. In 2008, he preached that 'God expects us to rule this country because we are the only organisation which was blessed by pastors when it was formed. It is even blessed in Heaven. That is why we will rule until Jesus comes back.' When he appeared at the ANC's final rally before the 2009 general election, he was greeted thus, as reported by *The Atlantic*:

> 'A young woman toward the front of the crowd, on Zuma's left, held up a handmade cross, with his image and name at the top and a message painted in uneven letters: BLACK JESUS. Zuma

> raised his head, clasped his hands together, and bowed in her direction.'

Even as late as 2018, when Zuma appeared at the Durban High Court, the *Daily Vox* spoke to a laboratory technician from Richards Bay who began his defence of his hero with the un-ironic statement that 'Zuma is like Jesus to us'.

For 14 years the ANC gave us the clearest, most comprehensive explanation of what it was and how it worked. And for 14 years we told it to shut up and angrily asked each other: What is the ANC, and how does it work?

Some of the answers seemed pretty solid at the time. During the late 1990s, for example, opinion-makers in the media explained that the ANC was a proud liberation movement which had good intentions but was naïve about money and its corrupting power. In the early 2000s, the narrative shifted. Now, we were told, the ANC had graduated from liberation movement to being a political party that showed a taste for centralised power, disdain for critics, and an alarming tolerance for corruption. By the 2010s it seemed that the ANC had transformed from political party to banana republic junta, a floundering mess of a thing which had sold its moral compass for a few gewgaws and was in mortal danger of being taken over by criminals. In the last years of Zuma's catastrophic reign, I was not alone in insisting that the Gupta ANC was no longer either a movement or a party but had become a criminal organisation, a ruling Cosa Nostra dedicated to nothing but directing taxes and tenders through its patronage network to well-connected parasites.

In December of 2017, Cyril Ramaphosa defeated Nkosazana Dlamini-Zuma at Nasrec and the story changed again: now, a consensus of punditry explained, there were two ANCs.

The one was a political party, perhaps even an idealistic, progressive liberation movement, which quoted Mandela and Tambo and talked about non-racialism and unity. It had also apparently discovered a cure for chronic laryngitis and perfected groundbreaking stem-cell research involving the human vertebra: all of a sudden, 'elders' who had mysteriously lost their voices ten years earlier started talking again, and politicians who had been almost entirely invertebrate for a decade grew a new spine and stood splendidly upright, despairing about how bad things had got despite their best supine efforts.

Up against this party of political reformers and medical geniuses was the 'fightback' mafia, a shadowy group of godfathers still intent on enforcing the old ways and keeping the patronage flowing, and, coincidentally, keeping Zuma out of jail. Often the comparison with the Mafia was quite literal: many of the ANC's methods seemed to come straight out of the Cosa Nostra handbook, whether it was muscling in on infrastructure projects and inflating costs or hinting at a violent response from its pet unions should it not get its way.

As this narrative took hold in the South African press, the view of Ramaphosa split into two wildly divergent camps. To his supporters, Ramaphosa was a saviour. Middle-class South Africans have a curious habit, when they abandon objectivity and reason in favour of political infatuation, of ditching surnames and using only the first name of their crush: within days, Ramaphosa was 'Cyril', a jovial, smiling, jogging, high-fiving Obama-lite who was dead set against the corrupt old ways. To his critics, he was a wolf in sheep's clothing. The right seized hold of a passage from the memoir of IFP MP Mario Oriani-Ambrosini in which he claimed that Ramaphosa had once revealed to him a master plan whereby 'the black majority would pass laws transferring wealth, land, and economic power from white to black slowly and incrementally, until the whites lost all they had gained in South Africa, but without taking too much from them at any given time to cause them to rebel or fight'. (There was even a reference to our old fake science experiment of the frog in the hot pot.) Meanwhile, Ramaphosa's enemies on the left talked about the Marikana massacre and the impossibility of a billionaire oligarch having the interests of the country at heart.

I was sceptical of Ramaphosa. For years I have referred to him in columns as Cyril The Human Ball-Gag, thanks to all that time he spent smiling and nodding in the passenger seat as Jacob Zuma went 'Heh heh heh' and drove the school bus off the bridge. I also believe that the ANC has a momentum of its own that is paradoxically both frantic and glacial, like a block of Bully Beef being dragged slowly across a pavement by a column of ants, the result of its collective nature rather than the efforts of individuals. It was unlikely, I thought, that Ramaphosa could produce the sort of dramatic, euphoric change we had seen during the early 1990s in the Soviet Union, East Germany and South Africa.

As I watched him scramble up on top of the slab of corned beef and test the limits of his power – a cabinet reshuffle here, a raid on someone's already empty office there – a new allegory took shape. Perhaps, I hoped, Ramaphosa was a kind of modern Michael Corleone from *The Godfather*: a prodigal son, coming home from war, damaged but with his soul more or less intact, returning to the embrace of La Famiglia, resisting the darker lusts of his peers because he can see the bigger picture. He understands that the era of small-time hijacking and civil war is over. He understands that there is not only a vast fortune to be made by taking the family legitimate, but also a chance at sloughing off the small, petty, ultimately self-destructive habits of the past.

I preferred this narrative to the previous ones because it best expressed my view, or at least my hope, of where Ramaphosa was trying to take the ANC. I suspect that Ramaphosa thinks in slightly longer terms than his colleagues. Where Zuma's ANC often seemed to operate like a baby – picking up policies and plans like toys and then dropping them again; soiling itself regularly but not knowing how to stop doing it or how to clean up the mess; existing in a world of endless, urgent consumption, in which the whole point of other people was to satisfy its appetites at once – Ramaphosa gives the impression of someone who understands what a process is, and that it takes time. At my most optimistic I allow myself to imagine that Ramaphosa even has a long-term master plan; a slow, careful strategy of tiptoeing over and between the landmines buried by South Africa's colonial and apartheid history and Zuma's administration. Sure, in the end Michael Corleone loses everything. Hubris is destroyed by Nemesis. But, I thought, if Ramaphosa could avoid dodgy deals with the Vatican and stay away from opera houses, maybe it would all work out.

And yet something just didn't fit, either in my Godfather analogy or in the more widely accepted narrative of a reforming political party versus an entrenched criminal organisation.

It was, very simply, the nagging fact that professional criminals are professionals.

I know that mafiosos don't always get it right. They blab into wiretaps. They take the gun and leave the cannoli. Usually, however, they don't. Crime syndicates are in the world, rather than in prison or in holes in the ground, because they are run by efficient, highly motivated leaders commanding disciplined, ambitious, hardworking employees. They are, in short, good at crime.

The 'bad' ANC, on the other hand, is not good at crime. Not even a little bit. Indeed, its two greatest heists to date – the Arms Deal and State Capture – were planned and run by other people. Yes, the arms dealers who approached the ANC in the early 1990s and the Gupta brothers found extremely willing accomplices in South Africa, but to describe the Joe Modises and Jacob Zumas of this world as mafia kingpins is to credit them with skills far, far above their pay grade.

No, at best the corrupt ANC was a fresh-faced young wannabe, less Michael Corleone in *The Godfather* than Ray Liotta's Henry Hill in *Goodfellas*: a naïve young nobody desperate to wear a shiny suit and be respected by the sort of people who respect shiny suits. And once this useful idiot got the arms dealers and the Guptas through the doors of the warehouse, they threw him a roll of twenties and said, 'Here ya go, kid, go buy yourself a steak or a new dress for yer ma. Now fuck off cos me and the boys got work to do.'

Of course, the roll of twenties they were tossed would be a fortune to you and me. But it was a pittance compared to what the masterminds took out of the country. You can see it in what they left behind. I'm sure that whichever fire-pool installers and thatchers and chicken wranglers got the Nkandla gig tried their best, but that place is a dump. Nkandla might have a helicopter pad, but the only thing landing on it is tumbleweed. And while there are some dully luxurious estates in Saxonwold, they'd struggle to buy you a townhouse with a splash pool in Cape Town's posher bits. Private islands in the Caribbean or penthouse suites in Moscow and London this ain't.

Then there's the fact that this useful idiot, this sweaty-palmed slave to his banal little appetites, keeps tripping the alarm or getting blind drunk and roaring about his crimes to whoever will listen. The Mafia has relied for over a century on *omertà*, the code of silence which ensures that nobody talks. Yet the ink on some ANC scam is barely dry before the cadres are leaking and denying and asking their spin doctor *du jour* to tell the press that they were taken out of context or that the accusations are a racist smear campaign. Hell, ANC MP Andrew Feinstein even resigned from the party in 2001 when it wouldn't institute an investigation into the arms deal. The ANC might as well have hired a stripper to jump out of cake wearing a sash reading 'WE'RE DIRTY!' Jacob Zuma was in court before he even became president.

And speaking of judges, if the usual ANC suspects are such criminal masterminds, why are they the ones having to lie and fudge and hand sick notes to Justice Zondo while the arms dealers and the Guptas make snow-angels on piles of South African taxpayers' money? If they're so devious and slippery, why are they still here, launching pathetic fund-raising schemes like selling socks, rather than posing for photos with the Emir of Dubai as he hands them their Emirati passport, or shopping for an apartment in Paris along one of the boulevards popular with former despots?

No, look at the quality of the villains involved and the Ramaphosa vs The Mob analogy starts falling apart quite quickly. But the main problem with the analogy that claims that half or most of the ANC is literally a criminal organisation is that it can't explain certain traditional ANC behaviour.

For example, it can't explain the ANC's penchant for making a spectacle of itself in public, whether through internecine squabbles or pathetically obvious lies apparently produced by five year olds with their hands wedged in cookie jars. It can't explain why a number of genuinely decent, impressive human beings continue to stay with the party, even publicly defending it when it has done something inexplicably vile. It certainly can't explain why so many South Africans, many of whom are vocal critics of criminality, would keep voting for a criminal organisation. Perhaps most significantly, it can't explain the relative safety of the ANC's critics. It is terribly dangerous to be an ANC councillor in certain provinces, or to express an interest in becoming one, but (without wanting to tempt fate) judges, state prosecutors and journalists are not being gunned down or blown up, as was often the case in Mafia-controlled parts of Italy. Indeed, the most intense campaign of harassment aimed at South African journalists in the last few years has come from the EFF, not the ANC.

So if the current ANC isn't a very tedious remake of *The Untouchables*, in which a doughty band of tough guys is trying to take down the criminal empire of local Al Capones by using an arsenal of, er, stern hints, then what is it? Is there a way of thinking about this vast, sprawling and often contradictory confederation of progressive public servants, predatory charlatans, lackeys and idealists, oligarchs and charity workers which doesn't require a degree in politics?

I believe that there is. It's the one given to us by the ANC, on Monday, 15 March 2004, and repeated every few months for the next 14 years.

> *'The ANC will rule South Africa until Jesus comes back.'*

It was there in plain sight all along: not a political boast but a simple, honest statement of faith. And what it said, in plain, transparent words, was this:

1. The president of the country and of the ANC, and a substantial number of its voters, believe that Jesus Christ is currently in heaven, and getting ready to return to earth, as promised in the Bible, which they believe to be the literal word of God.
2. It is possible that Jesus Christ will return tomorrow or in 10 000 years. We don't know. But whether it is a day or ten millennia, the ANC will do its best to govern his

children, as it was charged to do when it received God's blessing by being founded by ordained ministers.

3. When Jesus Christ arrives, the ANC will gladly hand over South Africa to him to govern, and take its place at his right hand, or wherever he has put us in the seating plan.

Now, in Christian lore, there is a name for an organisation which regulates, governs and guides the lives of God's children as it and they wait for his return, and then steps back with humility and grace when he does finally arrive.

It is called 'the church'.

Jacob Zuma and his followers tried to tell us what the ANC is and why it operates as it does. He tried to tell us that it is a church, but nobody was listening.

As I mentioned earlier, it was a busy week when he said it the first time. But it was more than that. I think the message never got out because of who was reporting it.

Whenever a politician says or does something, a kind of Critical-Industrial Complex gets to work on his or her words or deeds, feeding them into the media machine, which turns them into noise, heat, anger, entertainment and money. This Critical-Industrial Complex consists mainly of journalists, analysts, academics, columnists and satirists. Those people can come from different backgrounds, social strata and political viewpoints, but they all have one thing in common: an affinity, to a greater or lesser extent, for writing. They may not consider themselves writers, but most are skilful readers and have, I suspect, a heightened awareness of and appreciation for writerly or literary techniques. This manifests as a soft spot for metaphor and allegory, and a deep abhorrence of the literal. To many people in the Critical-Industrial Complex, words are imbued with magic and power. They are never simply units of communication. And no matter how professional or clear-eyed they may be at work, many of them can simply not resist that deep, creative urge to rearrange other people's words in a way that is pleasing to them, to make clearer the meaning they believe the speaker or writer was trying to make.

Which is why, when someone says something, the Critical-Industrial Complex has a tendency to interpret it rather than to read it. You see it in something as basic as the journalistic habit of smoothing out and correcting people's quotes. If you've ever read two different reports of the same quote – let's imagine two articles about Joe Politician, reading, respectively, 'We deny these allegations' and 'These allegations are not true' – you can be fairly sure that what Joe actually said was 'Yes, I'm, uh, we, er, we're denying, those allegations are – they're not true.'

And so, when Jacob Zuma said 'The ANC will rule South Africa until Jesus comes back', the Critical-Industrial Complex heard something else.

I know I did.

What I heard was 'Let me see how far I can push my megalomania while still appealing to a largely Christian electorate and expressing the sort of brash, Big Man swagger that plays well with the groundlings.' I heard 'Heh heh heh'; a cynical catch-phrase repeated endlessly. I saw political grandstanding. Most of all, I heard a lie: Zuma, I was sure, didn't believe what he was saying.

In retrospect, and with my case of Parys Poepstring firmly diagnosed, I see that I was wrong. It wasn't a cynical catch-phrase, and it wasn't a deliberate lie. If I had read the words he actually said, rather than the words I assumed he was saying, I might have understood that Zuma was telling us that the ANC is a kind of parallel Christian church, thereby giving us a perfect explanation for what the organisation is and why it operates as it does.

It had been there all along, in all those endless comparisons, all those statements of faith that I had thought were metaphors or boasts. It had, I realised, even been there in my Michael Corleone metaphor. In the third film of the trilogy, Michael's final transition isn't from godfather to legitimate businessman: it is from godfather to god-fearing father, recognised and lauded by the Mother Church. La Famiglia is, at the end, transubstantiating into a part of the Catholic Church.

I am not suggesting that everyone in the ANC consciously believes that the party is the literal servant of a literal God in a literal heaven. But the ideological and emotional foundations are the same, and it doesn't take too dramatic a shift for a liberation movement deeply rooted in secularism, and imbued with a deep communist suspicion of God, to find itself so awash in money and so distanced from the lived experiences of the poor that it begins to view itself as a church: an arbiter of righteousness and wickedness, virtually infallible in its rightness; a protector of the weak against the enemies of goodness, who are, by definition, anyone who challenges its dogma or its saints.

We often wonder why the ANC doesn't seem to care about South Africa. I would suggest to you that the reason for this is that the ANC doesn't actually live in South Africa. It exists alongside it, much as the Vatican is in the middle of Rome but not technically part of it. Indeed, once you start thinking of the ANC as the South African version of the Catholic Church, a great many things start making sense.

Both churches are founded on one undeniable truth: that life is hard, but through loyalty, discipline and living in the way prescribed by the Church, it will be much better at some point. For the Church, that point is after you die. The ANC has been less specific, suggesting that 'A Better Life For All' might happen somewhere between now and death, although it doesn't promise that it is necessarily talking about your lifetime.

Both entrench their power, and the mythology which feeds that power, with a succession of popes, each of whom is chosen behind locked doors by a gathering of senior officials, themselves also elected by lower echelons. Each of these father figures ('Tata Madiba', 'Papa') brings his own character to his reign, nudging the church either towards 'tradition' (backwards by a century) or 'reform' (extremely cautiously into an earlier part of the current century). There might be talk of renewal but the point of the new face – painstakingly added to official portraits and gilded, ornate walls – is to show an unbreakable line going back to the original founders; of power born out of continuity.

Then there is sin. For the Catholic Church this is the fundamental human state ordained by God and therefore not something that can be judged or condemned by anyone except God. Since simply being born and being alive are sins, it is unreasonable to prohibit sin. Rather, sinners must confess their sins regularly, and be forgiven so that they can go and sin some more, that is, continue being alive.

The ANC has been less clear on whether it believes in original sin, preferring to focus on the less metaphysical, very real crimes of dispossession and oppression in South Africa before 1994. But practically it follows the Catholic Church very closely when it comes to the forgiveness of sins committed by its believers. Should some party cleric sin against the poor he or she has sworn to serve, a private confession, or at least a slightly less brazen denial leads to a brief withdrawal from public life, before the sinner is forgiven and reinstated, often in another parish.

This is how, for example, Gauteng Health MEC Qedani Mahlangu could be found responsible for the deaths by neglect of 140 mentally ill patients and promptly be re-elected to the ANC Provincial Executive Committee (PEC) in Gauteng. It is how Bathabile Dlamini, a belligerently incompetent vicar in the church of the ANC, could be found guilty of defrauding the taxpayer in 2006's 'Travelgate' scandal and be elected to the ANC's National Executive and National Working Committee in the following year, effectively becoming a cardinal. It is how she could be appointed minister of Social Development, run the social grants system into the ground, lie under oath to South Africa's highest court, be fired by Cyril Ramaphosa – and then promptly be hired by Human Settlements minister Lindiwe Sisulu to chair the country's social housing regulatory authority.

Just as the world is littered with disgraced thieves and predators wearing priests' collars, endlessly moved from one scandal to the next by the Vatican, so South Africa's political parishes are haunted by an endless procession of liars and hucksters, spending a little while in the provinces until the stench dissipates and they can return to Rome and the eternally forgiving embrace of the Mother Church.

Once ordained, nobody is left to wander in the harsh world with its cruel, secular legal codes and consequences. As political clerics have told us for years, it is cold outside the ANC. But this endless forgiveness is reserved only for those inside the blessing: leave the church and become a heretic, or challenge its power from outside its walls and you are beyond contempt. The ANC regards the Western Cape much as Rome regarded the Antipopes of Avignon. Mention the Cape Town government, and the ANC's democratic rhetoric quickly degenerates into the sort of sabre-rattling used by popes to launch crusades in the Middle East. When Jessie Duarte, the patron saint of shouting at journalists, told a Freedom Day rally in 2019 that 'we must liberate the Western Cape, we must liberate it now', she was preaching the ANC's fundamental, fundamentalist dogma that there is only one true faith and that the results of legitimate democratic elections don't matter.

Perhaps this is inevitable when you consider another similarity between the Vatican and the ANC, namely, that they each obey their own set of laws, rather than those of the country in which they are located. Italian law does not automatically apply to the modern Vatican, which follows a mix of God's purported laws and its own secular varieties. Likewise, the ANC has its own constitution, which, it endlessly demonstrates, takes precedence over the constitution of the Republic of South Africa. Certainly, Jacob Zuma was infinitely more faithful to the constitution of the ANC than the South African one he swore to obey: almost everything he did as president put the interests of his party above those of the country.

The similarities go on and on. Both churches are supremely conspiratorial, drawn towards secretive cults and sects, where intrigue is as potent as gospel and where possessing powerful magic can help you rise to the top: whether you are an archbishop fighting to keep the knuckle-bone of St Paul in your basilica, or Bathabile Dlamini fighting to return to the trough, you are both using *smallanyana* skeletons as currency. Both involve a tripartite alliance of sorts, with believers being very clear about the composition of the holy trinity while non-believers simply can't get their heads around what it is, exactly, the Holy Ghost and COSATU actually do in the whole setup. Both are profoundly patriarchal, offering endless lip-service to an idealised vision of motherhood and feminine strength while making sure women never become much more than handmaidens to power.

Notably, both the medieval church and the ANC have a deep suspicion of commerce. The ANC has made it clear for decades that business is not just an ideological enemy but a spiritual one too – a belief it shares, quite literally, with European Christianity in the 1300s. In *A Distant Mirror*, the iconic history of that 'calamitous' century, Barbara Tuchman points out that Saint Augustine preached that 'business is in itself an evil'. 'It followed that the banker, merchant, and businessman lived in the daily commission of sin and daily contradiction of the moral code centering upon the "just price",' writes Tuchman. 'This was based on the principle that a craft should supply each man a livelihood and a fair return to all, but no more. Prices should be set at a "just" level, meaning the value of the labor added to the value of the raw material. To ensure that no one gained an advantage over anyone else, commercial law prohibited innovation in tools or techniques, under-selling below a fixed price, working late by artificial light . . . As restraint of initiative, this was the direct opposite of capitalist enterprise.'

The ANC has not yet managed to set prices, but anyone who has ever tried to start or maintain a business in South Africa will know how successfully the party has prevented innovation. As for working late by artificial light, I suspect the popes of the 1300s would greatly approve of how ANC-run Eskom has introduced regular blackouts. Indeed, Tuchman's phrase – 'restraint of initiative' – is an almost perfect definition of the ANC's fundamental approach to economics.

Of course, it should be said that while the medieval church and the ANC were wagging their fingers at commerce and doing their best to cripple it, both were standing naked under an endless shower of money pouring in through taxes, tithes, rents, indulgences or plain old bribes. In this particular religion, it is only people who actually work for a living who should be prevented from getting rich.

For me, the analogy of ANC-as-church explains plenty. It explains how the party can claim to be inextricably bound to South Africa's identity and yet feel so entirely detached from its daily realities. It explains how it can endlessly preach about hope and redemption for the poor while it busily makes an already wealthy conclave of bishops and cardinals even richer, or, in the case of our education system, actively steals the future from South African children. And, to be fair, it explains how it continues to attract a small number of pious, humble servants who want to house the poor and heal the sick, even if it means working alongside predators and con artists.

But, for me, its greatest benefit is that it explains one of the great mysteries: why people continue to vote for the ANC, despite every indication that the ANC can't govern, because it doesn't really want to.

These voters are not stupid. They are not zombies or sheep or sufferers of Stockholm Syndrome or any of the other names slung at them by aghast, endlessly frustrated supporters of other parties. Instead, I think many are responding quite sensibly to a powerful and ancient incentive: economic self-interest.

In 2003, Thabo Mbeki suggested to the Black Management Forum that SA has 'two economies', an idea concretised the same year in a report by the Presidency and the Department of Social Development called *Towards A Ten Year Review*.

'The first,' read the report, 'is an advanced, sophisticated economy, based on skilled labour, which is becoming more globally competitive. The second is a mainly informal, marginalised, unskilled economy, populated by the unemployed and those unemployable in the formal sector.'

The implication was clear: there was no bridge between the two economies, and it was the ANC's job to build one.

Except there already was one. It had started being built decades before Mbeki was president, and, whether consciously or not, it was being built on a blueprint thousands of years old.

Because, of course, by the early 2000s, South Africa didn't have two economies. It had three. And if we'd understood that the ANC was a church rather than a political organisation, that would have made perfect sense.

In medieval Christendom, society was arranged into three rigid classes: the Third Estate, home to the merchant and peasant classes; the Second Estate, where the nobility lolled; and, acting as a bridge between both of them and God, the First Estate, or clergy.

The First Estate wasn't simply a conduit between God and humankind, however. It was, much more importantly, a golden ticket. In the strict class hierarchies of medieval Europe (and perhaps most other pre-modern societies) social and economic mobility was incredibly difficult. You tended to stay in the class in which you were born. But the church offered a third way: a means of escape from poverty and anonymity, by which the poor and powerless could become, at the very least, fed and educated and, at best, rich and mighty. For the pious and humble, it meant a lifetime of relative safety and modest rewards. For the lustful and ambitious, who had the wits and appetite to play the game of faith and become adept at the politics of piety, the church could raise them higher than princes and make them richer than Croesus.

Just five years after Pope Mbeki misdescribed South Africa's two economies, he was gone, supplanted by an almost perfect embodiment of the transformative power of the church of the ANC.

Jacob Zuma had been born into deprivation. His father died when he was five. His mother was a domestic worker. He had almost no education. And then, when he was 17, he joined the political clergy. The church of the ANC became his new home, and, 50 years later, it anointed him as Pope and ruler of his own country.

In the end, there was even a miracle, although Zuma never claimed it for himself personally. Two years into a 15-year prison sentence, a faithful and humble servant named Schabir Shaik was, reportedly, terminally ill. Zuma, now Pope, saw to it that Shaik was granted medical parole. But instead of dying at home, Shaik slowly recovered, eventually becoming strong enough to play golf and shout at journalists. In 2017, Dr Elizabeth Gwyther, CEO at Hospice Palliative Care Association, told Cape Talk: 'I would even contest that Schabir Shaik has a chronic illness that is under control and it is not something I would even define as a serious illness.' Today, 11 years after being so sick that he was sent home to die, Shaik is still with us.

If you're a secular pundit or a cold-blooded member of the Critical-Industrial Complex, you probably see a comically crude jail-break carried out by a gang boss to free one of his goons. But if you go beyond this atheistic view, and glimpse the all-encompassing, reality-altering power of the Church of the ANC, you might see an act of compassion and forgiveness transforming a terminal illness into something that a medical professional classified as 'not something I would even define as a serious illness'.

You might truly believe that in the ANC, all things are possible.

If we consider the possibility that the ANC is not a liberation movement nor a political party nor a criminal organisation but rather a kind of parallel Christian faith of the old world, it explains a great deal. It explains why people vote for it, even now, despite everything; how scandals seem to bounce off it like raindrops off the dome of St Peter's. Human weakness, after all, is infinitely more familiar and forgivable than Satan or Helen Zille. It explains why it remains a home for both good people and hollowed-out parasites. It explains its ability to preach about sin while protecting its own sinners. It explains how it can endlessly, subtly change shape and form without splintering: so far the only heretics to have left it have been the UDM (terminally ill), COPE (dead), and the EFF, a tiny sect howling in the wilderness.

Indeed, the EFF is following the medieval script almost perfectly, forming a breakaway cult like the Fraticelli of the late 1200s, renouncing the Mother Church as corrupt, decadent and inherently opposed to the poor. Like many of the millenarian cults claiming greater purity and a greater affinity with the poor, the EFF preaches an apocalyptic vision in which the only way to save the poor is to reduce a fundamentally evil world – one entirely rotten with capitalist exploitation – to rubble. Once this holy crusade is complete, and everyone is as poor as society's poorest members, then all will be equal in a Christ-like poverty and therefore a Christ-like righteousness. The only difference between fourteenth century cult leaders and the EFF's commissars, of course, is that you'll struggle to find any of our latter-day saints wearing rags and living in caves.

If we are open to the idea of the ANC as an old and deeply rooted faith, then we realise that South Africa's crisis of leadership is different to what we thought. The question is not how we transition from bad government to good government. The question is how we transition from a theocracy to a democracy. Specifically, we must ask how, or indeed, if, this church can be nudged out of its gilded conclaves and secret chambers into the bright, harsh light of a modernity and relatively efficiency.

This is a vital question, because the ANC is going nowhere. It remains an astonishingly potent machine for self-advancement, far more effective, in fact, than South Africa's economy, where the Second and the Third estates eye each other resentfully and blame each other for the mistakes of the First. Mismanagement, corruption, junk status and Covid-19 have pushed the economy to the brink, but barring the total economic collapse of this country in the next few years, the ANC seems certain to win the 2024 elections. If collapse is averted, and small, faint advances are made, it will win in 2029 as well. In other words, we can be relatively sure that if South Africa doesn't slide off a cliff towards becoming a failed state, we will have an ANC government for at least the next 14 years.

Perhaps only its priest class can nudge this vast, complex, secretive, contradictory faith in a more pragmatic, secular direction.

Perhaps its millions of devotees don't want to reduce its office-bearers to the status of mere service providers, preferring to keep some of the mystery and majesty intact. After all, how do you dismantle a faith without losing faith in all sorts of other things?

Then again, the almighty Church of the Middle Ages, which ruled not just a continent but the hearts and minds of millions of people, today occupies just 44 hectares on the western edge of Rome. In some matters it is still obeyed – its edicts on abortion and contraception still defy international borders – but in most, it has been forced into a grudging détènte with the urgent, grimy realities of modernity and political power. If we're lucky, we might begin to see evidence that the ANC is slowly passing beyond its medieval stage, where corruption, coercion, extraction and hypocrisy make its piety a sick joke, and slowly entering an early Renaissance, a time of careful compromise and negotiated power. If we're not lucky, well, we know what that looks like. Either way, the ANC will be with us for many, many years; and if thinking about the party as a church helps make those many years slightly less vexing – if, like faith, it offers some comfort in stressful times – then perhaps it is no bad thing.

And if that doesn't help?

There's always prayer.

Chapter 7

SOE What? A Parable in Two Parts

So far in this book I have been extremely critical of the ANC. But at this point, in the interests of fairness and objectivity, it is important for me to tell you that I do actually have one thing in common with the ruling party: I also don't know anything about state-owned enterprises.

The benefit of this is that I can sleep at night. The downside, however, is that anything I write about them runs the risk of being as illuminating as Medupi power station after 'quite a long and big rubber stuff'[9] has torn.

Still, as my therapist tells me three times a week, I can't keep denying that I have, in fact, worked for one of the most infamous SOEs. So, instead of suppressing those experiences, perhaps it's healthier for me to share some of them with you. Because, for better and for worse, working for an SOE, albeit tangentially, taught me a little bit about this country: about how dysfunctional it can be, but also how that dysfunction can bring out the best of us. It taught

9 Eskom Acting CEO, Jabu Mabuza, October 2019

me about why we are where we are. And it gave me a tantalising glimpse of where, with plenty of luck and very different government, we might still go.

Part 1: It's So Much Worse Than You Think

High on a hill in the grasslands of Africa there sits a vast, crumbling temple, built by dead kings in service of an ancient and vengeful god. By modern standards it is brutally ugly, an immense monolith designed to strike terror into all who saw it, and to keep its high priests safe deep inside its warren of corridors and shrines and burial chambers. Beneath the monolith you can still find the sprawling remains of a large compound, where priests boomed and supplicants grovelled, around which extends a rusting fence of spikes. And if you know where to look, you can find, on that fence, a tablet carved with ancient symbols:

SABC

Like many ancient places of worship, the temple on the hill at Auckland Park has served a pantheon of gods. Its original builders – pink-faced pharaohs in porkpie hats – worshipped a god called Hendrik whose philosophy was based on benevolent hate and highly intellectualised cretinism. In the 1990s, it was taken over by the Cult of the Rainbow, itself quickly supplanted by the See-Nothings, a nihilistic group of fundamentalists who found righteousness and redemption by ignoring events its kings found unpalatable. Millenarian fantasies abounded: the ravages of the god-king Mugabe were declared benevolent, while the early escapades of the robber-baron Zuma were intercepted by soothsayers as 'Radical Economic Transformation'. For a short time there was talk of a Reformation. Banished clerics were allowed to return. But the temple's ancient system of tithing – 'It's The Right Thing To Do' – had broken down completely, and worshippers were finding new gods, such as the dismal pantheon of DStv and the foreign deity Netflix.

Inevitably, it began to fall into ruin. Its walls still gave sanctuary to the otherwise unemployable, but today, if you climb that great hill, you will find only a cathedral of mediocrity; the spiritual home of failure.

Not all of its oldest traditions, however, have crumbled. One of these is the garrison of guardians who watch over the temple's various entrances, a sort of Swiss Guard, if Swiss Guards received almost no training and, instead of guarding the Vatican, were keeping half an eye over an abandoned paint factory near a swamp.

The guards of the temple are impassive. They sit behind great desks, silent as stone sphinxes, gazing into the mists of bureaucratic eternity, or at a copy of *True Love* magazine. Like many such officials, they have taken a vow of silence: they communicate only in sighs and eye-rolls. There is almost nothing you can bring into the lobby of the Auckland Park temple that will disturb the serenity of the guards. Should some wild-eyed villain wheel a wooden crate up to the X-ray machine, its planks branded with Russian lettering and the three-sided nuclear symbol, the guards will simply turn their 1 000-yard-stare onto him and ask if he has an appointment.

'Yes!' he will cry. 'In hell!'

The guards will gaze at him and his glowing, ticking crate, and then ask: 'Which floor?'

'W-what?'

'Which floor is hell?'

'No, it's a – it's a figure of speech.'

An eye-roll and a sigh. 'Figures or speeches? Because figures is Accounting on 3 but speeches is Communications on 6.'

'No, I'm saying I'm going to blow up – '

The guards will raise a finger. 'Just wait.'

A phone will be picked up, numbers dialled.

'Hell. Ja, he's got an appointment in hell.'

Just then another man might arrive, a twitchy-lipped, red-eyed creature in a trench-coat.

'Special delivery?' he will hiss, fingering a greasy envelope.

'What's in the envelope?'

'Anthrax!'

'There's no Ann Thrax here.'

'No,' he will croak, his eyes wild, his breath rasping, 'but there's about to be!'

The fingers go up. The phone is dialled.

'Ja. Ann Thrax. No, he says she's still coming. New appointment. No, I don't know. No, I don't know. No. I don't know. No, I can't ask him because he is on leave. Ja.' A long pause. Then the guards will look up. 'Okay, fourth floor. Go through.'

They are unflappable. They do not flap. Not an eyelid. Not a fingertip.

Until, that is, you produce . . .

A laptop.

To walk into the SABC with a laptop slung over your shoulder is to know what it was like to be a gunslinger pushing through the swinging doors of a saloon in the Old West. A hush falls over everything. Women hurry their children into side offices and peep through hastily shut blinds. Somewhere a rattlesnake twitches its death-maracas. An eagle shrieks once, its shadow flitting across the lobby. For the first time that day, the guards freeze. Fixing you with a steely Eastwoodian glare, they ease their shooting hands down towards the walkie-talkies on their hips.

'Well, looky here,' they breathe. 'Seems we got ourselves a little MacBook over here.'

'Seems like it,' you will say through clenched teeth.

'Okay, pilgrim,' they murmur. 'Here's how this is gonna go.'

'I'm listenin'.'

'You're gonna ease that little ol' MacBook out of its bag, nice and slow, and then you're gonna slide it on over here.'

'You gonna make me?'

'I don't know,' they'll whisper. 'You gonna make me make you?'

'That depends,' you say, squirting tobacco juice into a nearby pot plant. 'You gonna make me make you make me?'

I know that I am mixing my idioms here and indulging in some terrible clichés, but given that I'm writing about the SABC, I feel that this is not inappropriate. Besides, 'Are you gonna make me make you make me?' is the spiritual mantra of most television production in South Africa. But I digress.

In the end, you will concede: you've got a pitch meeting in 15 minutes. At which point the guards will gingerly turn over your laptop, handling it like high-schoolers dissecting a toad, and carefully write down its serial number.

I have never heard a clear or plausible explanation for why the guards of the temple at the SABC treat laptops with such extreme suspicion. I assume it's because management believes the building contains intellectual property – and I use that phrase in its loosest possible form – that is worth stealing. Perhaps, in the minds of these apparatchiks, the world is a place in which HBO and Netflix are always trying to get their hands on the latest television gold mined in Auckland Park; in which American TV executives sit gloomily in their boardrooms, dismissing pitch after pitch as they wait for that stolen laptop to arrive . . .

'How about a show in which a high school science teacher becomes a meth-cooking crime lord?'

'Well, it's no *Isidingo*, is it?'

'No, but– '

'You're fired.'

'Okay, so, we've got something else. On the fantastical continent of Westeros the Starke family rules the north while the brutal and decadent Lannisters rule the south and – '

'Gerald?! Is that Gerald!? You did it! Make way for Gerald! Quick! Open the laptop . . . Shit, there's a password. Try 1234 . . . Yes! We're in! Oh my God, it's the holy grail. Open this one! This one! . . .'

> CONCEPT OUTLINE FOR UNTITLED SABC GAME SHOW IN WHICH PEOPLE STACK CHAIRS AS TEHY TRY TO REMEMBER THEIR FAVOURITE KNOCK-KNOCK JOKES.

'Yes! Yes! This is what I'm talking about, people! Goddamn, this is *gold*!'

I suspect the real reason for the laptop paranoia, however, is the same reason they don't let the internet into North Korea. Imagine coming home to Unit 3674-B#4 in Kim Il Sung Towers, 209 Kim Jong Un Lane after a long day in the dirt-sifting factory, and accidentally streaming *MasterChef Australia* and discovering that the Glorious People's Revolutionary Diet For Shining Health and Eternal Happiness, comprising one bean and some cement moulded into the shape of a pork chop, is not, in fact, the staple of French restaurants.

Can you imagine the existential crisis that everyone above the third floor at Auckland Park would plunge into if they were ever exposed to consistent quality? Would anyone be able to go back to work after tasting of that forbidden fruit? Would they even be able to get out of bed? Of course not. The SABC understands that it has to quarantine itself against virulent quality from the outside world. A single case of HBO would quickly escalate into full-blown Netflix after 48 hours. After 72 hours, nobody would be in the building.

I am exaggerating, of course. Most SABC executives are immune to outside pathogens.

I saw this first-hand some years ago. Through a series of extremely unlikely events, a script that I had written with my friend, the comedian and actor Alan Committie, found itself in front of the eyeballs of a certain Englishman who, we discovered, had helped put Monty Python together in the 1960s. Even more surprising, this certain Englishman liked the script so much that he wanted to meet its writers. And so, when he came to Cape Town as part of an international comedy-producing roadshow, he invited us along and I met a puckish dynamo of a man who might, in another age, have tamed horses in the morning before cataloguing butterflies in the afternoon.

Now, however, it was lunchtime, and he dragged me by the arm towards an SABC representative, allegedly a commissioning editor, who was entirely focused on nursing a sandwich. This script, my British gent told this person, was marvellous and needed to be produced. How about a co-production between the SABC and a BBC or an ITV? He was old pals with Cubby and Jingo and Waffles, and in fact he would be at Lord's with Bunty from the Beeb just next week so he could have a word and get the ball rolling.

She looked alarmed. 'Er . . .' she stammered. 'Well. Er. You see, these things are complicated. The money . . .'

'Oh,' he said breezily, 'I'm sure most of the money would come from the UK side.'

'Yes,' she muttered, 'it's just . . . we don't really . . . I can't . . . I don't have . . . It's difficult . . .'

And that was that. Not even a hint of a pretence to engage in a façade of deal-making. There wasn't even a standard brush-off about putting it all in an email or exchanging details. It was almost exhilarating, watching the creative process die at conception not because of malice or arrogance but because it might require initiative or individualism.

Which brings me back to the guards of the temple, and how I can tell you without exaggeration that they are almost entirely unflapped by anything that isn't a laptop. I know this, because I helped shunt a wedding cake through security at Auckland Park, both tiers of it, including the little plastic bride and groom on top, and nobody blinked because they were all too focused on the serial number of my computer.

The cake in question was, to be fair, a cheap trick. Alan and I were part of a team that was pitching two shows to the SABC. One was set in a high school. The other, the selfsame show which failed to launch at that roadshow, involved weddings. And so, in the hope that it would make us fractionally more memorable than the other dozen teams presenting that day, we wheeled in a wedding cake.[10]

As soon as the gathered executives realised that the cake was real and not just a cruel hoax, they fell upon it with cries and cheers. We smiled and nodded – Yessss, my pretties, gorge, gorge on the sweet, sweet cake and let your veins fill with sugar and a sense of obligation! – and shuffled our papers, ready to pitch. But the eating went on. And on.

'Should we . . .? Shall we, er . . .?' we asked, and they wiped the icing from their faces and cried, 'Bo, bo, we still eabing!' and started in on the second tier, abandoning a plastic knife in favour of simply yanking off chunks with their hands.

When we finally started telling them about the wedding show, they gazed at us as you would gaze at people who had just fed you 25 kilograms of cake; with a mix of snoozy gratitude and heavy-lidded, slack-jawed numbness. I'm not sure any of them heard a word we said, as sugar crystals rattled in their eardrums.

---

10 In case you're wondering why we didn't take a prop to invoke the high school experience: the SABC is already a grim institution through which tired, sad children trundle for a few years before leaving, so anything we brought would just have looked like SABC property.

The show was not commissioned.

Fortunately, the sugar had started wearing off by the time we started the high school pitch. Executives jerked awake and began to make notes. Some laughed at our jokes. At least I think they were laughing at our jokes. It is also possible that they were just chuckling contentedly to themselves, remembering how much they were being paid for work that could be done by a pug with a crayon duct-taped to its belly and set loose to wander across a floor covered in bureaucratic forms.

We wrapped up our pitch and opened the floor to questions. Some were excellent. Some were straight out of a satire of corporate paralysis: what takeaways were our deliverables going to action in terms of how our mission statement impacted on the broadcaster's mandate to provide blue-sky programming at a grassroots level?

One member of the panel, however, didn't laugh or look up or speak. She sat, alone and aloof, glaring at her cellphone. Every so often she would type something on it, and her perfect nails would go tap tap tap. Nobody on her side of the table dared look at her. She exuded status, or the corporate equivalent of it, which, at the SABC, is bad-tempered solipsism.

The questions petered out – 'Synergy . . . demographic . . . or . . . positive . . . world citizen?' – and silence fell.

'Anyone else? Anything more?'

And then the woman on the phone finally looked up and, with authority that set the room scintillating the way a church organ shakes the pillars of a cathedral, she said: 'Yes.'

Her subordinates froze. Had they missed something? Were they about to get the electric nipple clamps? Again?

I, however, had never had the electric nipple clamps, and so, not being terrified, my mind was clear and relatively open, which means I can still remember exactly what she asked. Indeed, I will remember it for the rest of my life.

'Apart from what you've told us today,' she said, 'what is your show about, and why should anyone watch it?'

I smiled and waited for everyone to laugh, and went down the row of faces, looking for some hint that this was some sort of industry joke that I had misunderstood. But everyone was stony faced. One man hunched over a pad of paper, pen at the ready, like a student who has just realised the term started two months ago and he is now about to transcribe literally every word his teacher says if it will help him scrape through.

I glanced at my team and met only confused, incredulous eyes. Had she . . .? Had we . . .? Surely not. But . . . and yet? Was she asking us to do the pitch all over again, now that her WhatsApp conversation was over?

Next to me, I felt Alan become warm and then hot, and heard the faintest whistle as steam began to escape from his ears; so I gripped his leg under the table and began to tap-dance.

Well, I said. Gosh, I said. Where to start? Firstly, we were *incredibly* grateful for her question. It was a great question, and, I think we all agreed, it really put a beautiful conceptual bracket around everything that had just been said over the last 20 minutes. But it was more than a bracket. It was an opportunity to revisit what we had just said, to really, you know, examine it, in a way that was both a summation and a proactive shift towards the next phase of the conversation. Because it wasn't enough that we were simply on the same page: we needed to be on the same line on the same page, and, most importantly, in the same font. So thank you for that, really. Namaste. As for the excellent interrogatory thrust of the question, which had brought such value-added *je ne sais quoi* to this creative gathering, I would simply *love* to elaborate.

What was our show about? Well, 20 minutes ago we told you that our show is about funny people in a high school. But really, now that you have given us this time to introspect, perhaps our show is about people being funny in*side* a high school. And now that you mention it, that creates an incredible synergy because people being funny has quite a lot of overlap with comedy as a genre, which – again, such creative synchronicity! – is the genre you asked for.

As for why people should watch it, well, that's as much about you as it is about us. Every executive in this room thrives on risk. That's why you're here. It literally doesn't get more dynamic or challenging than the senior suites at the SABC. In fact it had inspired us. To be better. To reach higher. To take the ultimate creative risk. When we'd first sat down to figure out the show, we'd laid out all the usual options. We could make a show that nobody would enjoy. We could make a show that everybody could ignore. Or – now stay with me here, people – we could *make a show that some people might enjoy*. And that is what we decided to do. We put all our chips on the table, we looked up at the brightest star we could find, and we aimed our dream-ship straight at *a generally favourable response*. Why should people watch this show, you ask? Because we believe that if they do, they will experience feelings of faint but undeniable *enjoyment*.

It didn't go exactly like that. I'm not brave enough to be explicitly sarcastic. But I did tap-dance as hard as I could, and I did cover those bases: thank you for the opportunity to repeat ourselves; here's the pitch, exactly the same as last time, except with me pretending that it's different so that you can feel that you've asked something important; a grateful conclusion.

In the end, she nodded. I'm not sure if it was because she liked what she'd heard or fallen asleep. It didn't matter. A nod was the thing. Her colleagues exhaled. The show was commissioned.

There was half a tier of wedding cake left, and our partner from the production company decided it would be a nice gesture to take it down to some of the people he knew who worked in the SABC's drama-producing department, by which I mean the department that produces all the slightly predictable drama you see on TV and hear on the radio and not the accounting department or the managerial suites, which produce all the extremely predictable drama you read about in newspapers. And so we pushed our trolley of badly mauled cake into a lift, and descended into darkness like a mood slipping into despair.

I have heard it claimed that the SABC's larger properties were designed by the apartheid government in such a way that a platoon of Reccies or a poly-shorts-clad death squad could defend them, or at least delay the advance of the Total Onslaught, in a sort of Stalingrad-like, corridor-by-corridor retreat, giving PW Botha enough time to tell the *volk* to die fighting and Tannie Elize to pack all of her hats into boxes and hop the first flight to Mauritius.

I don't know if that story is true, but I can report that the endless, twisting, disorienting passages under Auckland Park are about as creatively inspiring as dying in a race war. By the time we reached the little row of desks and cupboards, and were greeted with faint hellos, and handed over the cake, I was thoroughly depressed.

And yet, when it comes to the SABC – as with all our SOEs – you can always go lower.

On one of the cupboards, a single sheet of paper had been pinned up. Printed in large letters was a motto. It was probably meant as a joke. Perhaps it was a strange effort at motivation. But really it could have been the mission statement of every state-owned enterprise in the land. It read:

THE ONLY THING WORSE THAN HAVING A JOB
IS NOT HAVING A JOB

• • •

Part 2: It's So Much Better Than You Know

It was a beautiful highveld morning, one of those where the great vault of bright sky seems to draw you upwards and outwards, promising you that today is not just *the* day but *your* day. Birds sang all around me. An ornamental fountain plashed and glistened nearby. And I stood on the lawn of a Johannesburg guesthouse and screamed and screamed and screamed.

If I'd had any perspective at all, which, just then, I didn't, I might have reflected on the possibility that this moment was always going to happen. I might have thought back over the five or six years of my television writing career and realised that it was less a career than a sequence of sporadic bursts of frantic, confused effort, separated by very long expanses of nothing. It was less a solar system than a scatter of small comets, wandering across a cosmos of unanswered emails and silent telephones and unsuccessful pitches.

Indeed, if I wasn't screaming so loudly, and starting to worry if I was getting spit into the microphone of my cellphone, and if that might short-circuit the phone and cause me to hang up before I had a chance to scream some more, I might have remembered that I had done my best to kill my TV writing career almost as soon as it had begun.

In my defence, I hadn't known that I was trying to kill it, mainly because I didn't know anything at all.

I had written one show, the Blackadder-esque *Van Der Walt's Fault,* also with Alan, when I got a call from one of the producers of a very well-made, glossy, big-budget drama on SABC3. (I don't remember the year this happened, but the words 'big-budget' and 'SABC3' in the same sentence will date this story well enough.) The show's head writer was moving on, and was I interested in taking over?

I flew up to Joburg like a clown fired out of a cannon, and was immediately whisked off to a coffee shop by the producer, who, I discovered, was the sort of person who checks his watch all the time to make it clear that your existence is a slight inconvenience to him. Within two checks of his watch – 20 seconds at most – we had got down to business.

'Tell me,' he said, shifting in his chair in that eager, lascivious way tycoons do when they're about to tell their children that they've been disinherited, 'how you would improve the show.' He waved his hand, possibly as a pretext to checking his watch again. 'Wave a magic wand. Go for it.'

Well, I stammered, the show was great, but if I had one criticism . . .

God, how young I was.

Criticism?! Where did I think I was? The UCT English department? Nobody says 'criticism' in showbiz. If you have something to say that isn't gushing praise, you call it a 'note'. This way it sounds very, very small, like a PostIt. Because small is good. You can't write long, gloomy criticisms on a PostIt. You can't kill a buzz on a PostIt. All you can write is 'More!' and 'LOL!' and 'Yas!' A 'note' keeps the wheels turning and shows everyone you're a team player. 'Criticism' merely reveals that you're a pretentious malcontent who's somehow drifted across from a world of zero-stakes, pseudo-academic wankery. 'Criticism' is a warning, pinned to your tatty overcoat, that reads 'DOES NOT PLAY WELL WITH OTHERS'.

Sadly, it was all true. I didn't play well with others. I was a product of an academic system in which 'criticism' was a word with almost religious power, something I carried into the dark places of the world, such as Joburg production companies, and held up like a crucifix to protect myself from team players and happy, wealthy, productive people.

And because I had avoided those people for as long as I could, I didn't speak their language.

I didn't know, for example, that when he asked me how I would improve the show, he wasn't asking me how I would improve the show. He was telling me that it was a very good show, that I was lucky to be involved with it, and that, if I proved my worth, I might be allowed to tinker with it ever so slightly. The right answer wasn't 'It's good but . . .' The right answer was, 'You're asking me to improve on perfection, but if you want to make it perfect in a very slightly different way, we should schedule another meeting in a week, because that's how long it's going to take me to find something to improve on.'

But I didn't know any of that then. And so I blundered on.

My one *criticism*, I said, was that the show sometimes felt a bit static and shouty. My abiding impression, I expounded, was of characters trading barbs across a desk. I would recommend opening things up a bit, I continued, perhaps doing the old *West Wing* walk-and-talk so that characters could have conversations while moving between –

'Fuck off,' he said, sort of coughing it out, as if he was dislodging a kind of sweary frog from his throat.

At the time, it seemed like a quite rude thing to say. I think I blushed. But if I'd known more about the world, or at least more about television, I would have realised that it was probably a pretty fair comment.

I would have known, for example, that 'static and shouty' isn't a criticism. It's not even a note. It's a ringing endorsement. I would have known that characters trading barbs across a desk was the First Commandment of Making Television On A Budget, a gospel preached every single day in South Africa's vastly successful soap operas. I would've understood that, by suggesting *West Wing* walk-and-talks, I was demanding tracks for tracking shots or a squillion-rand steady-cam. I had basically told him that his show needed squadrons of fighter jets firing missiles at a robot squid battling a giant radioactive sperm whale.

After he told me to fuck off he said a little more, mostly about how pleasant Joburg was this time of year and how much he admired the writer who was leaving the show, and I mentally shredded every other ~~criticism~~ note I'd brought with me, and we drank our coffee and the meeting ended and I never heard from him again.

I did, however, hear from other producers, and over the next few years I wrote enough scripts for television and film to convince myself that I had a sort of career as a screenwriter – a career that was now ending in explosive fashion on the lawn of this guesthouse on this lovely highveld morning.

In my defence, it had been an unnerving few months. Creative control of our show had gradually become creative collaboration, then creative consultation, then creative contribution, until finally our project was somehow handed to a tin-eared hack with the comic sparkle of a prolapsed anus, who delighted in lecturing us passive-aggressively on how to write funny jokes.

On this morning, I had had my expectations whittled down so far that I had accepted the smallest possible promise: that a driver would be sent to pick me up so that I could watch the start of the shoot on a show that had once, long ago, been partly mine. But the driver was now two hours late, and so I had cracked, and poured out all that frustration and creative grief onto the person who was heroically holding me at bay, humming and cooing reassuringly in my ear.

In retrospect, being marooned at the guesthouse probably saved me from even more grief. Witnessing my prolapsed boss flounder with even the most basic elements of comedy was like watching a manatee who has gone from snoozing in a bayou to being inexplicably and nightmarishly selected to play in the World Championship of Billiards. He was really something. I mean, if this guy had directed a comedy like *When Harry Met Sally*, cinema history would look radically different right now . . .

'Meg? Billy? A word? Now I know the script has this scene ending with Meg having her big fake orgasm in the diner and then the lady at the next table saying, "I'll have what she's having," but I think we owe it to the audience to play the scene to its natural end, you know? Like they say: always leave 'em wanting less. So how it's going to play now is, Meg, you do your big orgasm, then Billy, you smile at her, then we go over to the lady and she looks at the waiter and says, "I'll have what she's having," but then, instead of ending the scene there, the waiter says, "Madam, she is having a pastrami on rye. Would you like that? A pastrami on rye?" and the woman says. "Why, yes, thank you, that sounds lovely, although please tell the kitchen to hold the pickles, because I don't like pickles," and the waiter says, "Of course," and then we stay on her as she reads a paperback until her sandwich arrives, maybe five minutes later, and then she takes a bite and says, "Hmm, that *is* delicious," and *then* we cut.'

All of which is why, if you'd asked me on that bright Johannesburg morning, or a few days later when I finally flew home in pieces, what I thought of South African television, I would have screamed at you for almost as long as I screamed at that poor production person. In fact, I'd probably have screamed very similar things for a good couple of years after that.

Now, however, I have calmed down. I have had certain facts explained to me. And I can tell you without a hint of snark that South African television is much, much better than you think. In fact, it's goddamned miraculous.

To appreciate this miracle, you first need to understand how television is made. The science is fairly complicated, but basically you take a large pile of money, shovel it into a special incinerator, which then projects the light from that burning money onto a screen. The more money you set on fire, the brighter and more impressive are the images on the screen. Good actors, directors and writers are a bonus, but what you need first and foremost is cash, in enormous quantities.

Now, some television is surprisingly expensive. Some is surprisingly cheap. For example, by the end of its reign *Game of Thrones* cost an average of $15 million per episode. This sounds like a lot, until you remember that *The Big Bang Theory,* a 24-minute sitcom filmed on a cardboard set, cost $10 million per episode. And even that looks reasonable next to the final season of *Friends*: the $10 million each of those episodes cost in 2003 is about $13 million in today's money. The Tom Hanks-Steven Spielberg war series *The Pacific* cost $20 million an episode, a bargain compared to the $4 trillion the United States spent fighting the actual war. *Breaking Bad,* arguably the greatest television series ever, cost just $3 million an episode, while *NCIS,* at one stage the planet's most watched television drama,[11] costs around $2.5 million. *Downton Abbey* looked glorious and lush, but by all accounts it cost a piddling $1.5 million an episode.

All of which is a roundabout way of saying you can spend as little or as much as you want on television. If you are paying your stars $1 million an episode, as was the case with *Friends* and *The Big Bang Theory,* you're going to be at the upper end: the A-list cast of *Big Little Lies* saw an otherwise entirely conventional drama costing well north of $12 million per episode. If, on the other hand, you're using BBC character actors, and a British aristocrat has loaned you her

11 In 2014, Mark Harmon was issuing steely-eyed orders to his band of misfits in over 60 languages.

house to use as a set, well, your biggest expense is probably going to be aloe vera gel for anyone who's been burned by Maggie Smith.

In other words, it is almost impossible for me to give you an accurate average figure for what it costs to project some high-quality, binge-worthy firelight onto your cave wall. But I don't think I'm speaking out of turn if I suggest that an hour of swords, dragons or spaceships costs somewhere around $10 million; that an hour of cops and robbers or drug-dealing schoolteachers costs about $6 million; and that 24 minutes of comedy costs around $5 million, depending on the fame of its cast and the voraciousness of their agents.[12]

Of course, some of that money goes to people who don't contribute anything meaningful to the process. I imagine that quite a lot of it is paid to drug dealers and then to rehab facilities. But the bulk of it goes into the quality you see on your screen. A multimillion dollar budget buys you good producers and show-runners, who in turn hire good writers, who have the time and space to develop good scripts. It buys you good directors and actors, and the time for them to rehearse and adapt the scripts. It buys you production designers who can make your show subtly memorable or startlingly new. It buys you lighting designs and sets. It buys you cinematographers, and the time necessary for them to develop a vision and a strategy for shooting each scene. Once the shoot begins, it buys you the best boom operators and steady-cam wranglers. It buys you multiple takes of scenes, and a meaty, intensive editing process in which the episode is cut and polished like a gem,

---

12 I haven't yet discovered why a sitcom, shot on two or three fixed sets, with a cast of at most six people, can cost more than a *Breaking Bad* but I assume it's because Americans once heard that laughter is the best medicine and should therefore be cripplingly expensive.

slowly changing from an amorphous rock into a glittering diamond. Finally it buys you publicity and, if you believe the cynics, industry awards, which buy you more publicity.

Before I understood that television is the light emitted by burning money, I used to wonder why South African TV was so bad. Why, I would ask anyone who would listen, do local shows look so shabby? Why is the lighting either a blinding, thermonuclear flash or a gloomy fog that washes out all nuance? Why is their pace so leaden? Why do so many of the actors look like they're making up their lines as they go along? Why couldn't we just copy the Americans? I didn't need innovation: I'd settle for a competent facsimile.

What I really needed, of course, was a basic understanding of maths. And the basic maths of local television is this.

A half-hour of comedy, produced to a standard we accept as 'world class' or at least binge-able, costs around R60 million.

The last SABC sitcom I wrote had a budget of R150 000 per episode.

Development, production, cast, catering, costumes, all of it.

My criticism of local TV had not only been ignorant, it had been wildly unfair. I had, in effect, developed a taste for a certain kind of cake baked by the Hollywood Bakery across town at a cost of R600 per cake, and then demanded from my local bakery next door that it recreate my favourite cake with ingredients that cost R1.50.

And yet, the little bakery next door hadn't given up. It could have put a sign up in its window reading 'PLEASE NOTE THAT IT IS LITERALLY IMPOSSIBLE TO BAKE A CAKE FOR R1.50'. But it didn't. Instead, its staff had shrugged, sighed, made a plan and baked something. It wasn't the creamy confection produced at the Hollywood Bakery. It was slightly smaller, and a little bit chewy and left a bit of a taste in the mouth. But it was a cake, dammit. And they'd done it, almost miraculously, for R1.50.

I don't want to excuse some of the cynical, deliberate mediocrity that flourishes in South African TV. There is one production company, for example, which cornered the sitcom market in the 1990s based on a simple and depressing model: no matter how cheap and nasty you were prepared to go, they could go cheaper and nastier, on shorter notice. And it showed in their final products. Jesus, it showed. Likewise, there was no excuse for my prolapsed director not to have read our scripts and, when he encountered words he didn't understand, like 'comedy' and 'timing', looking them up in a dictionary or asking me to explain them.

But for the rest, however, I now get it.

When your budget is R60 million, you can put together a team like the one I outlined earlier. But when it's R150 000 you do not get producers or show-runners, you get triage nurses. Instead of directors, you will get frazzled multitaskers, a sort of showbiz version of a single mom trying to scrape by with no time and less money while smearing Vaseline onto the ears of a child who has got its head wedged in a gate. You will get writers and actors, but since soap opera is how actors and scriptwriters stay alive in South Africa, you will only get what the soap machine can spare, at which point you will be faced with another problem.

Soap opera has a curious effect on anyone who works in it for a few years: like the Roman javelin thrower in the Asterix story who has one hugely over-developed arm and an otherwise withered body, people who work in soaps become very good at some things and strangely incapable of doing others. Ask a soap writer to plot out a 30-character, six-storyline mega-saga about feuding families, and they are like a coked-up Elton John at a keyboard, banging out hours of explosive melodrama faster than you can say 'I had amnesia while I was held captive on the island but now I've remembered that I am your birth mother, Griselda!' But ask them to write a joke and you get, well, explosive melodrama. Actors who have spent years in the soaps, likewise develop odd tics, such as a penchant for paraphrasing the script or leaving out certain lines. This makes sense in the soap world, where story and intensity of character is much more important than wordplay; but it can lead to awkward moments on the set of a sitcom. Well, awkward for the writer, because at that point the director is shouting, 'I'm happy! Moving on!' because the difference between the original line and the newly invented, slightly flabbier version isn't so dramatic that it's worth falling even further behind schedule by doing it again.

Finally, the whole thing will be rushed across the desk of a skilful but desperately over-stretched editor who will perform battlefield surgery on its most creaky bits and give it a cursory polish, at which point it will be released, with no publicity, and that's that.

Yes, there's an awful lot you don't get with a budget 0.25 per cent of the American standard. But here's what you do get.

You get the industry veteran opening his home and his family to me and more or less adopting me for the duration of a shoot. You get the director, someone who doesn't have to talk to a writer let alone ask his opinions, inviting me to sit next to him and peer into the monitor, and asking, 'So, what do we think?' You get the camera operator I worked with on a nature documentary series, murmuring reassuringly to a mother baboon because the afternoon light was starting to glow perfectly and he wanted to soothe her long enough to get the most beautiful image of her he could. You get the producer of that show, his face lighting up with childlike joy as he explains to you the magnificence and variety of a mollusc called a nudibranch. You get the ageless, chain-smoking set designer and her team of grinning, semi-feral prop- and décor-finders, rummaging contentedly through car-boot sales and dumpsters to find that one, perfect period piece for that desk in the background of that one shot that might get cut from the final show. You get the costume designer, agreeing to work more or less for free because she has the time and likes your show. You get the immense gaffer, built like a slab of granite, rewiring entire buildings in half an hour using nothing but duct-tape and testosterone. You get the continuity expert, sitting with her clipboard and her stop-watch, her mind like the Hubble telescope, taking in every detail so that she can stop a take with a terse reminder that Extra Number 3 needs an Elastoplast on her fourth finger because she had one there yesterday. You get the actors; warm, fragile, beautiful, tormented, light and shade flitting over them, with their astonishing ability to go inside themselves and drag it all out in full view, for hours on end, under hot lights and inside scratchy clothes, for shockingly small amounts of money.

You even get the production assistant who listened as I screamed at him, telling me that I was heard and that my feelings were understandable and he was sorry I was so sad rather than that I needed to calm down and get over myself.

I have worked with a small handful of very special pricks in South African television, but for every one of them there have been a hundred of these strange, nomadic, indefatigable, infinitely generous people, drawing together like a band of shabby superheroes in the shared hope of making just a moment of magic; of baking a cake – a bit lumpy, a bit doughy, but unmistakably a cake – for R1.50.

• • •

We know that South Africa's state-owned enterprises represent an existential threat to this country. Our best journalists have produced hundreds of thousands of carefully researched words describing in forensic detail the destruction of the SOEs and the danger they represent to the future of all South Africans. We know that some

SOEs have been allowed to crumble by treasonously negligent politicians and bureaucrats. We know that others have been hollowed out by some of the most focused and lucrative looting since the frantic final hours of the apartheid regime. We know that some are still clearly considered to be almost magical sources of patronage and extraction, still staffed by individuals who put personal, short-term gain above the survival of South Africa. As Adriaan Basson reminded us earlier this year: 'Remember the rapturous applause [Brian] Molefe received when he returned to Eskom for a short stint in 2017? This was after he had been implicated in state capture and malfeasance. Those hundreds of singing, dancing Eskom employees are still at Megawatt Park. They didn't leave the building with Molefe.'

We know that, thanks to treasonous self-interest like this, the SOEs have become the economic version of vast unexploded bombs buried under our country: unstable, unpredictable and, should they all detonate in a chain reaction of failure, utterly obliterating. South Africa, at least as we currently know it, will not survive the total collapse of the largest SOEs.

The last few years have shredded the strongest nerves and depressed the most buoyant spirits. Covid-19 plunged us even deeper into crisis. All kinds of bills are due, and there are no more IOUs to be written. But as the media endlessly remind us of the rot and cynicism and arrogance that have brought us here, I think it is also important to remember – or cling to – the fact that down in the muddy hole where these immense, complex bombs smoulder and creak, there are thousands of South Africans doing their utmost to defuse them; bloody-minded, skilful, relentlessly forward-looking, supremely practical people determined to make the damned things safe.

Many of us are deeply despondent, a sensible response to the

Zuma years in whose wake we were still spinning even as the coronavirus hit us.

But I know that we are also resilient, blessed with a gritty grace that comes to the fore when things get difficult. We work hard, often without expecting great rewards, and make something out of very little. We make a plan.

We will have to make some big ones. Once South Africa has struggled past the fallout from Covid-19, it must free itself from its compulsion to prostrate itself before patently untrustworthy and incompetent leaders. We must make difficult choices around economic justice. Climate change will require fundamental changes in how and even where we live.

But if we can survive the SOEs, I believe we have a fighting chance. Perhaps that's the naïve optimism of someone who writes fancies and jokes for a living; someone who worked briefly with the SABC. Perhaps if I'd worked for Prasa or Eskom instead, I might be far more gloomy than I am.

But even though it's much worse than we think, I can't help feeling, despite everything, that we're much better than we know.

Chapter 8

Love and Marriage, Politics and Sport

Twenty years ago I spoke sport.

It hadn't been by choice: I had got a job as a sports journalist, a post which required me to travel internationally every day, leaving my Cape Town suburb each morning to cross the Claremont border post into Newlands, a small country populated by enormous white youths called Bazza endlessly courting tiny blonde women called Tasha, ruled by a parliament of former Springboks, all of whom were called Chalky.

As is the way with the languages you learn because you have to rather than because you want to, I never achieved fluency in sport. A few seconds into any conversation with a sportsperson, I saw them retreat into that patronising wariness of the first-language speaker waiting to hear the inevitable mix-up of tenses or syntax.

To be fair, my accent was quite good. As a child I enjoyed mimicking certain accents – whether it was Har Medjestair the Queen or Shine Warne the Strine crigdah – and I found it quite easy to make the extended, nasal vowels and softened consonants required by sport.

The grammar and idiom, however, remained forever out of reach. Just as I had struggled with German's *der, die* and *das,* I never knew whether it was 'bru', 'bro', 'buggah' or 'boet'. Indeed, I usually stumbled at the very first hurdle, opening with 'Harzit!' when the social setting and status of the sports-speakers present clearly required me to use a more formal greeting, such as 'Buggah, haryoo bin keepinhay?'

Likewise, only native-born sportspeople know the subtle distinctions of nomenclature. Nothing singles you out as a second-language speaker like using first names when you should use nicknames – 'Wayne! Duane! Shane! Harzit, mar buggaz?' rather than 'Bazza! Chalky! Shithead! Nought, bru, watchoo fuckfaces doonear?'

Still, I muddled along, and slowly learned enough sport to realise that I often had to look beyond the literal meanings of words to understand the sense of what was being said.

As an English speaker raised in the British linguistic tradition rather than the American one, this was quite familiar to me. Speakers of American English are like golden retrievers: everything is out in the open, as complex and subtle as a chewed frisbee. When they ask you, 'How are you today?' – and they always do, for some reason – they are asking you how you are today. But when speakers of British English say, 'Hello' they are saying: 'There, I have met the basic requirements of etiquette, which means we can now agree that we will not speak to each other again, unless we are trapped here by an earthquake, in which case we might feasibly share 10 or 15 more words, possibly about the lax building codes in parts foreign.'

So it is with the South African dialect of sport. Everything means something else. Let me give you an example, based on the sort of sports that might be spoken in your average post-match interview.

WHAT THEY SAY	WHAT THEY MEAN
'Ja, look, the guys are absolutely gutted . . .'	'We never had a hope of winning this one, and the fact that we got through it without injury to our most expensive players is a massive win for us, plus there's the fact that this franchise competition no longer has the status it once did, so this loss today is more or less meaningless in the endlessly repeating soap opera of sport. All in all, a solid day's work.'
'. . . but they gave 110 per cent.'	'The guys gave the physiologically and psychologically sensible 60 per cent, then Coach took another 10 per cent, mostly with some very hurtful personal remarks, and that leaves about 30 per cent in the tank for a little cry in the showers followed by some brooding and drinking.'
'Ja, for sure, it's a case of back to the drawing board . . .'	'Coach is going to make us stand with our backs to his drawing board then throw us with a brick.'
'. . . and really focusing on getting the basics right . . .'	'When he throws it he whispers, "Taste my pain!" and then he does this thing where we're not sure if he's laughing or crying or both.'
'. . . and building ahead of next week.'	'Mostly just dodging the brick and making sure the sponsors don't see us cry in the shower.'

'The knee? No, fully, the knee is actually feeling great.'	'I can't feel the knee. At all. I'm not sure if it's the meds or if Doc maybe amputated halfway down the thigh. I'm too scared to look down, because if Coach sees fear in my eyes he's going to get the Punishment Nozzle and make me wish it was just the brick.'

It didn't always go exactly like this. Every so often, honesty tried to crack through the euphemism and double-speak. I was at one press conference, for example, where West Indian cricketer Brian Lara was facing the media after the umpteenth embarrassing loss of an awful tour. For 20 minutes he was asked the same two questions: why did your incredibly crap team lose again, and can you see the future and tell us for how long you're going to stay crap? Lara batted away each question with eloquent patience. The guys were disappointed. The guys had to work on their skills. The guys had given 110 per cent but it wasn't enough. The guys –

And then some hack in the back row asked the same two questions, yet again, and I saw Lara teeter on the edge. In that moment, his face wasn't speaking sport. It was speaking English. And what it said was:

'Oh, you're asking me about habitual losing? You, in the back row, working as a content mule at an exploitatively low wage for a no-name website that's been running at a loss for years? You, whose existence is now a series of airports and hotel bars, are asking me about what it's like to slide into failure? You, someone who demands humility from sportspeople, are asking me what every single other person in this room has asked except *you're* asking it because you think you're so magnetic and charismatic, and your knowledge of sport so immense, that I might look up and see you and think "Shit, *this* guy really knows his stuff, maybe I should tell him what I've refused to tell everyone in this room for the last 20 minutes?" You and your colleagues are starting to notice that I'm getting sullen, and you're starting to jot down things like "hostile" and "icy", as if *I'm* the asshole here?

'Well, let me ask *you* something. Imagine that people cared enough about your crappy job to want to watch it broadcast live on TV. Imagine that every time you had a paper jam, or the office server crashed, or you misattributed a quote, or you split an infinitive, the whole country went, "Ooooh, that makes me feel terrible because it undermines the sense of self that I have built on the success or failure of this one particular sports website!" Imagine if every time your sub-editors put the wrong picture on an article you'd written, or nobody noticed it because there aren't subs anymore because your team is crumbling just like mine, I went on TV and talked about how it might be time for you to step down and stop being a shit sportswriter. Imagine if, at the end of every week you'd scraped through with demoralised or incompetent colleagues, producing mediocre work, littering the internet with mistakes and banality, I called a press conference, televised in at least two countries, and asked you for 20 minutes, "Why is your work so shit?"

'So now let me ask you, Mr Back Row: how sunny and chatty do *you* think you'd be right now?'

But of course Lara didn't say any of that, because he was a professional. Instead, he said that he was disappointed, obviously, and that the guys needed to ask some tough questions and dig a bit deeper . . .

Yes, sports is a language veiled in secrecy, double meaning and, sometimes, outright untruths. And because so much of its meaning is projected, implied or inferred from context, it allows enormous amounts of bullshit to be spoken without anyone really knowing the difference.

For example, you can wake up in a dumpster wearing someone else's bloody clothes, with no memory of how you got there or even your own name, but if you stumble through the gates of a cricket stadium and mumble 'What day is this?', you will be welcomed and offered a drink because everyone will assume that what you're really saying is 'Given the rain and the lack of intent shown by the batting side, I must say I'm starting to doubt if there is enough time left in this Test for us to see a result.'

In this language, you can say almost anything and mean something else or nothing at all.

Except, that is, when it comes to one statement.

When speakers of sport say this one thing, they are speaking as plainly and transparently as they know how. They say it as if they are nailing an edict to a church door. And what they say is:

Politics should be kept out of sport.

When you consider the existence of someone like Fikile Mbalula, this statement seems to make perfect sense. Recall, for example, Mbalula's most important contribution as Sports minister: calling Bafana Bafana a 'bunch of losers'. Now, I don't deny that Bafana Bafana are a terrible, terrible football team. At the start of this year they were ranked lower than Iraq, a country which has spent most of the last two decades being bombed into rubble by the United States and blown apart by sectarian warlords. But next to Mbalula, Bafana Bafana are Liverpool, FC Barcelona and Real Madrid rolled into a single phalanx of footballing demigods, concussing goalkeepers and tearing holes in the back of nets. Mbalula is part of an organisation which, in footballing terms, loses 1-100 every time it runs onto a field, 70 of those coming via own goals before it finally gets on the scoreboard thanks to a ricochet off a dog that has wandered onto the field in the final minute. Mbalula is well qualified to talk about losers – he works with scores of them – but when he recanted a year later and called the national football team a 'bunch of winners', one had to ask: how would he know?

But of course, when sports fans demand that politicians stay out of the games they love, they're not really talking about objectionable personalities or stupid comments about winners and losers. In South Africa, what they're talking about is quotas, the on-again, off-again semi-policy introduced in the 2000s, sort of, whereby sports teams that represent South Africa at provincial or international level are forced, or strongly urged, or formally requested, or politely asked, or gently nudged, to select a certain number, which varies all the time, of black players, whereby 'black' means black African or 'players of colour', depending on how recently the current Sports minister has read their own policy statements. Or something.

The vagueness and elasticity of the policy hasn't stopped it from being bitterly divisive, perhaps inevitable as it has forced a confrontation not between two sets of sports fans but two entirely different – and mutually exclusive – worldviews.

For the first group, sport is a spectacle, largely removed from society's day-to-day concerns (and blessedly far removed from its politics) in which two elite players or teams compete at an extremely advanced level to wrestle fractional advantages away from each other. Since it is, by definition, an elite activity, only the best athletes should be selected.

For the second group, sport is not a clash between genetic freaks inside a bubble of money and privilege, but rather an extremely potent nationalistic ritual with the power to inspire and unify society. As such, it should fully represent the society in which it takes place, even if that requires the state to force a semblance of representivity onto it.

Where these two worldviews meet, there is only screaming. That's because they're not really meeting. They've merely approached each other, like two spaceships from opposite sides of the galaxy which have slowed to a stop a safe few thousand kilometres from each other, erected their force fields, set photon torpedoes on kill, and opened a hailing frequency through which, as I said, they are now screaming.

The noise and belligerence of this standoff can sometimes make it seem like neither side has anything sensible to say. But if you left the screamers to their screaming, and instead smuggled the brightest and best off each ship and set them around a table on the dark side of a nearby moon for a kind of Sports Summit, I believe you'd hear some pretty good arguments for each position.

For example, the No Politics In Sport delegation might say that, while it understands the necessity for nation building, it doesn't understand how nation building is helped by assembling a team that, at least in theory, has surrendered some of those fractional advantages before it has even walked on the field and is therefore more likely to lose than to win. A losing team, after all, is not one that unites or inspires a society. As for representation, they might argue, people don't care what teams look like as long as they win. They might point to the National Basketball Association or the National Football League in the United States, where an overwhelmingly white fan base supports teams that feature disproportionately high numbers of black players, all selected on merit: around 75 per cent of players in the NBA are African-American, despite African-Americans comprising just 13 per cent of the overall US population.

For its part, the Quotas delegation might agree that selecting purely on merit is an admirable idea – *if* all eligible talent has an equal shot at being noticed, developed and selected. But, they'll say – and rightly so – South Africa is not such a place; that the institutions and systems that produce the country's elite sportspeople still tend to be occupied and maintained by largely white Old Boys' networks that still, whether consciously or not, recognise and reward white talent more easily than black talent. They will argue that, even if this system notices and selects black players, those black players will spend much more time warming benches than their white counterparts. In other words, the traditional production line of elite sport cannot be trusted to police its exclusionary tendencies, which means that the state must do so by doing what states do: legislating.

These are the broad strokes, but each side has many smaller, specific gripes that it throws into the fray. I find myself floating in space more or less exactly between the two. I believe that merit must be the founding principle of elite sports *and* that normal sport is impossible in an abnormal society like South Africa. But I nevertheless find myself rolling my eyes hard at the politicians who tell us that quotas are about achieving representation. Because, of course, a genuinely representative Springbok team, which accurately reflected the demographics of South African society, would include:

- 8 women
- 4 players younger than 14 and one older than 60.
- 3 players who were getting paid and 12 who had no formal contract
- 4 players living in extreme poverty.

Perhaps most importantly of all, 14.9999 players out of 15 would not have the physical ability to play international rugby. Even if the

Springboks were a perfect reflection of the racial demographics of South Africa, the fact remains that almost every single one of us is excluded from playing for them because the first time we got tackled we would explode like a sachet of tomato sauce being run over by a car. I would be very surprised if there are more than 50 young men in South Africa who are big, fast, resilient, co-ordinated and fit enough to play international men's rugby and not have to be stretchered off within seconds. In terms of raw physicality, 99.999 per cent of South Africans are not represented every time the Springboks run out to play.

Inevitably, when politicians fudge their definitions and fiddle their numbers, confusion and acrimony will reign. Consider, for example, a complaint we hear from the No Politics In Sport faction on those occasions when Bafana Bafana does not field a white player. Why, the quota critics ask, do quotas only seem to apply to sports dominated by white players? Where are the threats to suspend the South African Football Association from international events until it selects a demographically representative white person?

The trouble with this line of questioning, unfortunately, is that it requires medical atrocities to be committed. At last count,[13] whites comprised 7.9 per cent of South Africa's population. There are 11 people in a football team – 7.9 per cent of 11 is 0.86. In other words, if the national football team is going to be truly representative, it needs to select just over four fifths of one white person. SAFA's choice is clear: either it needs to surgically remove enough body parts from its white players that they now qualify as 0.86 of a person and can compete for selection fairly and squarely, or it needs to do the humane thing and select no white people at all.

Unfortunately for SAFA, demographic trends are going to make

13 Stats SA midyear estimate, 2019

these decisions increasingly distressing. Stats SA figures show that whites are dwindling away as a proportion of the population, with the current crop of white children 14 years and younger comprising just four per cent of their age cohort. In other words, when they start becoming available to play for Bafana Bafana inside the next decade, SAFA will find itself unable to select more than about half a white person – little more than a torso or a pair of legs and buttocks. To be fair, I'm not sure a pair of dismembered legs, lying bleeding on the halfway line, could be very much worse than most Bafana Bafana players, but still, you have to feel for the officials making these calls.

Of course I'm being facetious. Dismembered legs would be quite a lot better than most Bafana Bafana players. Also, my gripe about the fuzzy definition of representation is, admittedly, somewhat pedantic. The decision to use race as the key indicator of inclusively and representation might sometimes sound crude or divisive when it is presented by crude, divisive ANC Sports ministers, but ultimately it is a pragmatic and sensible one. South African society before 1994 discriminated against people on the basis of sex, gender, age, language and socio-economic class, but it was race, above all else, which decided whether citizens were allowed to pursue their ambitions and fully realise their talents, or whether they were shut out.

Still, despite its clarity and pragmatism, using race as the defining factor in quotas has triggered some extremely confused reactions among those who continue to denounce political 'interference' in sport.

Consider, for example, the intellectual dumpster fire that sparks up every time two indisputable facts bump up against each other. The first is that, until political pressure became too great, South African sports teams obeyed a strictly enforced quota system which required them all to be 100 per cent white. The second is that many of those quota teams and quota players are still idolised and remembered with intense nostalgia and admiration by the very people currently denouncing quotas. Now this is very odd. To object to quotas post-democracy while treasuring your memories of quota teams pre-democracy is, you must admit, a fairly feeble position to take. So feeble, in fact, that you must forgive me for assuming that your objection isn't so much to quotas as a principle (which it clearly isn't, since you were such a big fan of them back in the day) but rather to the presence of black people in sports that were, until change was forced upon them, exclusively white.

This kind of confusion and prejudice have, in my opinion, allowed many people who believe that merit trumps politics to forget that South African sport has already accepted, celebrated and then mourned a player who was selected not on merit but for his value as a nation builder.

His name was Hansie Cronje.

Cronje was a mediocre Test batsman. Technically unsound against short, quick bowling, he was soon found out and moved down into the middle of the South African batting order, from where he cobbled together a career that, barring one or two memorable flourishes, was substantially below average. His conversion rate – the frequency with which he scored a Test century, the all-important yardstick of a specialist batsman – puts him squarely down among those unlamented Proteas players who, most local fans would agree, either never converted their talent into results or were never good enough in the first place.

Cronje, however, was never selected as a specialist batsman. He was selected as a symbol who was just good enough to stay in the team long enough to achieve political goals that were more important than sporting ones.

In the early 1990s, the South African national cricket team had charmed its way back into the global game, relying on beginner's luck, the fearlessness of naïvety and inexperience, and, in the lanky frame of Allan Donald, one of the best fast bowlers in the world. But by 1994, the United Cricket Board (formed three years earlier as an amalgam of the racially segregated boards which had previously run the game) could no longer rely on amateur theatrics and the mercurial ebullience of Jonty Rhodes. As the country went to the polls to reinvent itself, the UCB, likewise, needed a new direction and a new political strategy that would allow it to achieve three vital tasks.

The first was to move decisively away from ageing players whose careers were inextricably linked to the isolation era. The second was to position itself firmly behind Nelson Mandela's nation-building project. And the third was to bring the white Afrikaner cricketing establishment into its new, tentatively progressive, sort-of-multiracial project. Cronje could not have been more perfect. Young but relatively sophisticated for a sportsman, a white Afrikaner from the Free State but overtly enthusiastic about the new dispensation, he was, by the less radical standards of the mid 1990s, the ideal figurehead to stand beside Madiba or to receive the jubilant embraces of Archbishop Desmond Tutu.

On his day, Cronje could be a good captain, although I would argue that he was made to look much better than he was by having the once-a-generation pairing of Donald and Shaun Pollock raising hell for him.[14] But if we accept that a quota player is one who has been selected predominantly to embody a new political reality, to

14 In 37 Tests under Cronje, Donald and Pollock took 328 wickets together at a rate of one every eight overs. With respect, it is quite difficult for a captain to look ordinary under those conditions.

promise of national unity, and to draw a certain demographic into the game, while having their personal failures explained away or tolerated because they're doing the political job so well, then Cronje was undoubtedly a quota player. And if Cronje could become one of the most popular sporting figures of his time, before he sold out the trust of the fans, then perhaps quotas – or selection based on factors other than merit – aren't the work of Satan their critics claim them to be.

All of these arguments, however, are getting in the way of a fairly simple truth: that politics can't be removed from sport, because modern sport, both as a corporate product and as a competition between countries, is entirely and fundamentally political, and no amount of grumbling will make that fact go away.

It is politics, not vague camaraderie, that makes the Olympics happen every four years, and that decides where the Games will happen. It was politics, not the love of competition, that saw the US and the Soviet Union pump millions into developing their sprinters and gymnasts, turning athletes into Cold Warriors. It is politics, not some idealised, nostalgic fantasy of schoolboy rivalry, that fuels and facilitates international sport. In South Africa, it was politics that prevented the black majority from representing their country in the sports they loved. It was politics that punished South Africa for that crime by banning it from international sport, and it was politics that saw it restored.

Keep politics out of sport, they say; but would they have said the same to Steve Tshwete when he risked his political reputation, and quite possibly his personal safety, to have secret talks with Ali Bacher about planning the rehabilitation of South African cricket? When the government of India made the first moves in restoring cricketing relations between our two countries, would the No Politics lobby have demanded that the politicians stop what they were doing?

And how, exactly, do you keep politics out of sport when it penetrates every aspect of human life, as invisible but relentless as the neutrino particles that blast out of the sun and pass through our very cells? How, for example, was Mfuneko Ngam going to keep politics out of sport?

Ngam was one of the brightest prospects in South African cricket after readmission. A beautifully balanced run, a classically slinging action and searing pace elicited comparisons with past greats, and in his first Test series, in 2000, the 21 year old went through New Zealand's batsmen like a flame-thrower through an ice-cream cone. And then, after three Tests, it was all over. Doctors revealed that Ngam was extremely prone to stress fractures in the bones of his legs, a condition, they explained, that had either been caused by genetics or by poor childhood nutrition. If the latter was to blame, then Ngam's sporting career had been ended by socio-economic conditions entrenched by politicians in the Eastern Cape a century before he was even born.

To demand that politics be kept out of sport is to demand that oxygen be kept out of lungs, that blood be kept out of veins and that passion be kept out of arguments. Because the most immediate thrill of international sport is a political one. Putting your arms around strangers and weepily roaring, 'We beat England!' isn't about who kicked which balls where. It is a moment of unapologetic, euphoric nationalism or patriotism; one in which our nation state took on their nation state in a ritualised form of warfare, and *we beat them*, and now everything is perfect.

It's why we unconsciously begrudge sportspeople their individual rights, believing, deep down, that they are the property of the state; soldiers in a kind of parallel army that defends our national pride rather than our borders. When Trevor Noah builds a career in South African comedy clubs, benefiting from South African comedy writers and South African broadcasters, and is eventually hired to host *The Daily Show* in the United States, we celebrate his ambition and hard work, and marvel at the riches he has secured for himself. But when Kyle Abbott builds a career in South African domestic cricket, benefiting from South African coaches and South African broadcasters, and is eventually hired to play for English county Hampshire, sports fans condemn him for 'using' the local system and becoming a mercenary interested only in himself and personal gain. Both men have followed very similar paths, building their professional brands at home until they are offered serious money in a major currency overseas. And yet our responses couldn't be more different. Noah has made us proud. Abbott has betrayed us.

Politics is the lifeblood of international sport. The fact that clots like Mbalula sometimes form in that circulatory system doesn't change the fact that the political impulse, and specifically the nationalistic urge, is the animating energy of the great sporting spectacles we admire.

All of which is why it might be time to try to persuade those who angrily insist, 'Politics should be kept out of sport!' to accept a slightly expanded, and substantially more honest version of that war cry: bad politics and opportunistic, D-grade politicians should, where possible, be kept away from sport so that energising politics and pragmatic, deal-making politicians can perform their essential role in creating the arena in which the best take on the best.

I don't expect that this will satisfy all the Mbalulas in the ANC, and it may well anger those on the other side of the argument who still believe that professional, international sport is magically organised by a committee of invisible high school teachers. Agreeing with both and with neither might sound like fence-sitting. But I prefer to think of the fence as a very narrow strip of common ground. Because I believe that both sides of the argument are trying, in their own way, to create the same thing: community.

When fans cry, 'We beat England!', the word that carries the most power isn't 'England' or even 'beat'. It is 'we'. The 'we' in sport is the golden thread that binds together the political and the personal, the public and the private, the rational and the emotional. The promise of community is stronger even than the desire to win. Indeed, I know a couple of fans who have spent a lifetime supporting a losing team, not because they believe their team is about to string together a streak of wins but because it offers them a community of like-minded people and the opportunity to invest in its particular mythology; to find a role in sport's great soap opera in which they can play the eternally wronged Cliff Barnes to the endlessly smug JR Ewing.

It is the 'we' that can make militantly Marxist South Africans feel not just affection for, but a deep bond of comradeship with 11 millionaires running around on an icy field in Manchester or Leeds. It is how this white boy raised in apartheid South Africa could believe that black cricketers from Trinidad and Jamaica and Barbados were the greatest and most beautiful athletes in the world.

The Politics Versus Sport argument will go on, with neither side willing to concede. But perhaps that's how it's supposed to go. Because perhaps, in the end, it's not a political quarrel between two camps but rather a strange sort of sport; fiercely contested by two communities, each bound together by that glorious 'we', each with its own set of projections, its own heroes and villains, its own all-encompassing, all-explaining mythology. Two teams playing an endless game, each giving 110 per cent, and then coming back the next week to do it all again . . .

Chapter 9

How the Other Half Lives

So far in this book I've written a great deal about the ANC but said almost nothing about the other parties. This is because the other parties aren't killing South Africa.

Yes, the Democratic Alliance is collapsing under the strain of maintaining the pretence that it isn't Helen Zille's personal project and that she is still the same person who fired its growth 20 years ago. Yes, the EFF's election manifesto is *How To Create a Failed State For Dummies*. And yes, a weak, fractured or, in the case of the EFF, allegedly corrupt opposition is a danger to a country because it is less likely to hold the rampant ruling party to account.

But right now, most of the day-to-day criticism of the opposition, however valid, sounds about as useful as a medical intern tapping a bloodied surgeon on the shoulder and saying, 'Doctor? I know you're currently assessing this patient who was hit by a train and then rolled into a field where he was driven over by a combine harvester and then nibbled by rats, but I'm looking at these X-rays and I think you need to know that this patient has quite a nasty sinus infection which, left untreated, might get into the brain and – oh okay, I see the head's off, so, okay, cool cool cool . . . '

Still, in fairness to the pundits who keep coming back to them, we have to admit that the DA and EFF do make themselves very hard to ignore. The DA's leadership meltdown in 2019 was as dignified and discreet as a family spilling out onto a Brakpan street to slap each other with Crocs. Before she retreated into a private account, Helen Zille's Twitter persona had become an endless shriek for Hugo to *bel die polisie*[15] as a sizeable faction inside the DA abandons its dreams of national power and instead focuses on competing with the Freedom Front Plus.

Then again, perhaps this kind of embarrassing display is what happens when you try to live a double life for too long.

The DA, in its heart and soul, is a bureaucrat. It feels keenly the unfairness of not getting the respect it deserves. It often sighs or rolls its eyes. But, as the faintly disappointing child of faintly depressed Calvinists, it is nevertheless at its desk at 8:00 am sharp and never takes a sick day. It works quietly and hard: what it lacks in brilliance it makes up for in diligence. It keeps excellent records and perfect accounts. It forgets nothing, unless ordered to do so by its boss. It deeply distrusts outsiders or people who ask questions: the only thing that leaks in its world is the brown, government-issue air-conditioner mounted up in the corner of its brown, government-issue office. It is reliable. It is professional. It believes with burning conviction that it is correct on almost all matters: it listens to people for only as long as it takes to formulate a response and explain to them why their feelings are invalid. And it is as charismatic as the dead pot plant on the corner of its brown, government-issue desk.

---

15 In case you missed it, google 'Hugo, bel die polisie' . . .

This is a problem, because people don't want to vote for a T-crossing, I-dotting pedant with vast institutional knowledge but no social skills. They want to vote for a radiant, magnetic rockstar; part reconciler, part warrior-prophet, who combines, in one, shimmering persona, the best aspects of their consoling mother, their strict father and their childhood sweetheart.

This is very upsetting for the DA. As it puts on its brown tie in the morning, making sure the bottom is the appropriate height above its brown leather belt, it allows itself to wish for a moment that it lived in a world in which people loved it for how well it did its job. If only, it sighs as it clocks in at 7:55 and heads for the lifts, sexy and popular people would offer to buy it a drink when it told them how often it had dragged the ANC to court. If only, it thinks, as it takes its exactly-one-hour lunch by itself, it could post its perfect auditors' reports on Tinder instead of a profile picture. If only, it sighs as it gets into its pyjamas that night, this was a world in which listing the many concessions one had forced from the state, and the many abuses of power one had delayed or stopped, was an effective form of foreplay.

But this is not that world.

And so the DA does the only thing it can. It goes out and, burning with embarrassment, hires a sequined tuxedo, like the one it once saw in a magazine when it went on holiday to Hartenbos. It asks the young clerk if it's what the kids are wearing, and she makes a serious face and says, 'Tooootally.' This reassures it. It then goes to a shoe shop and is persuaded to buy a pair of extremely expensive sneakers which the salesperson assures it are 'on fleek', which it assumes is a kind of payment plan. It tells her that it doesn't have a fleek card. She giggles and murmurs, 'No shit.' It doesn't understand.

That evening, it goes to the club where the other political parties hang out. It orders a drink with an umbrella in it – that's what Mom and Dad always had on those holidays at Hartenbos – and watches the political players in their expensive suits and pointy shoes laughing and dancing and glad-handing their way around the floor; the ease of their smiles and the perfect timing of their facile jokes and oleaginous pick-up lines. It watches how they touch the voters, and knows that if it tried to touch them like that it would be arrested. At some point it tries to dance, and a kind-looking person comes up and says, 'I love that you don't care what people think about you!', and it retreats back to the shadows. Here it finds a small group of people who look tired and responsible, the way people should, and it haltingly tells them about its perfect audits. They raise their eyebrows and say, 'Wow, cool', and they all exchange numbers. But there is a clear understanding that nobody is getting naked later. Still, it's a start. And so, as the weeks turn into months, the DA comes to this club, over and over again, its sequinned suit and earnestness setting it apart, to watch the populists do yet another blazing dance routine and go home with a voter on each arm, whispering into their ears that they're going to give them everything they've ever dreamed of . . .

Nobody can go on like that, trying to be an austere, monkish guardian of democratic processes as well as a light-footed, sweet-talking lech. The DA was always going to crack.

The EFF, on the other hand, has never pretended to be anything other than what it is: an old-timey millenarian cult built in the image of and in service to Julius Malema and his disciples. Released from the restrictions that bind actual political parties like the DA – implementable polices, economic reality, the laws of physics – it is free to roar any fantasy, threat or populist catch-phrase it wants. Venezuela is an economic model that must be emulated! Busisiwe Mkhwebane is a splendid choice as Public Protector! VBS bank is being victimised by white people and must be protected! Cyril Ramaphosa won't become president! Anton Harber and Thandeka Gqubule were Stratcom agents! Pravin Gordhan must be defended, no, wait, Pravin Gordhan is a dog of white monopoly capital!

It doesn't matter if any of it is true or not. It doesn't matter if its claims and predictions are debunked or proved to be nothing but opportunistic hot air. It doesn't matter if it is forced to pay damages for libel. For the cult, whose leaders are only interested in recruiting the sort of people who join cults, all that matters is that the message goes out, broadcast by a media kept constantly wrong-footed by Malema's Angry/Forgiving Patriarch routine. Cult members will do all the rest themselves, jumping through all sorts of psychological and emotional hoops to make sure that they are conforming to the high priests' version of reality. Debunked claims and failed predictions are ignored. Adverse legal findings are blamed on biased judges. Allegations of corruption are dismissed as a conspiracy. And all the while, the party roars and threatens and grumbles, speaking almost endlessly and saying almost nothing.

One of things the EFF has told us with monotonous regularity is that it is a 'government in waiting'. In this instance I agree with it. The EFF *is* a government waiting. And waiting. And waiting. This is why the party leadership has been careful not to put a date on its ascent to power. It has done extraordinarily well to claim 10 per cent in just its second general election, but if it continues to shoot the lights out and grows by a phenomenal 20 per cent every five years, it will be in government in 45 years. This in itself will not discourage Julius Malema, who will be 84 at that stage and therefore just reaching puberty by the standards of African strongmen, but you understand why they're not naming dates.

Admittedly, that figure is misleading. Parties do not grow in a linear fashion but rather rise and fall on prevailing economic and political tides. In its current shape the EFF is an ethnic nationalist party which draws its energy from an engine fuelled by utopian magical thinking, militaristic posturing, violent rhetoric, and regular claims that it is the victim of a shadowy conspiracy by Gordhan, South Africans of Indian descent, white people, journalists, or whichever other minority is the most politically lucrative that week. A country that gave such a party 30 per cent of the vote would be well on the way to giving it 40 per cent; and a country that gave it 40 per cent would be so broken and full of rage that it might very soon do away with elections entirely, having decided that democracy isn't really working.

If, on the other hand, the EFF suffers its worst nightmare and is forced to do some actual governing – of a particularly unlucky province, perhaps – it will be revealed very quickly indeed as an organisation that can't govern because that was never the plan. Malema is a creation of the ANC, and, like the ANC, he is much more interested in being in government than in doing any actual governing. It is easy to promise the earth when it's not yours to give, but the moment the EFF has to deliver anything more substantial than paranoia, conspiracy and a caricature of revolution, its profound limitations will be on full view.

Indeed, we've already had a sneak preview of these, courtesy of the EFF's role in foisting the UDM's Mongameli Bobani on the unfortunate residents of Nelson Mandela Bay. Within months of this cynical manoeuvre, the metro was collapsing and the EFF was explaining that Bobani had been everyone's mistake (the benefit of being in a coalition government) and that the dog had eaten its homework. Its first significant act, when given a little bit of power by voters, had been to demonstrate that it is the ANC but with a lot more shouting; a party that, in the grand traditions of its grandfather, Jacob Zuma, will condemn the 'masses' it pretends to love to corruption and incompetence if it means securing a scrap of power for itself and lucrative positions for its leaders.

That, however, is all I want to say about the opposition, because I've already fallen into a trap I had hoped to avoid: talking about opposition parties exactly how they want us to talk about them.

It's there in the first paragraph, where I mention the ANC, then the DA, and then the EFF. 'South Africa's three largest parties,' the media would say, as if we're all off on a game drive trying to tick the Big Three off our list of political animals. It's everywhere, that one-two-three list, partly because it appeals to a certain kind of logic, but mainly because that's how the parties themselves want us to refer to them, all bunched together like Olympic medallists on a podium.

The trouble is, it's a deeply unhelpful way of thinking about the ANC, DA and EFF. It is, in fact, a trifecta of misdirection. The 'three largest parties' exist only as a mathematical idea. In reality, what South Africa has is a ruling theocracy which deigns to contest secular elections, then more acres of daylight, and then the angry cultists in their thought-proof bunker who comprise the largest of the 46 small, tiny and microbial parties that contested the 2019 elections.

It can be difficult to see this arrangement, mostly because we are not encouraged to see it: like children growing up looking at the Mercator projection of the world map, we have been conditioned to believe that Greenland is bigger than Africa and that the ANC, DA and EFF dominate South Africa's politics and are therefore entitled to dominate our public life. But, luckily, there is a much more accurate, and therefore necessary, way of eyeballing the true lay of the land. And it's a method entirely endorsed by the DA and EFF themselves.

In January 2020, Education Minister Angie Motshekga proudly announced to the nation that the class of 2019 had shot the lights out: for the first time in democratic South Africa, the overall Matric pass rate had risen above 80 per cent. It was wonderful news for hundreds of thousands of children as well as the nine operators of the steam-powered Inflate-O-Matic machine in the basement of the Education department, which raises the final Matric mark to politically acceptable levels by adding actual marks scored to imaginary marks assigned, subtracting the current level of despair in state schools, dividing by the number of days teachers are absent, multiplying by the average income of Education ministry staff, and then calculating the square root of just how stupid Angie Motshekga thinks we are.

I'm joking, of course. The state doesn't cook the Matric marks by using a steam-powered machine. It does it by making children study Maths Literacy instead of actual mathematics, by offering Life Orientation (the scholastic version of Oprah yelling, '*You* get an extra 80 marks and *you* get an extra 80 marks! You *all* get an extra 80 marks!') and, most effectively of all, simply making sure academically weaker children never get the opportunity to write Matric, either by holding them back in Grade 11 until they improve or drop out, or by letting children fall through the cracks and out of the system.

And they are falling out by the hundreds of thousands. For years, education experts have been sounding an increasingly urgent alarm, pointing out that only about half of the children who start Grade 1 make it to Matric. That's about half a million Grade 1s who never become Grade 12s; half a million young lives flicked off the conveyor belt every year onto an ever-growing heap of wasted potential.

This appalling rate of attrition has given rise to a strong argument that the official Matric pass rate trumpeted by the state is merely a reflection of how the surviving half – carefully curated and artificially selected – is performing. To figure out the true effectiveness of the primary and secondary education systems, they argue, we need to follow the entire cohort of Grade 1s who started school twelve years ago and see how many of that initial group went on to pass their Matric exams.

Which brings me back to the DA and EFF, both of which issued press statements in January endorsing the logic outlined above, demanding that the real pass rate be measured by using the number of *potential* matriculants rather than the number who finally got there.

I agree with both of them. This is absolutely the best way to gauge the education system. It is logical. It offers a much clearer and more accurate picture of the state of things. It does away with political posturing and pompous claims. Which is why I think it's time we applied it to election results, too. If we want to assess how popular particular parties really are, it makes no sense just to tally up votes cast for them without looking at the bigger picture. This, after all, is the electoral equivalent of only counting marks scored by children who made it to Matric while ignoring those who fall by the wayside. Instead, we should rather look at the entire cohort of South Africans who are eligible to vote and see which proportion of them endorses each party.

Once we go this route and calculate election results based on the pool of eligible voters rather than the pool of people who found someone to vote for, the numbers stand in stark contrast to the claims of the 'Top Three' that they represent most citizens. What the general election in May 2019 revealed is that the ANC is supported by 27.9 per cent of voting-age South Africans, the DA by 10 per cent, and the EFF by 5.2 per cent. Put another way, 72.1 per cent of eligible voters do not endorse the ANC, 90 per cent do not endorse the DA and 94.8 per cent do not endorse the EFF.

These figures might sound startlingly poor, but South Africa's political parties are not unique when it comes to winning over relatively small numbers of citizens while pretending that they enjoy almost universal acclaim. In 2019, even *The Guardian* declared Boris Johnson's win a 'landslide', despite the fact that only 27 per cent of eligible voters had supported him. We are often told that Americans are more divided now than at any time since the Civil War, glaring at each other across a political and ideological divide which has touched almost every citizen of the Republic. And yet in 2016, when the dust settled after one of the most high-stakes and acrimonious elections in generations, Hillary Clinton had been endorsed by just 26.3 per cent of eligible voters, while Donald Trump could claim only 25.1 per cent.

Looking at political popularity in this way draws back a curtain on the mass of potential voters who live beyond the glare of the electoral cycle. And it is immense: in 2019's general election, half of South Africans who could vote, didn't.

There is a school of thought that insists this group doesn't matter. If you don't vote, this argument goes, you don't get to complain. It encourages us to believe that those standing out there in the dark have willingly surrendered their agency and therefore, like people who have slipped away in the night leaving no forwarding address, no longer matter.

I must confess that I believed this line for some time. But I have since come to realise that simply ignoring the half of South African voters who don't participate in elections is just as shortsighted, and potentially dangerous, as ignoring the half of South African Grade 1s who don't reach Matric. Worse, I have realised that I was merely parroting a line fed to me by politicians. Because, of course, non-voters don't matter to politicians. This is why abstaining from voting is a pointless form of protest. Politicians are, by definition, only concerned with what voters think. By refusing to vote, all you're doing is giving already neglectful politicians official permission to ignore your needs and opinions entirely.

I have spoken to resolute non-voters who believe that by abstaining they are forcing politicians to see them and their deep concerns about the political system. I understand their desire to protest, and we can all understand their dissatisfaction with the parties on offer, but I can't help feeling that abstaining from voting is like boycotting a party to which 30 million other people have been invited and hoping that the host will lie awake all night, worrying about why you didn't pitch.

In 2019, an Afghan politician named Ashraf Ghani won just 5.2 per cent of eligible votes in that country's election. Today, that politician is referred to as Mr President. Under the current system, fed to us by politicians and their media spin doctors, it doesn't matter that Ghani won an election in which almost nobody voted. All that matters is that he won 50.64 per cent of the votes that were cast somewhat freely and mostly fairly. South Africa's legion of non-voters could double in size, but someone is still going to be president when the votes are counted.

So why jump through all these arithmetical hoops to try to point out that legitimate election results are still legitimate but just in a different way than we thought?

The first reason is that we need to step back from the toxic narratives, cooked up by professional gaslighters and circulated by cynical politicians and credulous followers, that dominate our thoughts and conversations. Which means that we need to notice if politicians are urging us to ignore or even deny the reality of half of our compatriots. Shining a light on those outside of conventional party politics will no doubt annoy those people whose careers depend on looking important, but if we are to gain a clearer picture of this democracy, I believe it is essential to acknowledge that half of us are not participating in the democratic experiment in South Africa, either by choice or because it is too difficult or dangerous to vote. Indeed, if the Independent Electoral Commission counted citizens who voted with their feet rather than with a ballot, we might even have to consider the paradoxical possibility that democracy, at least in its current state, is not the most popular form of government in this country.

The second reason is about self-care. Every day, political parties bombard us with an endless, often subliminal barrage of claims about their importance. Dominating the headlines, sucking up far more oxygen than they are entitled to, barging through our collective consciousness like one endless, eternal blue light convoy, their sheer prevalence in society encourages us to believe their claims that we need them; that they deserve their immense salaries and perks; that they are, in short, too big to fail.

The media is, unfortunately, complicit in this, although this is not entirely the media's fault. It is the job of journalists to get close enough to politicians to expose their hypocrisy and reveal their abuses of the public trust. But access comes at a cost, and that cost is endless, often uncritical coverage. The EFF has played this game particularly well, consistently getting more airtime than the DA, a party which represents twice as many citizens.

Acknowledging the missing half, and seeing what those percentages really represent, is a way of turning down the noise and deflating that immense balloon of pomposity and entitlement that looms over our political landscape. Suddenly, the 'Big Three' stop being immutable laws of political physics and become the representatives of relatively tiny segments of the South African public. Suddenly, the people who present themselves as a politburo of Easter Island heads carved by the gods and worshipped by an awed nation, start looking more like what they're supposed to be: service providers who can be fired when they're not doing their job and replaced by other, better service providers.

Such thinking can only benefit democracy as a whole, but I think it also offers important benefits to our private, personal mental health. If you have allowed the EFF and its stenographers in the media to convince you that it is, in fact, a 'government in waiting' that enjoys the support of 'the masses', its threats to seize and implode the economy can sound like a gathering political storm. But if you know that Julius Malema is talking to five per cent of the population, those threats start sounding like what they are: a brand of political theatre being performed for a loyal but tiny group of fans. Likewise, the almost trebling in size of the Freedom Front Plus in May 2019 might have alarmed you. This, after all, is a party founded to promote the establishment of a secessionist ethnic *volkstaat*, and one that, in 2003, welcomed the remains of the Conservative Party, itself formed in 1982 because it considered PW Botha's apartheid regime too liberal. You might have feared that such a surge represented the rise of the white right in South Africa. And yet it is important to remember that the 414 000 people who voted for the FF+ represent just 1 per cent of eligible voters. Even if you assume (incorrectly) that only white people voted for the FF+, then at absolute most just 12 per cent of eligible white voters put their cross next to Pieter Groenewald's face. If the FF+ represents the white right, and the white right is rising, then it has risen only to ankle height.

I don't want to dismiss rational fears about the potential for highly racialised nationalism or even fascism to take root in South Africa.

I don't want to discount the power that politicians do hold. South Africa is still covered with the scars of what happens when democracy is perverted and abused by minorities. In 1948, the National Party used an already farcical 'democratic' system to seize control of a country of 12 million people with just 401 834 votes.[16] I want the media to keep hounding politicians, even if it means having to listen to the pompous sanctimony that is the price of that quid-pro-quo arrangement.

But I also want to stay alert to the relentless inflation – of reputations, of threats, of party narratives – which masquerades as gospel truth every day. If I'm going to read the promises and pronouncements of the 'Big Three', I must also remember that these are parties rejected by the vast majority of South Africans, and reinterpret those claims from that perspective. If I'm going to worry about the rise of populism, I also owe it to myself to keep asking: yes, but how popular are the populists? If I am going to be wary of fascistic tendencies in some of our more belligerent megalomaniacs, I want to keep asking: 'Okay, "Commander-In-Chief", but you and whose army?' And if I'm going to accept that it is a crisis when our education system dumps half of our children along the way, I also want to keep asking: why the great silence about the half of South African adults who are not participating in our much vaunted democracy? Where are they? Can they be brought back into the system, or have they abandoned the democratic project for good?

If I'm going to nudge myself towards a clearer, more balanced, and ultimately calmer perspective on South Africa, I must resist the

16 They didn't even win a majority among the tiny minority of citizens allowed to vote: the United Party won 524 230 votes, but, much as Clinton won the popular vote in 2016 but lost the electoral college, the UP failed to secure as many seats as the NP.

addictive drama of the 25 per cent, the 10 per cent, the 5 per cent, and the 0.1 per cent who control them all and get rich from them.

And I must start wondering, honestly and with an open mind: how does the other half live?

Chapter 10

The Penalty of Death

In the first season of *Star Trek: The Next Generation*, the voyagers of the starship Enterprise find themselves on Rubicun III, a planet populated almost entirely by blonde fitness instructors wearing the 1987 version of athleisure.

The citizens of Rubicun III, who call themselves the Edo, spend most of their days jogging briskly from point to point like extras in a straight-to-video remake of a Leni Riefenstahl film. The Edo also have a lot of sex, although, this being a family show in the days before *Game of Thrones*, this seems to consist mostly of nuzzling necks and stroking knees. As you might expect from people who have never gone longer than eight minutes between orgasms, everybody is very relaxed, and the crew of the Enterprise find themselves welcomed and invited for some flirty jogging.

But things are about to go very wrong. During a game of catch with some local Edo teens, Wesley Crusher, the starship's resident boy wonder, bounds across a shrubbery and crashes through a small greenhouse. Moments later, a very stern policeman-slash-personal trainer jogs up and prepares to administer Wesley's punishment: death by lethal injection.

What Wesley hasn't realised until now is that Rubicun III is policed not by buff personal trainers but by a roving 'punishment zone' which wanders randomly but lethally across the planet. Any crime committed inside this zone is punishable by death, no matter how small the infraction. It is straight out of the wildest curmudgeonly dreams of Walt Kowalski in *Gran Torino*: a slightly annoying teen is about to be legally executed for trespassing on someone's lawn.

The beefcake tasked with administering the lethal injection is sombre, even sad. Taking a life is a terrible thing, but he understands that the needs of the many outweigh the shocked pubescent protests of the few. When the ship's senior officers are alerted and start trying to negotiate Wesley's pardon and release, the Edo leaders make it clear that they are not bloodthirsty or even draconian. The punishment zone might pop up arbitrarily, but the rules are very clear: overstep, and you are killed. Also, never skip leg day.

In the end, the episode chickens out of any real exploration of the politics and ethics around capital punishment. The Edo turn out to be the slightly cultish servants of a small extraterrestrial ball of light, a sort of orbiting Tinkerbell, which they worship as a god and which, presumably, demands that they bump off teens who ruffle the topiary. The crew of the Enterprise make it very clear that they don't approve of capital punishment, but also don't want to violate their Prime Directive of not interfering in the ways of other civilisations. Well, except for rescuing Wesley.

A very brief and superficial foray into internet Trekkie lore taught me that the episode is not generally liked, presumably because of its jumbled plot and strong focus on the importance of cardio. Still, before the episode 'collapses under the weight of its own ridiculousness', as sci-fi writer Keith DeCandido put it in a 2011 review, it does offer one a peculiar parallel with South Africa: a view of a society which believes the death penalty is not just necessary but is also a fundamentally civilising force in society.

For the Edo, and for many of the South Africans who want capital punishment brought back, the execution of criminals is not a barbarous act. Those who legislate it or carry it out are not monsters. Wesley was not going to be executed by a mob but by a representative of the state who fully understood the gravity of what he was about to do. Every day I see angry South Africans on Facebook urging the state to 'just shoot the bastards!', but I'm sure if I asked them to explain the practicalities of what they were imagining, they would insist at the very least on some sort of hastily assembled firing squad acting on behalf of the justice system. This is not the Wild West, after all. No, both the Edo and many South Africans believe that executing law breakers is a just and civilised method of creating and maintaining a just and civilised society. Both believe that a society can kill people and remain well adjusted, mentally and emotionally stable, and harmonious; that murder by the state leaves no blood spatter on the rest of society.

At this point I feel I should apologise for luring you here under false pretences. I've set you up with sexy aliens and cheesy but endearing 1990s sci-fi, and suddenly here we are, talking about the death penalty in South Africa. But perhaps that's the nature of crime and punishment in this country: one minute it's fun and games, the next we're having angry conversations about awful things. We live in an extremely violent country where life is often shockingly cheap. It is natural to feel helpless, anxious, angry or fearful. The issue of the death penalty is not going to go away any time soon. And since we're going to keep talking about it – either to denounce it or to demand it – I think it's worth thinking about it, and people's motives for supporting or opposing it, a little more carefully than we might around the dinner table or braai.

I am not, however, going to pretend to be a neutral observer of this issue. I believe that the death penalty is not a solution to any of South Africa's problems, and that calling for its return is a mistake. But I am also not going to tell South Africans who want it reinstated that they are monsters. So instead, let me explain my position as clearly as I can. If you oppose the death penalty, all this will be preaching to the choir, but if you want it reinstated, perhaps some of what follows might sway you, or at least give you pause for thought.

The first thing I must acknowledge is that my view is that of a small minority. As much as liberals might take it as a given that the death penalty is wrong, this is not the belief of the overwhelming majority of South Africans.

I used to think that it was only elderly white people who supported capital punishment, perhaps because I only ever heard elderly white people vocally endorsing it. But I was mistaken. It is possible that most elderly white people want the death penalty reinstated, but so does a very large chunk of the rest of society. In 2013, when marketing research company Pondering Panda polled the opinions of 6 900 South Africans between the ages of 18 and 34, over three quarters wanted the death penalty reintroduced. South African Millennials and Generation Zedders are living in the twenty-first century and straining towards the twenty-second, but when it comes to crime and punishment most seem firmly rooted in the first or second.

Not surprisingly, political parties are pricking up their ears. The African Christian Democratic Party has campaigned on the death penalty ticket for many years, but it is being joined by newer allies with their eyes fixed hungrily on the youth. In 2018, the IFP's chief whip in parliament, Narend Singh, said that 'an open and frank discussion must be had in our country about this matter as South Africans are becoming more and more fed up with the scourge of violent and sexual crimes'. In 2019, shortly before the general election, the African Transformation Movement (ATM) appeared on the scene, similarly committed to killing bad people.

Indeed, in the final months of that year the question of the death penalty had forced itself to the centre of national politics. The murder of UCT student Uyinene Mrwetyana cracked through the surface of the country's despair around the endless torture and murder of women by South African men, and released a geyser of rage. Protesters outside parliament and online petitions were adamant: violent crimes against women should be punishable by death. The clamour grew so loud that the state was forced to respond, reiterating that it would not be reinstating the death penalty any time soon.

For many angry citizens, this response was outrageous. At best, it sounded like yet more ineffectual hand-wringing from a government hopelessly overwhelmed by the wave of criminality swamping the country. At worst, it seemed like callous disregard for the fear and trauma of South Africa's women.

But the state was right. It can't reinstate the death penalty.

The first reason is basic human fallibility. If police were incorruptible, evidence indisputable, forensic science infallible, eyewitnesses photographically accurate, lawyers unable to lie and the law they argued as immutable as the laws of physics, then maybe, just maybe, some proponents of the death penalty might be able to argue that society should start having a conversation about capital punishment.

But of course none of those scenarios exist anywhere in the world, least of all South Africa. Practically, the death penalty cannot be imposed by the state because the risk of getting the verdict wrong is so great, and the consequences of executing an innocent person, or at least one who is not guilty of a capital crime, too high.

Then there is the question of what, exactly, the death penalty is for.

Its supporters present two answers: deterrent and punishment. The first of these is simply not true. It has been established beyond reasonable doubt that the only thing that deters criminals is the possibility of being arrested, successfully prosecuted, and sentenced to real time in jail. In South Africa, that possibility is so slim as to be non-existent. According to constitutional law expert Pierre de Vos, somebody committing murder in South Africa has an 11 per cent chance of being sentenced and jailed. In other words, a murderer sitting in jail has been very, very unlucky. In crime fiction, the perfect murder is one that is carefully planned, every detail considered and every clue carefully erased. In South Africa, it sometimes feels like the perfect murder is walking up to someone in a crowded street in broad daylight, stabbing them with a knife on which you have engraved your name, address, ID number and blood type, before posting a selfie of you with your victim on Facebook.

I suspect that many of us have had our perception of crime and the likelihood of punishment badly distorted by Hollywood. In Western pop culture, a killer is still crouched over his victim when he hears the wail of sirens. The details of the plot differ – he might get caught or get away – but almost always, he has to run. The police are everywhere: skidding to a stop in a scrum of patrol cars; thundering overhead in helicopters, searchlights glaring; pounding down alleys, guns drawn. Indeed, there are often so many police converging that they get in each other's way, piling up in a gridlock of cruisers, SWAT vans and orange tape.

Watch those films and TV shows for long enough and it's easy to start believing that policing isn't enough. After all, if a criminal can expect that army of squad cars and helicopters to descend on him just moments after he's committed his crime, and he does it anyway, policing clearly isn't a deterrent. Society needs something more drastic. In Hollywood, that fearful fantasy has given rise to an entire mythology around extra-judicial execution, ranging from the lone gunslinger in Westerns to the maverick cop (*Dirty Harry, Lethal Weapon*) and rage-filled vigilante (*Death Wish, The Equaliser*) to one-man armies like the ultra-violent caricatures portrayed by Chuck Norris, Sylvester Stallone, Arnold Schwarzenegger, and, more recently, Keanu Reeves in his blood-drenched *John Wick* series. Some are presented as heroes; others are antiheroes. But all, without exception, are executioners exempted from legal and ethical concerns. They can kill scores of criminals in cold blood because, the myth insists, they must: extra-judicial murder is the only thing that can hold back the tsunami of indiscriminate violence, its perpetrators so blind with murderous blood lust that, like kamikazes or suicide bombers, they will all deliberately run – one by one – at the guns, blades or fists of our heroes.

To a certain extent, I think that this Hollywood logic has taken hold here. I keep hearing that our criminals are 'fearless' and 'brazen', words that conjure nightmarish connotations of Mad Max-style anarchists smashing their way through police roadblocks or attacking police patrols with assault rifles. Certainly some South African criminals do engage in military-style firefights with police. But for the most part, the 'fearlessness' of South African criminals is probably quite literal: they have nothing to fear, because the roadblocks and patrols simply aren't there. The wailing sirens and helicopters never arrive. It is no more 'brazen' to commit violent crime in South Africa than it is to jaywalk. And in a society in which punishment is an almost inconceivably unlikely outcome, the nature of the punishment is almost irrelevant: South African's Police minister could threaten criminals with prison, being publicly hanged, drawn and quartered, or teleported to Mars. All would provide the same deterrent: none whatsoever.

So if the only real deterrent to criminals is thorough policework, what about using the death penalty as a form of punishment?

Here, too, things get tricky.

Punishment is the act of exacting a price for causing harm to others, but when we demand the death penalty are we demanding retribution or revenge?

Modern justice is extremely cautious about meting out anything that looks like revenge, and with good reason. Firstly, revenge, almost by definition, legitimises an endless cycle of violence in a way that retribution does not. Imagine a society in which revenge is not only tolerated but is lauded as the only way to restore honour and see justice done. If a member of the Smith family kills your brother, you are not only entitled but expected to kill that Smith. At which point another Smith will be entitled and expected to kill you. And so on and so on, until nobody is left. Retribution, on the other hand, sees the state stepping in to break that cycle. If a Smith kills your brother, the state does harm to that person on your behalf and short-circuits the feud so nobody else has to die.

The second, and perhaps more obvious problem with revenge is that it implies passion, which is the last thing we want in a justice system. Justice, if it is to be worth the name, has to be dispassionate. This is why crimes are tried by judges and not the aggrieved parties, and why punishments are decided by a complex code of laws rather than the emotional needs of the victims or their families. It might not be satisfying, but it is better than the alternative, which risks a swift descent into vigilante justice, revenge- and 'honour'-killing, pogroms against scapegoated minorities – in short, the killing of innocent people.

The trouble with these arguments, however, is precisely that they are unsatisfying. To the person who has lost a loved one to a violent crime, dispassionate philosophy must seem insultingly cold-blooded and supremely impotent. When our people are violated or taken from us, we don't want legal research about deterrence. We don't want lectures on how the law has evolved and left behind the bloody, fallible urges of past centuries. At that moment, those bloody urges seem perfectly sensible, and those bloody acts entirely justified.

It is difficult to fault this reaction. I certainly don't judge anyone, shattered by a crime, wanting violent revenge. I am opposed to the death penalty, but I know that if I faced someone who had done something appalling to my family, I would want that person tortured, quite possibly to death. We are often told about the healing power of forgiveness, and popular culture is full of stories where the bereaved and the violated slowly rise above their rage and grief and move on, but I think it takes a very rare person not to go down the route of bloody vengeance.

Which is why, if you believe that the perpetrators of certain crimes must be put to death, I know it will take more than an intellectual argument to change your mind. If you have decided, for your own reasons, to set aside the research about deterrence and to embrace capital punishment, fully and openly, as a form of revenge, I understand the emotional impetus behind that decision.

But if that is what you've decided – that an eye for an eye is a sound way to run a society – then I must ask you to grant the rest of us three favours should your dystopia ever come to pass.

The first is that you don't ask the state to do your killing for you.

People who want to give the state the power of life and death believe they are making themselves safer. They're not. What they're really doing is gambling, based on current information and hope, that the state will remain as benevolent and liberal as it is right now, rather than become, say, apartheid South Africa or modern China, and merrily start using the death penalty to legally murder political opponents. Of course, states that are mutating into malevolent dictatorships don't need the permission of their citizens to institute the death penalty – they do that all by themselves – but why would you thrust a weapon like that into the hands of the state before it's even asked for it? Why would you willingly surrender the one, vital defence you have against the sort of violence meted out by the powerful and the untouchable for thousands of years? Why do you assume that it won't ever be used against you? 'Because I'm not a violent criminal,' you say. But when the state turns on its people and gives itself the power to start defining new crimes, you don't have to be a violent criminal. All you have to be is the wrong colour or religion, have the wrong friends, love the wrong person, read the wrong books, or just be in the wrong place at the wrong time.

Perhaps this won't sway those who can't imagine a world in which they are falsely accused and wrongly convicted of anything. So perhaps I should go on to my second favour and ask, if you are determined to execute someone, that you do it yourself, or at least be present when it is done by someone else whose services you have acquired.

In his 2019 feature on the rise of the ATM in *New Frame*, Dennis Webster recounted his meeting with the party's provincial chairperson, Veliswa Mvenya, who confirmed ATM's support for the death penalty.

This support, however, hadn't yet produced any firm ideas about how the deed should be done: Mvenya was clear that people would be executed, but insisted that it would not involve hanging. Why? '"Hanging is too . . ." Mvenya's sentence trailed off as she screwed up her face,' writes Webster.

Webster didn't press her to complete her thought, but I'd like to know: hanging is too what? Too upsetting for those watching, as the hanged person's eyes bulge out or their neck snaps or they twitch for a while before they stop moving? Too slow? Too reminiscent of what the apartheid state used to do? Perhaps shooting, then. Or does that also risk being an aesthetically displeasing mess, with all the brains and blood and faeces? If only it could be as clean and humane as on Rubicun III, yes?

Again, I concede that I might be preaching to the grimly converted here. If you are ready to pull the lever or trigger yourself, or order someone else to do it as you watch; if you have decided that the trauma of committing murder yourself will be outweighed by the sense of justice having been done and a monstrous wrong avenged with blood; then that is between you, your psyche and the prevailing legal system of the day. But if the aesthetics of execution bother you; if you want criminals killed but not in a way that is nauseating to you; if any single mode of execution makes you think, 'This is too . . .', then you have no business whatsoever demanding that someone else does the killing while you sit far away, protecting your eyes and soul from the scenes you have demanded must take place.

Finally, I have one more condition that I must, unfortunately, demand if you are going to insist that capital punishment is a workable system: if you believe in God, you must immediately recuse yourself from the entire debate and have no part in anything to do with the death penalty ever again.

I understand that this last demand might be tricky. Many of the most vocal supporters of capital punishment are religious people: the ACDP, for example, presents a world view proudly founded on the Old Testament, a book famous for its endorsements of genocide and extra-judicial killings. Remember the bit in Genesis where God tells Abraham to murder and burn his only son and Abraham says, 'Okay, but how about we first have a sort of trial to establish whether this is a reasonable demand that has some basis in law, given that right now this whole murder-your-child-to-prove-you-love-me thing is looking pretty needy for someone who claims to be an omnipotent superbeing, and, now that I'm thinking about it, raises a few red flags over the whole question of whether you are, in fact, God or just a really nasty hallucination?' Of course you don't. Because all that Abraham says is, 'How high do want me to stack the braai wood once I've knifed my child, boss?'

Religion's deep affection for murder, however, isn't the main reason the religious should be kept far away from the death penalty. No, my main concern is that I'm not sure they understand what death is.

If you genuinely believe that there is an afterlife, then you believe that when a person dies a substantial part of them continues living somewhere else. If your faith is fundamentalist, this afterlife might see the dead reunited with dead family members, living in metaphysical reconstructions of actual houses they once lived in, or involving an unexpected hookup with large numbers of virgins. If your faith is more esoteric, the personhood that exists in the afterlife might be more diffuse and generalised. But for most faiths, the dead continue living, forever.

Death, in other words, is not a final, total obliteration but a transition from one sort of life to another. This means that when a religious person calls for someone to be executed, they are merely calling for that criminal to be relocated – to go on living somewhere else, out of sight. And we already have a punishment like that. It's called 'life in prison'.

But of course prison doesn't feel like a harsh enough sentence. The point of the death penalty, for its supporters, is that it is the most severe judgement we can pass on a human being. Well, except if you believe in God. Because if you're religious, you believe that there is only one true judge: the Almighty. And the existence of that celestial Supreme Court means that a legal verdict and a sentence of death passed down in an earthly courtroom is more or less irrelevant. All that it's doing is acting as a kind of revolving door, shuttling wrong-doers straight into the courts of supreme justice, where God, not humans, will pass judgement.

In fact, to demand the death penalty as a true believer is to take a position of almost complete passivity. You are demanding so little (according to your belief system) that you might as well not support the death penalty at all. You have taken no position, made no difficult choices, shouldered no burden. You have demanded that a killer be held responsible for taking a life, but you have refused to take any responsibility whatsoever for his killing.

No, people who don't understand that death is final, and who pretend to be interested in justice while offloading it all onto an invisible, unreachable, unchallengeable judge, should recognise that they are hopelessly out of their depth when it comes to capital punishment and they should step back and stay silent.

Perhaps what I'm asking is impossible. South Africa remains trapped in the grip of extreme, apparently systemic violence, and we will continue to be shocked into rage and grief by the worst crimes. Which means that millions of citizens will continue to demand revenge via the death penalty. As I've said, this is an entirely understandable response. But perhaps, instead of arguing with each other about the death penalty, or, in the case of its supporters, calling for its return, we would all be better served by uniting in demanding more pragmatic and effective responses from the state than executions.

For example, if I were going to raise my voice or fists to the state, instead of demanding that it changes the Constitution to take back the power to execute me, I would rather demand that it implements the Constitution we currently have. Instead of calling on the police to 'kill the bastards', as Deputy Security Minister Susan Shabangu did in 2009, I would rather see a police force, purged of corrupt officers and trained to collect and process information and evidence, tracking and arresting the bastards in a way that secures convictions and creates a deterrent. Instead of paying attention to the vengeful gimmicks of the ACDP and ATM, or any other party busily monetising the fear and trauma of South Africans, I would rather see funding and airtime given to those researchers who are starting to find patterns in the crime statistics, identifying hotspots and trends that could potentially lead to more targeted policing.

If I am going to demand things from the state, I would certainly prefer to demand, instead of death, a criminal justice system in which a life sentence means life, and in which rapists and murderers are not paroled. I would rather demand a massive programme of education aimed at men and boys, targeting the patriarchal assumptions and normalised misogyny that continue to hide behind 'tradition'. I would rather demand that the state stops referring to the murder or rape of women with passive euphemisms and shameful omissions, describing women as victims of an apparently perpetrator-less crime. I would demand that it acknowledges that the problem South African women face is South African men; that South African men are waging an undeclared war against them. I would demand that femicide is made as high-profile a crime in South Africa as racism, and make sure that the people who will inevitably object to this understand that yes, men murder far more men than women in South Africa, but men don't murder other men because they believe they own them.

I concede that these demands might sound naïve or even futile. The ANC government is a cult of entropy and passive patriarchy. It can't even keep the lights on, so how could any sane person believe it could develop an excellent police force or change men's hateful attitudes to women?

But if South Africans are going to keep calling on the state to reintroduce the death penalty, then those who oppose it must keep calling, too, to point out the dangers and contradictions inherent in such a call. Because in the end, our safety and the success of our country will not be measured by the number of evil-doers we put to death but by the number of innocent people who are spared from evil deeds in the first place.

Chapter 11

On Immigration

Immigration is a topic that vexes many people. I don't know why, because to me it seems quite simple.

I think that rich countries that don't want poor immigrants living and working in them should be allowed to keep them out.

In fact, I think they should be allowed to build a great big wall around themselves. If they have a coast, they should be allowed to patrol it night and day, arresting anyone who comes within sight of their precious land.

Once they have secured their borders, they should be allowed to deport every person not born in their country, if they so wish.

And when they have sent away everyone not born to native parents on native soil, they should be allowed to celebrate their way of life, and congratulate each other for freeing themselves from the oppressive yoke of living in the world.

They should be allowed to grow old in the country of their birth, talking to their children in other countries (who are not, they insist, immigrants hoping for a better life but are instead 'global citizens') and asking them how to find a good plumber because for some reason there don't seem to be any in their town anymore.

When they fall and break their hip, they should be allowed to go straight to the front of the queue in hospital. Yes, there won't be anyone to help them, but simply going to the front of the queue will almost certainly make them feel a bit better as they wait for five days to see a specialist.

And once they've healed up nicely – well, mostly – they should be allowed to travel through their country, although not by train, because those aren't really running anymore, or by air, because they've shut down most of the airports because of staff shortages. But the most important thing is that when they travel around their country, they should be allowed to hear their own language spoken. Every third day, when they finally see another person.

Yes, they should be allowed to grow old – independent and free.

And when the last of them calls out, asking for someone to lift him back into his bed, he should be allowed the complete silence he always wanted, hearing nothing but the whispering of the native wind blowing through native trees, and the deep stillness of a nation left finally, blissfully alone, with all that space it always wanted, with nothing between its white, white bones and the ice-cold night sky.

Chapter 12

La Dolce Vita

In this chapter I am going to be writing about rich people. This is tricky, since 'rich people' is a very vague term and open to all sorts of abuse and misunderstanding. It is easy, for example, to create false dichotomies or to be guilty of hypocrisy. After all, I had the time to write this book, which means I, too, am rich. If you bought this book new in a bookshop, the chances are fairly good that you are also rich. Even if you stole it by downloading it in PDF format, it's possible that you are very, very rich. (In 2019, Julius Malema, a man worth millions, had no problem mounting Twitter to ask for a pirated version of Pieter-Louis Myburgh's *Gangster State.*) Which is why, for the sake of clarity, I think a short taxonomy of this species we call 'the rich' – *Decadentis Opulentis Opulens* – is in order, so that you and I can both be very clear on what I'm talking about.

There have been many subspecies of *Opulens*, that ancient amphibian that first dragged itself up out of the swamp and onto dry satin thousands of years ago. Many have gone extinct, killed off by natural predators like in-breeding, syphilis or failing to pay off the right warlord. Some simply had it coming. *Opulens Guillotinus*, for example, was a hyper-predatory subspecies which existed in Europe until the eighteenth century, rashly constructing enormous burrows out of gold and marble right out in the open with gates that were easily scalable by French peasants. In 2008, *Opulens Lehmanensis*, a small but jubilantly psychopathic subspecies that lived in skyscrapers on Wall Street, was on the verge of extinction until it was artificially inseminated with a vast bailout from American taxpayers, the unholy union spawning yet another subspecies, *Opulens Vampiricus Zombii*.

Today, however, the *Opulens* species can generally be divided into five main subspecies, presented here from most to least rich.

Opulens Abstractus. By far the richest of the species, they have evolved to avoid the fate of *Guillotinus* by existing at no physical address, their domicile represented only by a post-box in the Cayman Islands. After all, it is difficult to remove a head you can't find. Indeed, *Abstractus* are so rich that they have almost dematerialised, their physical human bodies being only a fractional part of a gigantic entity which exists only in derivatives, collateralised debt obligations, stock options and litigation.

Opulens Transparens. The invisible rich exist in the material world, but in places very few people have seen or even know about, and leave no trace of their activities, mainly because they own all the newspapers. If you are personally invited by *Opulens Transparens* to its estate, island or alpine bunker for the weekend, and are told to enter via the front door, you are either extremely rich yourself or are about to get fired. If you are personally invited by the assistant of the secretary of *Opulens Transparens*, and are told to report to the tradesman's entrance with your passport and a large plastic sheet, you need to change your name and move to Nepal at once.

Opulens Fugens. Not wealthy enough to dematerialise or decamp to an island, this subspecies – the furtive rich – lives hidden in plain sight. Having seen *Guillotinus* stripped of its assets, beheaded, and, much more upsettingly, made to pay tax and get a job, *Fugens* has evolved to be less expansive than its truncated ancestor, preferring densely wooded habitats surrounded by high walls and electrified fences, and avoiding contact with anyone except other *Fugens,* which it marries in order to preserve its wealth and recessive chin.[17]

Opulens Humilitas Bogus. Also known as Fauxhemians, *Humilitas Bogus* has refused to learn the lessons of *Guillotinus* and has not developed a fear of the less rich, insisting instead that it is a friend to the proletariat, blessed with empathetic or possibly psychic powers that allow it to feel a deep connection to all humans, which it demonstrates by slumming it in the sorts of yoga studios that have 10-year-old cars parked outside. It also has a highly developed environmental conscience, preferring to take only one air-conditioned tent to AfrikaBurn.

Opulens Precarius. The final, and largest, subspecies is that of the *Opulens Precarius,* the contingently rich. These are people who have a regular income, a reliable supply of relatively healthy food, shelter that they own or rent, and opportunities for education and travel. In other words, they are wealthier than the vast majority of humans and therefore technically rich. But they are also never more than three paychecks or two major medical crises away

17 In South Africa, some *Fugens* have left the forest in favour of grassy savannah called 'golf estates', but the less said about these wretched places the better. Golf estates are, after all, an immense failure of imagination upon which the very rich reveal their unique psychology: they could afford to build the Hanging Gardens of Babylon or Venice, but instead choose to recreate, on a vast scale, the dullest suburban garden imaginable – a huge lawn surrounded by shrubs – across which they wander endlessly talking about handicaps.

from catastrophe. Inevitably for such a large and wide-ranging subspecies, *Precarius* seems to include a number of variations. *Precarius Illusio*, for example, puts on a display of wealth that is based entirely on debt. *Precarius Inheritus* is a shabby-genteel creature, endlessly hibernating in a dim and musty burrow that was left to it by its parents that it can't afford to maintain but also can't afford to sell. *Precarius Condescens*, or very petty bourgeoisie, enjoys sniping at 'the rich' because it does not identify as rich but also cannot identify as poor. *Precarius Ex Matrimoneum* still has a sports car and a golf club membership but everything else went in the divorce. (I recently had an *Opulens* DNA test done – I got a printout of my bank balance – and I can confirm that I am a *Precarius Condescens Literaria Jackpotens*; someone who takes pot-shots at the very rich while hoping that his book will be a bestseller and transform him into a *Fugens*.)

As I said earlier, these are broad distinctions. The difference between the richest and least rich variations of *Opulens* is clear to even the casual observer, but it can be extremely difficult to tell more closely related subspecies apart. Certainly, there are some basic rules of thumb. My wife Tanya believes that you can generally tell how rich someone is by how quickly they are exonerated after murdering their spouse. I, on the other hand, tend to believe that you can tell subspecies from subspecies by looking at the items they collect in their burrows and insist on calling 'art'. *Abstractus* and *Transparens*, the two richest subspecies, have tastes more or less in line with their species names. *Abstractus*, for example, will pay tens of millions of dollars for conceptual art that exists in no physical form – a cube of air, say, contained in a metaphysical box, displayed in a room that doesn't exist in a city constructed purely out of critical discourse theory. *Transparens* prefers pieces that exist in the material world, but only on certain wavelengths and at certain times of year, such as a hologram of their deceased mother, created by reflecting the sunrise on the anniversary of her death through a crystal made of her compressed remains.

I don't know the kinds of art preferred by *Fugens* and *Humilitas Bogus* in the wider world, but in South Africa they each have very clear tastes. *Fugens* is drawn relentlessly towards large, impressionistic bronzes of cheetahs. I don't know why this is the case but perhaps it sees something of itself in cheetahs, which are also highly specialised, largely opportunistic creatures bedevilled by in-breeding. The local strain of *Humilitas Bogus*, on the other hand, prefers enormous paintings of the faces – just the faces – of unnamed black women, painted by white women. The wealthier the *Humilitas Bogus*, the larger the face: some are two storeys high, laboriously manoeuvred into cavernous entrance halls by teams of stevedores. For *Humilitas Bogus*, the Anonymous Black African Woman As Décor is irresistible.

Because of its diversity, range and smaller budget, *Opulens Precarius* tends to scavenge a much wider and more eclectic selection of decorations for its burrows, but even so, a keen-eyed zoologist can pick out certain favourites: photographs of familial groupings of *Precarius*, all dressed in white or black; antique maps of Africa with Latin place names and an etching of a ship in the corner; an excellent and treasured painting or etching of the foreign city *Precarius* visited as a young person before it had offspring and a motor plan and things got dramatically more precarious; fetish objects such as Carrol Boyes salad spoons and metal geckos; or the sensible reminder, spelled out in large words screwed into the wall, to 'LIVE', 'LOVE' and 'LAUGH'.

The trouble with using art to tell who's who, however, is that you have to be physically inside the burrow of an *Opulens* to see it, and even then it's not foolproof. For example, if you wake up strapped to a block of marble, surrounded by people wearing nothing but Venetian masks, and then someone chants, 'Let the harvest commence!', and a nurse appears and pats you on the arm and says, 'This will only sting for a moment, dearie,' you would rightly assume that the marble block is some sort of decoration, but it would be almost impossible to know if you've become the centrepiece of a *Fugens* fertility ritual, a conceptual art piece for a *Transparens*, or an organ donor for an *Abstractus*.

Which is why I can't tell you if the people who gather in my street every morning are rich, very rich or extremely rich. But I can tell you that they are distressed. Very distressed. Extremely distressed.

The problem is the street, which, like many in Cape Town's city bowl, is fairly narrow, flanked by small houses and the odd oak tree bulging out of an uneven pavement. Indeed, if you didn't know it was causing such great distress, you might even think of it as quaint, a throwback to a time when cities were built on a more human scale and streets only had to accommodate pedestrians, horses and the odd cart. But at some point between then and now, something else arrived on the street: a private school for girls. Which means that, every weekday morning and a surprising number of Saturdays, hundreds and hundreds of schoolgirls must be driven down this very narrow street and offloaded into it. And that means the arrival of the cars, and the unhappiness.

You see, these aren't really cars. They are gleaming, gilded barns on wheels. The mighty Sports Utility Vehicle: as sporting as dynamiting fish in a barrel and as utilitarian as cocaine snorted off a model's midriff. The SUV is the orgasm at the end of capitalism's wet dream, the climax of a process that has taken the humble motor car and engorged it into a pornographic, pumped-up fetish of an original idea. Also, it's very safe. That's the line one always hears.

Very safe. It's technically true, I suppose. But it's also an understatement. The SUV is safe the way a nuclear-armed superpower is safe. If there is the chance of a violent confrontation between *Opulens* and non-*Opulens*, such as a head-on collision, then *Opulens* will literally crush non-*Opulens*, obliterating it in a screeching, rending, orgy of overkill. The SUV leaves nothing to chance: 50/50 survival odds are for people in Korean hatchbacks.

Most importantly of all, the SUV offers those *Opulens* further down the food chain a kind of camouflage, a chance to blend in among the *Abstractus* and *Transparens*. In fact, you might say that the SUV is an enormous pill; a big, beautiful sedative designed to ease away the gnawing class anxieties of everyone below *Abstractus*. If cars were honestly named, this year would see the launch of the Jaguar Valium and the Porsche Xanax.

And yet, as I watch the SUVs waddle up onto pavements in their futile efforts to get around each other, it seems to me that they bring no comfort to the people driving them. On the contrary, it seems as if their drivers' dreams – of ease, of space, of being unique and singly admired and accommodated – are shattered anew each morning, over and over again, by the terrible *narrowness* – the goddamned *quaintness*! – of that blasted street. Range Rovers rove nowhere. Discoveries discover nothing but the limitations of Cape Town's spatial planning. Fortuners rue their misfortune. Evoques evoke only the sense of an Emirati royal family trying to flee their imploding kingdom and finding that, because they've always had chauffeurs, nobody knows how to drive or how roads work. It is like watching a fleet of aircraft-carriers try to park in a bathtub.

It has become popular to depict the very wealthy as aggressive, entitled drivers, leaning out of their limousines to sneer or snap at the *hoi polloi*. To be fair, I do encounter this kind from time to time, usually a small man driving a large German penis extension. But this is an anomaly. In my experience, the people who cling to the steering wheels of the biggest SUVs, like bush-babies clinging to a banana leaf in the rain, are not aggressive. They are just upset. Terribly, terribly upset and confused. And I think it's important to understand why.

Imagine, for a moment, that you are an *Opulens* somewhere between *Transparens* and *Humilitas Bogus.* You live in house roughly the size of a cathedral, specifically designed so that you never have to see other people. One afternoon, while gazing up at your double-storey acrylic painting of an Anonymous Black African Woman, your WhatsApp pings. The au pair is sick. You will have to fetch your own children from school. So you leave your home office, walk around the bronze cheetah in the entrance hall, journey across second dining room, descend the spiral staircase to the guest mezzanine, circumnavigate the games room, hike through the main kitchen, cross the laundry room, and enter a garage considerably larger than most South African houses. Waiting for you in the middle acre of this garage is your SUV, into which you clamber, using the seatbelt as a rope as you climb hand over hand, eventually reaching the leather base camp that is the driver's seat, into which you sink and fire up the small dinosaur-fuelled power station that lives under the bonnet of the car. You cruise down a driveway that is visible from space, pausing at your front gate that is gaily dappled with the festive red laser dots of the Maximum Kill Logistical Solutions snipers who guard your property, wait for them to give you the all clear, and then you nudge forward into the street and –

Lilliput.

Tiny Town.

Honey I Shrunk The World.

It's horrifying, like falling off your comfy, king-sized bed into the hidden heart of a termite nest; a teeming, crawling world seething with tiny, tiny things. Tiny cars cluster around your hubcaps. How do they even make cars that small? What do they run on? Lighter fluid? Tiny hovels, some of them with only one bathroom, crowd in from all sides. And people can see you! And not normal people, either! Peering at you with their beady little eyes! But you can't escape, because the roads – oh Jesus, the roads! – are the tiniest of all! Torturous, winding, claustrophobic, *tiny*. Christ, your medicine cabinet is bigger than some of these intersections.

As I make my way through my *Precarius* world in my Hyundai hatchback, nipping around and between the SUV logjams like a tsetse fly flitting around a herd of water buffalo, or drive up onto the pavement to avoid being crushed by a tyre that cost more than my education, I can see them looking at me with that disconsolate, disoriented expression. As I reverse back up the road because there's an *Opulens Fugens* coming and there's only room for one of us and I don't want to rattle the already fragile *Fugens* nervous system any more than necessary, I can see them asking me: who did this? Who took the city of my dreams and shrank it? How did the episode of *The Crown* that runs eternally inside my head turn into this ludicrous Looney Tune? And you! You in your microscopic conveyance! Is that a car or a fairy chariot made from the carapaces of beetles and the wings of gadflies? What manner of thing are you that you can live here? Are you a native of this shape-shifting, daemon-haunted moonscape? And if you are, can you plumb the ancient, earthy wisdom of your people and tell me: *Why is this happening*?

This is the elemental cry for help that reveals the true crisis of the wealthier *Opulens*, the terrible confusion that lies in its heart; that makes it glance endlessly over its shoulder and peer anxiously ahead, groping for landmarks, fumbling with the map of its life. It is why it looks so tired and sad and confused as it steamrolls its way through the world. It is because *Opulens* doesn't know that it is *Opulens*. The rich don't know that they are rich. And because they don't know it, they have come to the logical conclusion that they are normal, which means that everything beyond their walls and the car windows has turned suddenly, absurdly, frighteningly abnormal.

Opulens Precarius can, sometimes, make a compelling argument for why it isn't rich, depending on what you mean by rich. It can tell you about the terrible stress of servicing debt and of clinging to the middle class in a way that can sound quite alarming as long as you're not someone who is not rich and who doesn't have the luxury of access to capital and therefore exposure to debt. But for all its protestations, *Precarius* is rich, which means it forms the base of a pyramid of endless, insatiable yearning and projection, each layer gazing upward, refusing to look at the world at its feet as it strains for something just beyond itself. *Precarius* can't own the home it wants, and so doesn't think it is rich. *Humilitas Bogus* owns the home it wants, but doesn't own the woodland it yearns to gambol through. *Fugens* owns the woodland but can't afford an island. *Transparens* owns an island but isn't rich enough to leave the material world and dissolve into pure maths. And *Abstractus*, which owns everything, clearly doesn't think it is rich enough because it spends most of its time using pure maths – and often impure maths – to avoid paying tax. And speaking of impure maths, this isn't just the envy of *Condescens* talking. In a 2019 survey by financial services firm Ameriprise Financial which included 700 Americans with more than $1 million in inevitable assets, just 13 per cent of those millionaires defined themselves as wealthy. Everybody else insisted that they were upper-middle class, middle class or even poor.

We have been trained (mostly, I must admit, by *Opulens Condescens* like me) to roll our eyes and despair at the solipsism, ignorance and self-delusion of the very rich. But I get it. Because feeling rich isn't about how much you have: it's about how much you have in relation to the people whose circumstances you aspire to. If you're an American worth $10 million, you are, by global standards, staggeringly wealthy. But if you are worth $10 million but want to be worth $50 million – if you gaze at the people who go to those parties or loll on those yachts and think, '*Those* are my people, and one day I will join them!' – then you are very likely to believe that you are not rich. Indeed, if you start feeling that distance between you and your chosen tribe as a lack or a loss, I can absolutely understand how you might also start believing that you are middle class or even poor.

Perhaps this is how so many South African *Opulens* can see poverty every day, be endlessly shown how their circumstances differ from those of the poor, and still not believe that they are rich. Because they aren't comparing themselves to the society in which they live. They are comparing themselves to the one in which they believe they should be living: a transcontinental, trans-hemisphere fantasy, a place made out of a pure projection and aspiration. *Opulens'* body may drive its SUV along highways in Johannesburg or Cape Town but its soul is altogether elsewhere, flitting between London, New York, Dubai, Paris and Los Angeles; searching for its dream tribe, the imagined people whose imagined lives and customs and homes exert the greatest pull on its ambitions and sense of self. In some cases, that spiritual home doesn't even exist any more. I have met South African *Opulens* who have constructed around them a magical fantasy of pre-war Europe, a town-and-country idyll in which the God-King-Empire trinity has not been challenged by ugly ideas like democracy or science; in which men are to be obeyed and women are to be looked at and bred; and in which it is entirely normal to refer to a black grandfather and combat veteran as 'the garden boy'.

All of which is why, when one breaks the rules of polite *Opulens* society and suggests that it is, in fact, very wealthy by the standards of its country or its continent, it will look bemused and reply, 'Yes, but those aren't really standards, are they?' To South African *Opulens*, it's a silly comparison, like telling a sick person that they should be feeling much better because they're not dead. When you believe that your once-and-future tribe lives in Kensington or Central Park West or Beverly Hills – or, in the case of many South African *Opulens Precarius*, in the suburbs of Sydney or Auckland or Toronto – the only comparison that matters is with them, there. And since you are not nearly rich enough to live with them, there, you must arrive at the logical conclusion that you are not rich.

So why point any of this out? What is the use of writing about the huge blind spots of a group of which I am myself a member, albeit fairly far down the food chain? Isn't this just hypocrisy, or an attempt at what the right calls virtue-signalling?

Well, I am a writer, and therefore I must admit that I am predisposed to some of the uncharitable and hypocritical traits of *Precarius Condescens*. But the point I'm trying to make isn't a condescending one. I genuinely don't think *Opulens'* denial about its wealth is entirely the result of greed or arrogance or some moral failing. Instead, I think it the inevitable result of having the means to inflate a bubble around ourselves and fill it with our projections of who we think we are and what we'd like to be; to float away from the world as it is; to start believing that the trappings of wealth are things like horse paddocks and infinity pools rather than things like household insurance, access to private medical care and a car.

I suspect this basic urge of *Opulens* – to emigrate psychologically to a land of its own aspirations – is why, when it is forced to notice the poor (a persistent buzz on the intercom, a tap on the car window) it glares at them with such suspicion or open hostility. It is not necessarily physical fear, although of course the memory of *Opulens Guillotinus* lingers. Instead, I think, those glares reflect the power the poor have to burst the *Opulens* bubble (and therefore do enormous damage to its soul) simply by existing. An *Opulens* may spend millions creating a perfect fantasy, and may protect it behind high walls and determinedly apolitical attitudes. But just one beggar at the gate sends tremors through all those carefully laid foundations; a vexing, jarring intrusion from the periphery like an alarm clock starting to interrupt a beautiful dream. No wonder the glares are so fierce.

Thinking about *Opulens* as a species lost in a collective dream has some obvious short-term benefits. Reminding myself that those above me on the food chain don't know that they are rich, and are therefore living in a state of almost constant confusion and disorientation, makes me feel slightly more kindly towards them, or at least less hostile, which in turn lowers my blood pressure. When I find myself parked in by two SUVs and am overwhelmed by the desire to key 'YUPPIES RAUS!'[18] into their paintwork, I try to remember that their drivers didn't do it because they're bad people. They did it because they didn't think my car was a car that might need to drive anywhere, much as you might see a crushed tin can lying in a gutter and rightly assume that it probably won't need space to reverse.

But that's as far as the consolation goes. Because if you are a human being on Planet Earth, there is nothing reassuring about the rich not knowing they are rich. Indeed, it may yet kill us all.

Ask the average *Opulens* what the greatest threat to this planet is and it will talk to you about viruses or nuclear war or an asteroid.

---

18 The battle cry of Berlin activists pushing back against gentrification, regularly spray-painted on apartment doors and any BMW or SUV that parks on the wrong street.

If it is a *Precarius*, it will probably tell you about climate change. If it is a *Fugens* or a *Transparens*, it might mention socialism. None of us will ever speak directly to an *Opulens Abstractus*, but if we could communicate with it via its lawyer's lawyer, it would probably reveal that its nightmare trifecta of threats is the closing of tax havens, the rise of clean energy, and women wanting to drive without a male relative supervising them. But put four vodkas into any of them and ask them the same question again, and almost all will tell you that the real crisis is . . . overpopulation!

You've probably heard this lecture yourself, perhaps delivered by an uncle who doesn't read books because everyone knows the real information is being suppressed by the government and only his favourite podcast, produced by a former currency trader called FreedomWolf69, cuts through the political correctness to tell it like it is. Citing the shoutings of FreedomWolf69 and a misquoted paragraph from 1968's *The Population Bomb* he once saw on Facebook, and drawing on his extensive racism and xenophobia, this uncle will explain to you that civilisation is about to end under a tsunami of differently hued babies. The pigmentation of the babies will depend on your uncle's particular brand of bigotry – sometimes the baby-tsunami is 'Asian', sometimes 'African', sometimes 'Muslim' – but I can pretty much guarantee that it will always have a darker skin tone than your uncle does.

Of course pronouncements about overpopulation can sometimes be useful. For example, if you find yourself with a stranger who starts talking about 'demographics' and how 'those people breed like rabbits', be grateful: they have just announced that they are a racist and a moron, and have saved you the bother of wondering if you should try to get to know them. Because the overpopulation bogyman is just that: a scary fairy tale. The global population rocket may still be climbing, but the boosters have been discarded and the thrusters are spent. Beyond Africa, the era of population acceleration is rapidly coming to an end, with some economists and analysts already starting to discuss the unprecedented question of the twenty-first century: how to keep global capitalism going as the number of taxpayers and consumers starts to level off and then starts tipping relentlessly – and permanently – downwards. It has already begun. Japan's population is falling at a rate of 500 000 a year. In parts of Central and Eastern Europe, bears and wolves are cautiously moving back into places they last ruled 1 000 years ago as rural towns and villages empty. China relaxed its 'one child' policy in 2013 and abolished it in 2015, but social engineering is not a genie one can put back in a bottle. Chinese officials hoped the end of the policy would produce a baby boom, but the opposite has happened: in 2016, 17.9 million babies were born, followed by 17.2 million in 2017, 15.2 million in 2018 and just 14.6 million in 2019. The generation raised either as only children or, in less strictly policed regions, as one of two siblings, now sees small families as much more desirable than large ones.

But even presenting these facts to population alarmists misses the point, because they are not engaging in a debate or presenting an argument. They are, instead, trying to create an enormous smokescreen to hide an inescapable truth: it is not overpopulation that will end humanity, but overconsumption of finite resources. And when it comes to overconsumption, it is *Opulens*, not the poor, who are doing all the consuming.

The facts are clear. If we agree that carbon emissions are a useful measurement of how much people consume – of how much stuff we literally burn up to maintain our societies – then there is simply no comparison between rich and poor. In 2009, the Yale School of Forestry & Environmental Studies reported that one American pumps out as much carbon as 250 Ethiopians. The United States, with a population of 327 million, consumes ten times more meat in a year than India's 1.3 billion citizens: the equivalent of one 330-gram steak slapped down in front of every human being in the US, every single day.

But of course it's not just Americans. *Opulens* spans the globe, gorging on resources wherever it finds itself. The armada of SUVs in my street is part of a global fleet over 200 million of such vehicles that now choke the planet, up from 35 million ten years ago. In the decade between 2008 and 2018, they accounted for the second largest rise in emissions after literal power stations and ahead of heavy industry, trucking, aviation and shipping. If the world's SUV drivers were citizens of a country (and I am arguing that, at least on a psychological level, they are), it would be the world's seventh largest emitter of carbon, larger than the UK and Belgium combined.

Each year the Global Footprint Network calculates something called Earth Overshoot Day, the date on which each country would exhaust the planet's ability to regenerate its ecological resources if everyone on earth lived like the citizens in that country. It will not surprise you to discover that petro-monarchies and oligarch playgrounds are gorging as if there's no tomorrow, which, to be fair, there won't be if they keep it up. According to the latest calculations, which started the consumption clock on 1 January 2020, the top fastest consumers of the planet's resources were Qatar (wiping out the earth by February 11), Luxembourg (February 16), the United Arab Emirates (March 7), Bahrain and Kuwait (both March 10).

Even these startling figures, however, overlook the real elephant being hacked up and eaten in the room. Earth Overshoot Day is calculated per capita, in other words, as an average of how much each citizen consumes. There are only 18 million people in the countries listed above. But just behind them, with consumption habits that would devour the planet by the end of April, is a mass of over

500 million, living in the US, Canada, Denmark, Australia, Sweden, Finland, Belgium, Saudi Arabia, Austria, South Korea and Norway. This vast bloc of the global rich is an immense, gleaming, diesel-powered drill relentlessly grinding its way through the planet. And as it grinds, it insists that it's the other 7 billion people who are the real problem.

I suspect that this project of buck-passing and blame-shifting is why, when climate activist Greta Thunberg scolded Donald Trump and the rich world at the United Nations in 2019, many of her critics demanded to know when she was planning to take the same message to China or India, countries which, to many *Opulens*, represent the real gluttons of global consumption. This 'gotcha!' argument is often based on prejudice, but also, I think, a lack of information, as the facts and figures get buried by Facebook's algorithms and confirmation bias. In this instance, however, there is simply no debate. The world-eating appetites of those two countries are dramatically smaller than those of the rich West: the Earth Overshoot Day of both China and India occur in June. This is not to say that an Overshoot Day in June implies sustainability. It doesn't. But if the rest of the twenty-first century is going to be a process of learning to live within our means, then it's the biggest spenders – the global 'shopaholics' taking home the most stuff – who represent the biggest problem.

Persuading *Opulens* to scale down its consumption will be extremely difficult. In some respects it may prove impossible. *Opulens* has evolved to require an ambient temperature of between 22 and 22.5 degrees Celsius, and yet many of the places it has chosen to live – northern Europe, North America, Australia, city-states in the Middle East or Asia – represent some of the harshest, most barren, hottest, coldest, driest, wettest and most humid places in the world. To maintain its optimal temperature and moisture content, *Opulens* has launched an all-out war against nature, burning billions of barrels of oil to force deserts to sustain golf courses, swamps to tolerate retirement villages, icy, barren steppes to allow cosy suburbs, and tropical jungles to be cool, mosquito-free idylls. Even a fractional scaling-down of this campaign to subjugate nature would make life unbearable for many *Opulens*. But before any radical leftists start celebrating the prospect of the global elite having to go without air-conditioning or golf courses, they might want to imagine the practical realities of such a shift: if you think climate refugees are a crisis, imagine the scene if the world's richest and most expansive societies – which also happened to have the largest armies, air forces and nuclear arsenals – decided that they needed to move somewhere more temperate. Say goodbye to Brazil, Argentina and India and say howdy and *ni hao* to the Relocated States of America and The New People's Republic of South China!

It is also extremely unlikely that *Opulens* will be forced to wake up and scale down due to pressure from outside its species. I think that some left-leaning opinionistas and academics take it as a given that the poor resent the rich and want to confiscate and redistribute their filthy lucre; that *Opulens* faces constant pressure to be less rich. But there is growing evidence that this is not the case, and perhaps with good reason. Humans have been trying to accumulate wealth and possessions since at least the establishment of agriculture 10 000 years ago. For the vast majority of us, wealth is aspirational. So when well-meaning *Precarius Condescens* fire up their laptops in ivy-covered university buildings and bang out explanations for why global capitalism is monstrous and why we need to abolish the billionaire class and tax *Abstractus* and *Transparens* until they bleed, it might sound very fair and sensible to their *Precarius* colleagues and some of their *Precarius* readers, but I can imagine that to many poorer people it sounds like a plan to dismantle the only system that can deliver on their dreams of wealth. In other words, a plan to wreck their longed-for future. During the nineteenth century, for example, Conservatives feared that introducing universal franchise would see the poor voting overwhelmingly for the rich to be taxed harshly and for their riches to be all but confiscated as part of radical redistribution. But it didn't happen, and still hasn't, at least not in the UK. In 2019, that country's Labour party, in the words of *The Economist*, 'went into the election offering the biggest transfer of power to the workers in history only to see more workers vote for an Old Etonian with the middle name of de Pfeffel than for Comrade Corbyn.' You might argue that, at least by global standards, there are very few poor people in the UK, and that even its working class is richer than the vast majority of humans, but still, it does seem to be the case that the loudest advocates of class warfare and radical redistribution are those lodged firmly in the global middle class.

Indeed, I believe that this is one of the things that *Precarius Condescens* pundits keep getting so wrong about the EFF. When Julius Malema and his comrades are seen quaffing champagne or wearing vastly expensive watches or driving huge SUVs, these pundits see hypocrites. But I suspect that many EFF voters see something completely different. To them, the bling isn't hypocritical: it is inspirational. After all, this is the Economic Freedom Fighters, not the Salvation Army. If you want economic freedom, who are you going to listen to? Some middle-class, shabby-genteel journalist or academic, driving a ten-year-old hatchback and wearing scuffed shoes, or the guy with a Breitling and a Range Rover?

Ultimately, however, the hardest barrier to break through will be the *Opulens* bubble; that almost impenetrable belief that its life is normal and that any suggestion that it consumes slightly less is therefore the same as Bolsheviks kicking down the door and forcing it at bayonet point to become a penniless match-girl freezing to death in a gutter. If Donald Trump had an epiphany tonight, perhaps after choking on a Big Mac and having his oxygen supply cut off for a few minutes, and declared that henceforth Americans were required by law to halve their consumption of meat, many if not most would believe that the End Times had come and that they were now doomed to a diet straight out of North Korea. I'm not sure they would believe you if you told them that they were now eating as much meat as the average well-nourished Norwegian.

It is this kind of mental splitting that leads to the bumper sticker I saw in Cape Town recently. On it, the Buddha sat cross-legged above the advice to 'Live Simply'. It was stuck onto the rear window of an SUV that costs roughly R2 million. I wanted to laugh, but of course it was not much more absurd than many of my own *Opulens* hypocrisies. It was just a particularly clear example of what happens when we emigrate away from this planet, with its finite resources and where half the human population lives on less than R3 000 per month, and move into a place of pure projection; of how we can be so disconnected from the world, and how much of it had to be blown up, melted down or set on fire to sustain a life we consider normal, that we can truly believe that we are living simply.

So how does the great downscaling begin? *Opulens* can't be forced to change. When backed into a corner, it will first buy the corner and rent it on Airbnb, then lawyer up, then use the newspapers and social media sites it owns to convince everyone that their demands are foolish or naïve, then explain that the real problem is the government, or plastic straws, or richer people, or the poor, or overpopulation, or people from Africa or Asia, or Muslims or Jews, and then, when all else fails, start a war. It also can't be frightened into changing. Apocalyptic warnings about climate refugees or societal chaos are less than futile. For a species that has ignored or dismissed half a dozen concrete realities before its first flat white of the day, hypotheticals and predictions are nothing but dandelions drifting past the window. Indeed, South Africa has proved that *Opulens* can live alongside grinding human misery and change almost nothing about the way it lives. It cannot be forced to think differently any more than you can force a sleeping person to dream what you want them to dream.

Nevertheless, I believe that *Opulens* can change, and will change.

It won't happen through introspection. It certainly won't happen through exposure to facts. Rather, I think, it will happen through flattery.

All of us fear that we will lose what we have. All of us are sustained by the dream that we will gain more than we currently have. To reach *Opulens*, therefore, one has to avoid making it feel that it is losing anything, and encourage it to believe that it is gaining something; that you are offering it the chance of making its bubble even more beautiful and its life even more elegant and virtuous. Until now, that process has been based on accumulation. Bronze cheetahs, paintings of Anonymous Black African Women, SUVs, the perfect travel selfie, you name it: if it can make *Opulens* feel better, richer, safer, more special – closer to its dream kin – then it is dragged into its burrow and manoeuvred into place next to all the other bubble-building trinkets. But accumulation has just been a means to an end. Ultimately, I suspect that *Opulens* will do whatever it has to to serve its dream. And this is how the world will be saved.

It will begin, late one evening, as a stream of pure data zipping between satellites, revealing to a disembodied *Opulens Abstractus* the disappointing news that his engineers have underestimated the scope of his brief and that his plan to retire to a space-bunker on

Mars probably isn't going to happen in his lifetime. Electrons will crackle and microwaves will hiss as he realises that he is going to be stuck on earth, at least for the next few decades, and that he might as well delay the damn rock's conflagration. And so he will take on human form – a host of lawyers – and appear unto a simple *Opulens Transparens* as he tends his flocks of mistresses on his island in the Caribbean, and reveal The Plan. And then *Transparens*, full of awe and wonder, will summon to his island the very furtive but very brilliant *Fugens* who runs his public relations firm for him, and tell her to travel back to her office in London or New York and, together with her team of young, hungry-eyed *Opulens Precarius Rapacius Advertisens*, hammer out the details.

And so it will come to pass, at first slowly but soon with gathering haste, that a new way of living will be revealed to *Opulens*. It won't take the form of a burning bush or a column of fire (except obviously in Australia) or as words written on tablets (because iPads aren't really a thing any more). Rather, it will drift down onto and into *Opulens* like an untraceable scent, a soft mist of revelation floating from the pages of *Vogue* and the front row at New York Fashion Week; drifting between beautiful ears and beautiful mouths at parties on Lake Como; clinging like sweat to the revellers on the dark, heaving dance floors of Moscow or Tokyo or Ibiza. It will grow and spread and swirl, until it reaches the habitat of *Bogus Humilitas*, carried between the pages of a copy of *Vanity Fair*, and then finally find *Precarius*, where it will form a gentle haze around Facebook and Twitter, talk shows and lifestyle programmes, and the smiling, orange-tinged faces on the cover of *Hello!* magazine.

And the mist will whisper, over and over again, so softly that *Opulens* will think it is the sound of its own thoughts: *the rules of the dream have changed*. We loved accumulation, but we no longer love it. Because you know who also tries to accumulate things? Non-

Opulens. The poor. And you're not poor, are you? No. You're the opposite. So what's the opposite of accumulation? Yes! Having less! And well done for working that out entirely by yourself, with no input whatsoever from this network of PR firms and advertising agencies and paid-for bloggers and 'influencers'. Not only are you clearly very intelligent, but it looks like you're a trend-setter!

And so it will go. Soon, *Opulens* will begin to believe that the only thing better than having a bronze cheetah is not having a bronze cheetah. The next logical step after an SUV? A small electric car! No! A bicycle! No! Living close enough to walk! There aren't any big houses within walking distance? Well, thank God for that: big houses are so mid-twentieth-century *Precarius*. Besides, all you really need these days is one small wall on which to hang the sexiest conceptual art new money can buy: a box-mounted printout of your most recent tax returns, with all charitable donations circled in green ink by a local artist.

I don't know what the *Transparens* and *Fugens* PR gurus will call their newly manufactured zeitgeist. Empathetic Minimalism. Compact Greatness. Real Wealth. Awe-Sterity™. It doesn't matter. All that matters is that it gives *Opulens* a new fantasy to emigrate to, just as consoling and affirming as the old one but with very different priorities, so that one bright morning I will be able to step out onto my street and find my hatchback boxed in not by SUVs but by a group of parents standing around it, shaking their heads in admiration . . .

'It's so *small*!'

'Look how little you can fit inside it!'

'God I wish I had one but Gary says we need the space.'

'Not cool, Debbie. Not cool at all.'

'No, it's so we can take our solar panels with us when we go to our holiday house in – '

'Your what?'

'Nothing.'

'You still own a *second house*?'

'No, I said, er, holy . . . day . . . house? It's what we call, er . . . church? When we go and give thanks for how lucky we've been to have so little.'

'I'm watching you, Debbie . . .'

And then I will politely ask them to step aside, and I will nudge my little car into the future, where *Opulens* is discovering that contact with slightly more reality is not a form of persecution; that lightness of touch has its own elegance; that moderation is not Marxism. And that, when it comes to living on this finite, tiny blue dot that is our only home in a dispassionate universe, a little bit less is much, much more.

Chapter 13

Robbing Us Blind

It has taken an hour, but now it's done. The men step back, wiping sweat off their foreheads and glancing at the paper cuts that criss-cross their fingertips. The Venter trailer is squatting low on its suspension, creaking under half a ton of money.

That's why it's taken so long. You can't just dump the R200 banknotes into it like in the movies where they throw millions into a sports bag. No, this takes precision. The notes have been counted out into small piles of 100 and then wrapped around with a paper strap. Ten 'straps' make a bundle, slightly smaller than a brick, weighing about a kilogram. And if it's all going to fit, and not rattle around during the journey, it has to be packed as carefully as you might lay a brick in a driveway here in Saxonwold. Every R200 000 bundle, carefully wedged into place. All 500 bricks. All R100 million.

Imagine what that looks like. Feel the weight of all that paper. That much cash has a strong smell, a musty, faintly chemical whiff that starts to feel like dust in the sinuses.

Now imagine that different men arrive, men in ill-fitting suits, wearing dark glasses and earpieces, who glance about uneasily as they gather around the trailer and carefully lower the lid and lock it down. Imagine the sweating men standing respectfully by, asking no questions, avoiding eye contact.

Imagine a large SUV with tinted windows being reversed up to the trailer. Imagine the men in suits scanning the perimeter one more time, and then piling into the car and dragging away all that money. Imagine it being driven around a corner and out of sight. The men who remain don't know where it's going. Perhaps out of the country. Perhaps to a private bank. Maybe it's all being chucked down a big hole or set on fire. It doesn't matter. All that matters is that it's gone. And that in twelve hours they're going to do it all again. And then in twelve hours after that again. And twelve hours after that.

Imagine that this scene happens twice every day. At dawn the men pack R100 million into a Venter trailer. And at dusk they do it again. And they haven't missed a day in 26 years.

I'm guessing I had your attention for most of that story. Packing R100 million into a trailer is the stuff of must-see TV. It's four seasons of *Breaking Bad* or *Ozark*. Doing it twice in one day, however, feels like a stretch. And doing it twice a day for 26 years just seems silly. It's too much. It's hopelessly unrealistic. Nobody does that.

That's the problem with trying to visualise the scope of South Africa's post-democracy plagues of corruption, economic illiteracy and cadre deployment. We can just imagine a Venter trailer full of R200 notes. But beyond that, it all starts feeling a bit abstract.

So here's another one, based in history rather than in Hollywood.

Every so often, a stoic South African has told me that what this country needs is our own version of the Marshall Plan, that extraordinary programme of reconstruction, funded by the United States between 1948 and 1952, that got Western Europe back on its feet after World War 2. The Communist bloc decried it as Yankee imperialism, but the results were fairly spectacular: seven years after the end of the most destructive and lethal war in human history, every single country in the programme had an economy substantially bigger and stronger than it had had before the outbreak of war.

Before we knew about state capture, my response had been polite disagreement. Yes, I said, it's nice to dream that South Africa could be reconstructed and experience the sort of transformation enjoyed by Germany, which went from being a burned-out wasteland to becoming one of the biggest manufacturers in the world. But, I said, it wasn't really a fair comparison. The United States poured about R2 trillion (in today's money) into Western Europe. And where would we get R2 trillion?

Now, however, we are starting to understand the immensity of the crime that has been committed against our present and our future. Because the truth is we've already had our shot at a Marshall Plan, and the ANC sold it for an evening of strippers and blow. Writing in the *Sunday Times* in 2019, associate professor at the Wits School of Governance William Gumede explained it simply and devastatingly: the amount squandered, stolen, handed to unproductive fat-cats or simply evaporated by the state and its corporate enablers since 1994 is 'almost the equivalent of the postwar financial aid' that the US used to reconstruct a devastated continent.

Whether you see those vanished trillions as creaking Venter trailers disappearing twice a day or as a Marshall Plan that never happened, the fact remains that the last 26 years have been an astonishing story of self-harm. In 1994, Nelson Mandela's ANC was the shiniest political brand in the world, fêted across ideological barriers in Washington, Tripoli and Beijing. It had both the mandate and the moral authority to cash an immense number of cheques, both political and literal. What Gumede described as South Africa's 'development trillions' were either in the bank, in an economy ready to be restarted, or were flooding in from eager international investors. Almost miraculously, the ANC had acquired a magic bullet that would deal a profound blow to poverty and injustice, slay fear and despondency, and jolt the country towards reconstruction.

So what did it do with its one, irreplaceable, hard-won shot? It decided that the best thing for everyone would be to fire it directly into South Africa's kneecap.

Just why it did this remains the subject of angry debate. Hanlon's Razor, a modern aphorism created by computer programmers in the early 2000s, warns us to 'never attribute to malice that which can be adequately explained by stupidity'. Certainly, some malice and a great deal of stupidity seem to cover most of the last 26 years. Where the ANC is concerned, we must also consider the role of infantile appetite. When a toddler lunges at a cake, yanking off a handful to mash into its face, and knocking over the rest to fall upside down onto the floor, it isn't being malicious or stupid. It is simply reacting as you do when you believe that you and your desires are paramount, and that everything within your reach was made for you.

This, however, is speculation. There have been no confessions from state captors explaining why they did what they did, no muffled admissions recorded via wire tap in Dubai massage parlours. We know that the 'normal' corruption which has filled front pages every Sunday since the 1980s suddenly mestastasised into a monstrous thing that may yet kill South Africa, but we still don't know, exactly, how much money was stolen and where it went.

So how corrupt, exactly, is our country?

According to Transparency International's 2019 Corruption Perception Index (CPI), South Africa sits fairly comfortably inside the less corrupt half of the global spectrum, tying for 70th place (where 1st is the least corrupt and 180th the most) with Romania, Hungary and Suriname. We are perceived to be slightly more honest than Jamaica, Bulgaria and Tunisia, and slightly dodgier than Argentina, Belarus, Senegal and Montenegro. Should you buy a used car from us? Probably not. Should you hurry your family to the other side of the street when you see us coming? Not really.

More importantly, should you base your view of South African corruption on this list? Absolutely not.

It's not that the Corruption Perception Index is inaccurate. It's just fatally incomplete. And in its current form it reinforces an idea which has taken hold in South Africa, an idea that will continue to prevent us understanding the corruption pandemic and figuring out what to do about it.

That idea, put simply, is that corruption is something only politicians and civil servants do. But to understand how corrupt South Africa is, we first have to understand why it's corrupt, and who's doing the corruption. And for that, the CPI provides only half the picture.

To be fair, it doesn't claim otherwise. It is very clear that it monitors perceptions about public sector corruption only. But to draw any kind of conclusions from this would be like a doctor only examining X-rays of a patient's left lung without examining the right. Because when it comes to corruption, public- and private-sector theft are the same disease.

The limitations of the CPI are evident right at the very top of the list.

In 2019, Denmark tied New Zealand in 1st place, revealing that its government and public service are considered the most honest and transparent in the world. Inevitably, such an accolade would lead many people to believe that Denmark itself is an incorruptible nation. 'If only South Africans could be more like Danes,' many in this country might sigh.

Well, there's good news for them. Because it turns out that some Danes are a lot like some South Africans. In 2017, it began to emerge that an Estonian branch of Denmark's biggest bank, Danske Bank, had been laundering money. A lot of money. Roughly €200 billion, in fact; which works out to more or less R4 trillion, give or take a few tens of millions.

Most of the money, investigators discovered, had come from Latvian, Estonian and Russian depositors. Igor Putin, cousin of Vladimir, was named, as was Russia's FSB, the modern incarnation of the KGB.

Because the branch was in Estonia rather than Denmark, and under the joint watch of the Danish and Estonian Financial Supervisory Authorities, both blamed each other for the vast corruption of the scheme, but soon the fallout all headed west: Danske's share price halved in 2018, CEO Thomas Borgen resigned, and a former finance director was criminally charged. The Danish prime minister said that he was shocked. (I told you some Danes are a lot like some South Africans.)

The details were complex, but the moral of that sordid story was clear: Danish bankers, regulators and no doubt a few politicians had somehow managed to miss the biggest corruption scandal in European history. A 'world class' business in a country regularly held up by South Africans as an example of ideal governance had laundered almost three times as much as the absolute maximum estimate of State Capture.

At this point I must pause to go and answer my front door, which is being banged on by a delegation of Danish politicians, accompanied by South Africans determined to believe the worst of their country, all of whom are outraged by me mentioning Denmark and South Africa in the same breath when it comes to corruption.

How dare you (asks the delegation, angrily thrusting its monocle into place and giving its cane a brisk twirl) compare illicit activity by one private company to the vast, systemic corruption of an entire political system? Besides, you diabolical stirrer, the nature of the crimes is completely different. State Capture stole hundreds of billions of rands from South Africans; Danske Bank's activities, while illegal, might actually have contributed to Danish wellbeing. After all, those billions of dirty roubles, euros and pounds kept hundreds of bank employees and dozens of cocaine dealers gainfully employed.

The best I can answer to that final claim is that State Capture probably boosted certain South African businesses, too. If you keep your estimates very conservative, and accept that R500 billion was stolen, and that just a fifth of that loot has stayed in South Africa, that's R100 billion that, even now, is being used to buy South African mansions through South African estate agents, brief South African lawyers to set up legitimate-looking shell companies, hire South African accountants to erase paper trails, contract South African heavies to lean on the guy who knows where the ledgers are buried, send their little tenderpreneurlings to South African private schools and buy the wife a Maserati for her birthday from a South African dealership.

As for the charge that money laundering by a private bank can't be compared to the dealings of a corrupt state, well, there's a less satirical answer for that one. State capture and white collar crime are usually two sides of the same dirty coin. The bulk of the money stolen by the Zuptas or funnelled to the families and mistresses of ANC politicians is not sitting in the national treasury of Dubai or the coffers of the state of Uttar Pradesh in India. It is sitting in private banks, private companies, and private property developments. It was private consultancy McKinsey that gouged R900 million out of South African taxpayers via Eskom before it was forced to hand it all back. It was private auditing firm KPMG that accepted R40 million to 'audit' Gupta-related enterprises and to destabilise SARS so that it could be opened up to predation. No, when it comes to systemic theft from taxpayers, there is virtually no difference between the public and private sectors. A case in point was the Danish scandal: many of the billions laundered by Danske Bank came from Russia, a state almost entirely captured by an extraction machine so complex and embedded that the difference between politicians and businesspeople is virtually undetectable. The whole thing is a Russian nesting doll of patronage, with business interests inside political power inside business interests.

Revelations about state capture in South Africa have forced us to become more aware of the role of big business in big corruption, but I think we still struggle to see it. And, in our defence, I think there are some pretty good reasons for why this blind spot remains.

Firstly, where corrupt politicians make us angry, corporate criminals just make most of us confused. When I've managed to read past the first dense, dry paragraph of the latest private-sector scandal, I've usually surrendered by the second, entirely overwhelmed by the sense that in order to read any further I need an MBA, a law degree or both. Indeed, in the months following the collapse of Steinhoff, during which everything went strangely quiet, Couch-Revolutionary Twitter kept insisting that Markus Jooste had bought the silence of the South African business press. I understand their suspicion, but I would argue that Jooste had bought that silence years earlier simply by putting together an impenetrable cobweb of numbers which fooled even the most canny investors. As veteran business journalist Bruce Whitfield told me: it is very difficult to report on a scandal when even the forensic experts are finding themselves baffled by what's in front of them.

The Joostes of the world are experts at confusing people, but I suspect another reason for our collective blind spot is our tendency to confuse ourselves when it comes to criminality and corruption. I know that South Africans feel extremely passionately about violent crime. I know that we get very angry when politicians or public servants steal from us. But even the most outraged South African would have to admit that we do, sometimes, have a very flexible relationship with crime and punishment when it suits us.

Consider the wretched case of Molemo 'Jub Jub' Maarohanye. In 2010, the performer got high on hard drugs with a friend, went drag racing and crashed his Mini Cooper into a group of schoolchildren, killing four and leaving two others permanently brain damaged. In court, he denied it all. He and his co-accused were sentenced to 25 years in jail. In 2014, this conviction was overturned on appeal and reduced to 10 years, starting in 2012, so effectively 8 more years. He was paroled in January 2015 and walked out of prison having served one year for each person he killed.

In some societies, that would have been the point at which Maarohanye disappeared. He would have slunk away from the public eye, and, if the media had mentioned him, it would have been as a classic case of justice denied. But just two years later, there he was, the subject of an astonishingly foul bit of tabloid journalism. Jub Jub, the reporter revealed, was managing to put back the pieces of his shattered life. So brave. So strong. 'The most important thing is forgiveness,' opined Maarohanye. 'It comes from God. So I forgave myself and God forgave me . . . It really doesn't matter what anybody else thinks because that gave me the energy and the ability to move on.'

So that's all good then.

At the time it struck me as the most grandiose kind of contempt and denial, but I was wrong. It wasn't just Jub Jub and God who had forgiven him: in 2019 it turned out that media giant MultiChoice was also keen to let bygones be bygones. Maarohanye was suddenly a B-list celebrity again, this time as presenter of a local copy of the sewer-dwelling American show *Cheaters*. Named *Uyajola 9/9* and broadcast on Moja Love, the show saw Maarohanye and his camera crew bursting in on people and then offering trite platitudes about how infidelity is harming society. If you were unlucky enough to see it, you would have come away deeply depressed. A few columnists expressed polite doubts about the rehabilitation of Maarohanye's celebrity, but that was the full extent of South Africa's objection. There were no calls to boycott Moja Love's advertisers, no march by the EFF on the offices of MultiChoice, and certainly no decision on the part of the production company to part ways with Jub Jub.

This is an extreme example, but South African life is full of wonky moral compasses. When the highest court banned corporal punishment in 2019, thousands of angry parents took to social media to say that they would ignore the law. When security guard Bathobile Mlangeni was alleged to have walked off with R4 million in stolen cash in February 2020, her neighbours expressed mild enthusiasm: one told Times Select that because the money was insured, 'everyone wins'. And that's before we get to the eagerness of many South Africans to abandon the rule of law completely when they feel their political idols are being threatened. In 2019, after Julius Malema tweeted a warning to his followers that 'the establishment has issued instructions to the #stratcom to rehash old stories' against EFF leadership, a certain Tatane replied: 'My president, even if the [sic] showed us your hand deep in the cookie jar, we're focused!'

Apparently having your hand in the cookie jar is okay if you're doing it to carbo-load ahead of a busy day of hawking your fake revolution.

Yes, sometimes it really does seem that, to many of us, a crime isn't really a crime if it doesn't harm us, or if we disagree that it is, in fact, a crime, or if we admire the person who committed it. And given the potential for such extreme double standards, is it any wonder that the crimes of smooth-talking sophisticates sometimes get written off as just a nasty misunderstanding?

Confusion – both intellectual and moral – are powerful contributors to our blind spot when it comes to the culpability of the corporate world. But I think another factor is the deeply seductive belief that the enemy of my enemy is my friend.

Over the last quarter century, an ideological, even archetypal, standoff has developed between government and business in South Africa. Its origins predate 1994 by many years. Some might argue that it has its roots in the Russian Revolution of 1917 or even the publication of *Das Kapital* in 1867. But whenever it started, by 1994 both sides were very clear on why the other couldn't be trusted. To the ANC, corporate South Africa was the predatory cabal that had funded apartheid and reaped huge profits from doing so. To business, the ANC was an economically illiterate gang of vandals that would strip the whole place and sell it as scrap. Since 1994, both have sniped at each other over the trench parapet. The ANC tells business it would like it more if it invested some of its profits. Business replies that it would invest more if it could be sure the comrades wouldn't just EFT it all to Dubai.

If the ANC had retained the moral high ground and continued in the 2000s as it had started in 1994, it might have been much easier for us to stay aware of the corporate world's dirtier habits. But the ANC's headlong rush towards failure has fired up that old 'enemy/

friend' binary with its appealing, simplistic logic: if government sees business as the enemy, and government is corrupt, incompetent, wasteful and antagonistic towards the hopes of ordinary South Africans, then surely business must be law-abiding, highly skilled, efficient and dedicated to a better life for all?

Finally, and perhaps most powerfully of all, I suspect that the corruption in the private sector has been pushed onto the periphery of our consciousness by the widespread belief that corruption is something that goes hand in hand with political power, no doubt entrenched by Lord Acton's famous observation that power tends to corrupt while absolute power corrupts absolutely. Business, always appearing to stand on the sidelines, earnestly and somewhat plaintively asking government to do this or that, seems to have very little power. And since it is power that corrupts, and business seems to have so much less than the politicians, how can we even begin to compare the two?

Acton's view of the corrupting influence of power is pithy, and satisfying in its gloomy finality. But I think we in South Africa would be better served by the more nuanced view provided by Frank Herbert, the science fiction writer who gave us *Dune*. Speaking to the BBC, Herbert said: 'The mistakes [of leaders] are amplified by the numbers who follow them without question. And charismatic leaders tend to build up followings, power structures, and these power structures tend to be taken over by people who are corruptible. I don't think that the old saw about absolute power corrupting absolutely is accurate. I think power attracts the corruptible.'

For me, the strength of Herbert's idea is that it widens our gaze and urges us to see more than the Machiavellian shenanigans of the power elite. Whenever I read Acton's maxim about power corrupting, in my mind's eye I see an individual politician writhing on the plush carpet of their office floor, clutching at their face and throat as they undergo a shocking and sudden transformation into a kind of lizard person . . .

'Deputy Minister, your two o'clock is – oh my God! Deputy Minister?!'

'Ssssave . . . yourselfff . . .'

'But – '

'It's . . . the corruption . . . It's finally got me . . .'

'But how?'

'Last week . . . When I was – gnnn! – promoted from MEC! Oh God, it's a tail!'

'Deputy Min –'

'Go! GO! Save yourself!'

Herbert doesn't see a bizarre affliction. For him, corruption isn't a mysterious disease that somehow infects the powerful. It is, rather, something carried by ordinary people, and then infinitely magnified by contact with power. Where Acton makes us think of a few hundred politicians, Herbert's vision presents an immense stampede: a host of flawed, ambitious, frightened, cunning people all rushing towards the great glowing, pulsing light at the centre. In Herbert's vision, corruption isn't a sinister transformation that happens to an individual behind closed doors, like Faust enjoying a late-night visit from Beelzebub. Instead, it is a process that requires a multitude. And where there is a multitude, even one rushing towards a single energy source, there is usually a wide variety of motives. After all, being attracted to power isn't necessarily the same as wanting to wield it. Attraction doesn't always involve ambition or obsession. No doubt some of those who are drawn towards power want to claim it and use it, but Herbert leaves space for many other motivations, such as those who yearn to be near it to bask in its glow but who have no desire for high office themselves. It is here – in this sprawling caravan that endlessly traipses after the powerful – that we find the private sector, biding its time in the knowledge that, if it plays its cards right, the politically powerful will put it in touch with an almost unlimited supply of money.

It is essential that we see corruption as a collective vice. If we are going to gain a more complete view of this country and the corruption that defines it at the moment, we can't just picture our least favourite politician. Instead, we must see him or her joined by Markus Jooste, and the stuffed suits who emptied out VBS Bank. We must see the crooked auditors and bought consultants in their expensive offices, and the union saboteurs and bagmen. We must see the blackmailed or bribed board members, and the minor-league tenderpreneurs dreaming of the day they get the contract to supply staples and paper-clips to dysfunctional government departments at a 1 000 per cent mark-up. We must see the cellphone giants robbing us blind, and the food-manufacturing cartels fixing prices, and other monopolistic corporations that use their size and influence to crush competition. We must imagine every employer who shrugs as they cheat day-labourers, domestic workers and freelancers out of their wages. We must picture the person next door – the one who's always telling you how corrupt Jacob Zuma is – lying on his tax return 'because they'll just steal it anyway'. We must see the bon vivant in the coastal holiday town, always eager to explain to you how the government is breaking everything, as he invites you to come and enjoy some of the undersized lobsters he bought from poachers that morning. We must see every person who ran the red light in the traffic this morning because the person in front of them also ran it, because it's not really illegal if both of you do it.

It is essential to see all of this for the sake of perspective. But it's also depressing as hell because it suggests that corruption is a deeply ingrained way of life in South Africa rather than the nasty anomaly we're always demanding be 'stamped out'. It suggests, in short, that corruption is here to stay.

I know this might sound fairly defeatist to many South Africans desperate for better times. I understand if some pragmatic, idealistic readers say, 'Fair enough, but if power attracts corruptible people, then surely we should try to prevent them from gravitating towards it? Instead of complaining about corrupt people, isn't our task to head them off at the pass and only allow ethical people into South Africa's parliament or boardrooms?'

I agree that would be grand, but I have to ask: what, exactly, would it look like? Do we drop a wallet on the floor during job interviews, leave the room, and see who pockets the cash? And what about all those genuinely idealistic, bright-eyed young things who honestly don't know how corruptible they are, and who believe that their desire for power is to make the world a better place? How can we tell, in 2020, that by 2050 they're going to be hollowed-out husks of pure greed? We can't. And besides, on a more practical note, do you know who'd be running government and business in this country if we waved a magic wand and rooted out every corrupt person in the system? About a hundred nervous wrecks, sobbing into their pillows and popping sedatives as they try to do the jobs of 10 000 chancers. Nobody else would apply, because incorruptible people don't want power. They just want their books and their friends and a good dog.

For some, the solution is to force good people into leadership. One suggestion I've heard a couple of times is a kind of lottery, whereby private citizens are picked to serve a fixed term in government. Patronage networks are unlikely to cosy up to newcomers they don't know they can trust, and most selectees wouldn't be in power long enough to set up their own get-rich-quick schemes. But a rapid turnover of personnel is the same reason this system would be a disaster: it takes time to learn how a bureaucracy or a business works. Replacing everyone every two years would be a vastly wasteful process of endlessly reinventing the wheel, as appointees spend most of their time at work just trying to figure out where to switch on the printer. It also goes without saying that this system would be extremely unpopular with citizens. Would you want to leave your current job (and, given the hours required, your family) and spend the next two years chairing the committee that oversees the purchase of furniture for municipal offices? Me neither.

I've also met some very *gatvol* South Africans who have gone to the other extreme. The cure for corruption, they insist, is to execute corrupt officials, like they do in China. The problem with this, however, is that in order to turn South Africa into the sort of country in which corrupt civil servants are put up against a wall and shot, all sorts of other people would also have to be put against the same wall and shot first, from academics and journalists to lawyers and business owners, or simply anyone who objected to the shooting. I'm depressed by corruption as much as the next bloke, but if my choices are South Africa as it is now and a totalitarian regime in which democracy is illegal, dissent gets you sent for re-education (or just plain old torture) and the justice system is a pen they hand you to sign a confession that's been written for you, give me our current mess any day. And if you think South Africa's most corrupt wheeler-dealers are nasty now, just imagine a scenario in which you can have your political rivals or industry competitors executed simply by revealing their *smallanyana* skeletons before they can reveal yours. No thanks.

No, the modern human world is built around very specific manifestations of power, which means that, unless we're all prepared to move into autonomous collectives, spending all day and most of our evenings recycling our poop into fertiliser and felting our pubic hair into clothing, politicians and their co-conspirators in business are here to stay. Corruption is going nowhere. Yes, it is important to keep denouncing it. It's therapeutic to demand that it be stamped out. It feels pragmatic to suggest governance lotteries or summary executions. But we have to acknowledge that we are a corrupt country, in which fraudsters are elected to high office or fêted at polo games, thieves are celebrated as heroes, criminals are courted by TV executives and gushed over by the tabloids, and laws are seen as more of a suggestion than an imperative. If you want to end corruption in South Africa, what you're really talking about is ending South Africa as it currently exists.

It's a conundrum. 'Stamp out' corruption completely, remove the animating energy of power and embark on a Great South African Leap Forward – a purging transformation of a society à la Mao Zhedong or Pol Pot – and the whole thing collapses in a heap. Shrug and allow corruption to spread unchecked through the public and private sectors, so that the state capture of the last 15 years becomes the norm, and the country becomes a failed state.

So what's the answer? I would argue that it lies somewhere between these two highly undesirable extremes is something I call 'sustainable corruption'.

Whenever I use this term, people think I'm joking or they're slightly shocked. Corruption, after all, is not a laughing matter. We all know that it hammers the poor and prevents societies from reaching their full potential. But corruption doesn't end countries. What ends countries is unsustainable corruption; in other words, when politicians and businesspeople steal too much and in effect kill the goose that lays the golden egg. In short, what the Zuptas were doing.

When South Africans despair about the levels of graft in this country, we often look longingly at countries overseas we believe have managed to 'stamp out' corruption. This is wishful thinking born of despondency. Corruption exists in every country on the planet, even the ones that have managed to convince us that they are squeaky clean. A Danish company laundered trillions of rands. Swiss banks are notorious for washing or simply hiding filthy money. Even as I was finishing this book, Airbus – a multinational corporation with a headquarters in France – agreed to pay R60 billion in fines to settle a case in which it had been accused of bribing public officials in France, the UK and the US between 2004 and 2016 to buy its aircraft and satellites.

There are, however, degrees of chutzpah and sophistication, and this is what I mean when I talk about sustainable corruption. What we need are not politicians and businesspeople who steal nothing. That would be an unrealistic expectation, setting us up for some major Parys Poepstring heartbreak. What we need are people who understand that there are limits to how much they can steal and how far they can hollow out a country before it all starts coming apart. Unfortunately, this will take time. I suspect that the world's 'cleanest' countries look that way because their elites are the inheritors of a long and august tradition of sophisticated corruption; a relationship with power, money and patience that you have to be born into. It is not something that former revolutionaries – born either into poverty or the middle class, and denied political power – can learn, even after 26 years. No, it starts in infancy, as baby oligarchs are bounced on the pin-striped knees of their fathers, or reach out for the monocles that dangle over their cribs. It comes to them in the fairy tales their mothers read to them: Snow White and the Seven Shell Companies in the Bahamas; Goldilocks and the Three Bear Sterns Executives Who Now Work for JPMorgan Chase; The Little Mermaid, a beautiful parable about how emotionally vulnerable people will put themselves through nightmarish pain and grief just to be close to the one per cent. Most of all, it comes to them in the folk wisdom of their people: give a man 10 per cent per year in kickbacks and you feed him for 10 years, at which point he gets called a looter and has to haul ass to a non-extradition country; but teach a man to accept two per cent per year and he'll not only be rich for a lifetime but when he retires he'll be called a humanitarian and a nation builder.

Growing a culture in South Africa of sustainable corruption – of finding leaders who realise that they should only hijack one or two SOEs rather than all of them – would not only help our economy but would also, I think, have a profoundly positive effect on our psyches. When I read about some new tender scandal, or the latest numbing account of yet more billions 'wasted' or 'lost' (as if the money didn't get paid to someone but rather wandered off into a forest), I obviously feel sorry for our battered little country. But I also feel angry because my intelligence has been insulted by a whooping court of gurning lickspittles. The looting in South Africa is so unsophisticated, so unapologetically ham-fisted and obvious, that I've actually begun to long for the sort of velvety, beautifully dressed, elegantly glib corruption that you might find in the head offices of a Danish bank or a European aircraft manufacturer. I mean, say what you want about Markus Jooste and Steinhoff, but at least Jooste respected us enough to put together a truly world-class scam. In a country in which the corrupt simply arrive with a brown paper bag and say 'Fill it up or else,' I can feel grudging respect for that kind of artistry, even if his house of cards did come cascading down in the end. As will everything else in South

Africa if we don't find a way of transitioning from crude highway robbery to elegant, sustainable theft.

So how does it start?

If we accept that corruption is an immutable law of physics in the modern world, how do we nudge it gently away from its current feeding frenzy towards a more elegant form of predation? How do we make sure that we only lose a couple of hundred billion over the next quarter century rather than trillions?

I'm not sure. But perhaps a first step might be to try, just once, just for *sommer,* to see what it's like to stop at a red traffic light.

Chapter 14

Back in The RSA

A big-budget Bollywood biopic about right-wing Indian Prime Minister Narendra Modi was always going to be controversial.

For starters, the 2019 feature film was named *PM Narendra Modi: Story of a Billion People*, which was a terribly cruel thing to do to the 999 999 999 Indians who might have gone to watch it hoping to see their story told as promised in the title.

Secondly, there is no singing or dancing in the film. Because it is about a nationalist populist rising to power, there is obviously an enormous amount of tap-dancing and busking, and pretty much everyone involved in the production is singing for their suppers, but there are no big musical numbers.

The main problem, however, is the obvious one: it is a two-hour praise poem to a sitting prime minister. This qualifies it as propaganda, although that word feels far too sophisticated to describe the sort of hem-kissing, rub-dust-onto-your-face fart-catching that only happens in medieval biographies and the ANC Women's League.

You won't be surprised, in other words, to learn that the film's release was met with condemnation and even an official protest in India's parliament.

What might be a little surprising, though, is the specific accusation levelled at *PM Narendra Modi: Story of a Billion People* (*PMNMSOABP*).

Nobody seemed to have a problem with it being propaganda. No, the problem was that it was propaganda released just days before an election Modi was contesting. Some of the accusations levelled at the film focused on the motives of its producers (the opposition Congress Party pointed out that the film was 'no artistic venture') but the main thrust of the resistance was not to have the film removed from view but to have its launch delayed until after the elections.

To be fair, if Indian lawmakers outlawed Modi-centric cinema there wouldn't be much left on the telly. In 2019 alone, audiences were subjected to *The Accidental Prime Minister*, a hatchet-job aimed at Modi's predecessor, Manmohan Singh, as well as *Modi: Journey of a Common Man*, a seven-episode streamed miniseries.[19]

As a white South African, however, I found myself morbidly

19 These are clearly not ambivalent productions, although, in the interests of balance, I should tell you that *Modi: Journey of a Common Man* has received a single review on the Internet Movie Data Base, written by a certain 'Awesome_Lily', which insists that 'there's nothing propagandistic about it'. ('Awesome_Lily' has written no other reviews on IMDb, presumably because s/he made the fatal mistake of starting the review by describing the series as 'must watch . . . even for Modi-haters'. For God's sake, Awesome_Lily. What were you thinking? Surely they told you the golden rule of political fluffing when you arrived for your first day down in the basement in the Positive Content Farm? Repeat after me: you never, ever acknowledge the existence of people who dislike the Big Man! 'Modi-haters'? Why not just set the PM on fire, you anarchist?)

fascinated by just how comfortable India seems to be with crude, almost naïve propaganda. I spent my formative years inside the vast, highly sophisticated project of thought control that took place under apartheid, and I am still trying to unpick the infinitely tangled strands of propaganda that exist inside me. Some are easy to identify. For example, when I was 10, I spent a term at a rural primary school where the teachers taught me songs about being loyal to the republic and my classmates taught me a fantastically racist parody of *Die Stem*. Even to a 10 year old, it felt like indoctrination. But there are other, much more complex memories, like holding my mother's hand in a post office and looking at the warning poster on the wall, showing the shapes and sizes of various explosive devices that 'they' might use against us, or being fed lunch at my grandparents' table and listening to a clipped British accent on the radio report on how many 'SWAPO terrorists' had been killed in such-and-such a skirmish. Today, these memories still have a paradoxical taste: of fear and comfort, violence and safety, absolute truths and deep distrust. That's the brilliance of that kind of evil: if it can mix its message in with a mother's touch or a grandparent's dinner table, hate begins to feel like love.

And the apartheid propagandists *were* brilliant. So brilliant, in fact, that they're still erasing and reformatting young minds even now, long after their regime has crumbled and most of them have died: every few months another white person, some not even born in 1994, will make headlines for spouting ideas and attitudes formulated in the nineteenth century but perfected by apartheid's brain-scoopers in the 1950s.

Naturally, they'll tell you different. Indeed, I've heard some insist that the real threat is from the government, which, they claim, subjects us to an endless stream of communist propaganda through its captured media outlets. It's a paradox: apparently the ANC can't get anything right *except* a highly sophisticated campaign of thought-control.

To be fair, the ANC did give it a go. ANN7 and *The New Age* were devoted little pooches, their ears cocked earnestly at every 'Heh heh!' of their master's voice, their tails wagging every time he tossed them a scrap. But since everything the ANC touches eventually turns to dust, they never managed to transform into sleek news hounds. In the end, neither developed into anything more than a cartoonish cavalcade of kowtowing courtiers. More sophisticated manipulation, such as full-length feature films, remains beyond the capabilities of our ruling cabal.

Back in 1993, before we knew any of this, I was sure that we were about to swap one brand of high-quality, high-concept propaganda for another. By the early 2000s, I imagined, I would be catching a Glorious Workers' Omnibus down to the Oliver Tambo Cineplex, and picking up my 3D glasses painstakingly modelled on Walter Sisulu's spectacles to watch a four-hour drama called *Patriotic Socialist Revolutionary Potato Farmers Crush Capitalist Imperialists Using Only a Trowel and a Copy of Das Kapital!*[20]

I should stress that this wasn't a kind of 'Rooi Gevaar' fear on my part. Far from it. As a child I was drawn to the Union of Soviet Socialist Republics like hypothermia to a Moscow drunk. I collected Soviet stamps, seduced by their austere beauty and cinematic imagery. I found a pen-friend who lived near Vladivostok, who wrote me polite letters in a beautifully repressed handwriting, the Cyrillic letters forced, not entirely successfully, into decadent Western shapes. He sent me postcards showing his town. It was staggeringly ugly, and when he asked for pictures of Cape Town, I was paralysed by guilt, and the correspondence died.

---

20 Still a better love story than *Twilight*.

Indeed, Russia exerted its strange pull on me right up until I went to the University of Cape Town and studied Russian Intensive for a year. That year taught me that the Russian sense of humour is as deep, dark and dry as a Siberian missile silo, and that I have no affinity for the Russian language whatsoever. Today, the sum total of my Russian is 'Ya ne znayoo' and 'Ya ne pannemayoo': 'I don't know' and 'I don't understand'.

Suffice it to say, in 1993 I had a fair idea of how the (recently collapsed) Soviet Union had rolled and unrolled. And since I knew what every white South African had been told – that the ANC's heart and soul were still encamped well east of the Berlin Wall – I couldn't help wondering just how comradely we were all about to get.

Yes, there would be a few years of a government of national unity in which the capitalist pigs would get a few token concessions, but after that? Would the Grade 1s of the new millennium be sent to immense primary schools, something between a chicken farm and a typing pool, where they would spend their days, 5 000 to a room, learning chemistry and welding bicycles together as they sang *Trotsky Sikelel' iAfrika*? Would their parents pass their time contently swirling test tubes, joyfully greasing giant steel-pressing machines and happily informing on their neighbours?

The transition made a certain grim kind of sense to me. Pretoria had told us what to think and believe. Now it would be Moscow. Instead of panoramic oil paintings of Voortrekkers walking barefoot over mountains, it would be panoramic oil paintings of the workers holding aloft the hammer of industry and the sickle of agriculture. It was going to be quite a spectacle.

Except it wasn't. Because none of that happened.

The Bold and the Beautiful wasn't replaced by *The Bold and the Bolshevik*. We got cellphone masts, not flagpoles. The only faces gazing down at us from billboards belonged to models slurping on a Coke. And when Big Brother was finally broadcast into our homes, he didn't appear as a huge looming face but rather as reality TV show about people pooping in the bushes inside the M-Net studio.

In retrospect, I suppose there are some fairly sensible reasons for why we weren't flooded with communist-style propaganda, and not just because the old Soviet propagandists were all discovering the joys of capitalism in jacuzzis full of champagne.

Firstly, the ANC turned out to be not so much communist as opportunist. Any income, no matter its provenance, was welcome, whether it was supplied by repressive Marxist regimes in the 1980s, European arms dealers in the 1990s, or Indian tenderpreneurs in the 2000s. For a few years the ANC pretended to be red, or at least pinkish, and later tried to stoke conflict between black and white via Bell Pottinger. But the only colour that ever really mattered was green. As for the South African Communist Party, well, instead of being a terrifying Fifth Column of the Red Army, it turned out to be a gloomy little student that lived in the mouth of the ANC and politely shared its food.

Indeed, the bookishness of the Tripartite Alliance also made it very difficult to impose a homogenising national myth on South Africa. Lenin and Stalin were willing to murder people who disagreed with them on even minor issues. The myth of Soviet unity and solidarity was based on assimilation and, when that was resisted, extermination. Murky rumours persist about ANC atrocities in its African camps, but for the most part it was a considerably less violent organisation than Stalin's party. And because it couldn't kill or banish its ideological opponents or rivals within its revolution, it had to accommodate them.

By 1994, the ANC was herding cats, trying to be a party for hardcore Stalinists, dedicated communists, eager young capitalists, conservative rural Christians, urban Muslims, Hindus and Jews, traditional leaders and small-town hustlers. There were simply too many moving parts requiring too much consultation to impose a single, grand narrative.

Then there was the awkward question of who, exactly, to put on the posters and the plinths. Soviet propaganda, like most of the powerful nationalist myth-making of the twentieth century, relied on the binary push-pull of warning against external enemies while celebrating (or inventing) domestic heroes and achievements. The message, constantly repeated in a dazzling and mind-bending variety of forms, from crude anti-Semitic cartoons to immense public works, was clear: the world beyond the borders of the Motherland was a Sodom populated by Western imperialists, fascist warmongers and scheming Jewish financiers, all endlessly plotting to rain down death upon the sons and daughters of the soil. Inside her borders, however, guarded by the square-jawed heroes of Stalingrad, the Union of Soviet Socialist Republics was a happy, progressive, egalitarian, peace-loving civilisation, in which brilliant scientists sent brave explorers into space, noble farmers worked tirelessly for the good of all, artists and architects celebrated their deep gratitude to the state and the land, and beautiful athletes showed the world what the Soviet body could achieve.

The ANC had none of these clear and potent binaries to draw on. The revolution had been negotiated. The enemy hadn't been crushed in a war and then sent into exile or to labour camps. It was still there, sitting across the boardroom table, an integral part of the economic machine that needed to be kept running. When the ANC purged the civil service to make room for its own, retrenched Eskom engineers and teachers were given packages rather than one-way tickets to Siberia. Whipping up some good old-fashioned anti-Semitism was also out of the question: Jewish revolutionaries and activists like Ruth First, Joe Slovo, Denis Goldberg and Ronnie Kasrils remained heroes of the South African Communist Party and therefore of the liberation struggle as a whole. The party couldn't even invoke the spectre of an international capitalist conspiracy: it is very difficult to convince your followers that Western bankers and European aristocrats are the devil when you are clinking glasses of bubbly with them at gala dinners hosted in your honour.

If potential villains were thin on the ground, the stock of unifying national heroes was more or less non-existent. The Soviet Union had almost buckled under the weight of statues celebrating its farmers, sports heroes and astronauts, but in South Africa the farmers were seen as ideological and economic enemies, the country's most famous international sporting brand was rugby, and our only astronaut – Mark Shuttleworth – was a white millionaire capitalist who'd bought his way into space.

In the end, a handful of Soviet tropes were imposed on South Africa. Rallies resounded with the grandiose, hollow rhetoric of the Eastern bloc, lauding the glorious movement and exhorting the sons and daughters of the soil to join the masses on their march towards ultimate victory. Red stars, sickles and AK-47s appeared on a few official logos. 'Cadres' and 'commissars' still delight in calling each other 'Comrade'. But that was it.

Without the subtlety and zeal of Soviet propagandists, or, for that matter, the creative sparkle and glamour of their counterparts in Hollywood, the new state was left to its own devices to cobble together a national myth using what it had: Nelson Mandela, an averted civil war, some unlikely sporting successes, a great deal of denial, and a country's earnest hope that things were about to get better. It wasn't much, but a good headline goes a long way, and when Archbishop Desmond Tutu christened it 'the Rainbow Nation', it was enough to make many people forget that a rainbow is an optical illusion.

Today, the Rainbow Nation narrative is in tatters as a younger, angrier generation demands to know just who, exactly, those famous negotiations were for. What seemed like essential compromises in 1994 are now viewed by many as cynical betrayals. Even Mandela's legacy is coming under fire from the raging revisionist left. It's becoming popular among EFF supporters, for example, to denounce Mandela as an 'Uncle Tom' who sold out black South Africans for a seat at the table of white Western capital.[21]

You don't, however, have to be an EFF cultist or a conspiracy theorist to see how easy it is to join the dots that condemn the Rainbow Nation era as a vast stitch-up. In 2013, the Pew Research Center showed that, after 1994, the average income of blacks increased slightly, but the average income of whites, which had been drifting lower throughout the 1980s, shot up. For all the talk of justice, almost nobody went to prison. It is easy to judge the past from the relative safety of the present. I also understand the decision to offer amnesty in return for information. But I wonder how different South Africa might be today if, in 1994, it had carried out a Nuremberg-style reckoning, whereby scores or even hundreds of apartheid's worst perpetrators were publicly tried and sentenced to lengthy jail terms. At the very least, it would have prevented a scene I saw a few years ago: Wouter Basson, the former head of apartheid's biological and chemical weapons programme and a man personally accused of having arranged the horrifying deaths of numerous enemies of the apartheid state, quietly having his groceries packed into bags by a Woolworths cashier.

That kind of moment feels like a stunning, even provocative

---

21 If you want to dip your toe into a truly nightmarish puddle, google the conspiracy theory that Mandela died in prison and was replaced by a puppet of the apartheid regime to do its evil bidding.

miscarriage of justice. And there have been many others. Eugene de Kock, one of the few killers to see the inside of a cell, was sentenced to 216 years but released after 23. We can talk about the complexities of compromise and forgiveness, but it is an indisputable fact that Nelson Mandela spent longer in jail than the man known as Prime Evil.

Yes, it's easy to understand why Rainbowism is a dirty word to many young South Africans who have grown up in a country ravaged by the social and economic crimes of apartheid and then either abandoned or pillaged all over again by Mandela's party.

The failure of our last national myth, however, shouldn't make us give up on them entirely. On the contrary, I believe it is important that we replace Rainbowism with something else, because, as much as myth-making can be used for evil, I know that it can also be used to create, at the very least, a sense of shared destiny. Sometimes, a pinch of propaganda is not necessarily a bad thing.

The trouble is, the only people trying to formulate a clear and appealing idea of who we are are Brand South Africa, the national tourism and marketing organisation. And it's not going at all well . . .

South Africa, they used to tell us, is Alive With Possibility.

It was a brave, almost revolutionary slogan, subverting traditional advertising models by promising almost nothing whatsoever. If you come to South Africa, it announced, there is a possibility that you will experience . . . something!

For example, maybe you'll go to a craft market and be persuaded to buy a towel with a whale on it that you don't really want but you haven't bought anything so far and this isn't the worst memento, even though it's pretty bad, but what if you don't see anything better?

Maybe you'll stand in a queue, and find yourself comparing it to the ones back home, and wonder if you're being unconsciously racist or classist by engaging in this amateur anthropology. I mean, if you're comparing queues, where does it stop? Measuring skulls? Transporting human cadavers back in the overhead locker?

Maybe you'll have a fight with your spouse because travel is stressful but our society insists we should be having fun when we travel, so neither of you feels you can express your tiredness and anxieties, and so when you say, 'I'm not sure if I want starters . . . I just can't make up my mind,' your partner will say, 'Well, *that's* a surprise' and you'll say, 'What does that mean?' and they'll say, 'Nothing, let's just order' and it will all kick off.

We just don't know. That's the beauty of possibility.

In 2011, however, the slogan was retired. Perhaps it was becoming increasingly hard to sell Jacob Zuma's South Africa as being alive with possibilities when it was so clearly being strangled to death by mounting probabilities. Perhaps it just sounded too much like an invitation to state captors and the Guptas didn't want any other international pirates muscling in on their private island.

Something called the International Marketing Council was commissioned to produce a new slogan, to be used by all South African organisations selling the country abroad, and, somewhere between R470 000 and R140 million later (reports vary), the new slogan was revealed: 'More Than You Can Imagine'.

Unfortunately, it soon turned out that the slogan was also more than government-hired copywriters could imagine: 'More Than You Can Imagine' was already the slogan of the US state of Maryland, the Scottish county of Clackmannanshire, and various businesses and PR campaigns around the world. Spokesperson Mzwanele Manyi took time off from his daydreams of shipping coloured people out of the Western Cape to explain that the IMC had 'done research, rigorous research, and came to the conclusion that it would be safe and presented (it) to cabinet'.

I assume this rigorous research involved googling 'What are the chances anyone in cabinet has ever been to Maryland or Clackmannanshire?' but either way, the new slogan was hastily shelved.

And so it was that in 2012 South Africa got its third tagline: 'Inspiring New Ways'. According to Brand South Africa CEO, Miller Matola, the new slogan was 'the culmination of many months of research into what thousands of ordinary South Africans believe captures the essence of our country'.

What a scene it must have been, that room full of copywriters, their nostrils festively dusted with cocaine, thumbing through pages of feedback from the South African public, their project leader yapping, 'Okay, people, let's get inspired to find new ways of saying "I need a job", "I need a house", "I can't walk alone at night", and "Jacob Zuma *se moer*". New ways, people! Inspiring, new ways! Hey, waaaait a minute . . .'

'Inspiring New Ways' was immediately condemned by ad industry veterans as meaningless and shallow, a criticism that Brand SA should have taken to heart because if anyone knows what it is to be meaningless and shallow, it is the advertising industry. To be fair, though, I don't think it was any more of a fence-sitting, agnostic cop-out than 'Alive With Possibilities'. If anything, it forced one to be a bit more creative. Inspiring New Ways to do what? See the world? Have a secret family? Dispose of bodies? Indeed, the new slogan seemed more alive with possibility than the old one.

Still, none of this answered my original question: Who are we? And so I turned to Google. I typed in 'South Africa is . . .' and was promptly told that our country is:

- truly an amazing country
- falling apart

- a dump
- burning
- a democratic country
- islands

That last one is probably the work of thousands of international visitors who have forgotten the word 'Robben', trying to plan their next holiday. But it struck me as the most accurate answer of the lot. Sometimes this country does feel like an archipelago of islands, each inhabited by different islanders, each with their own dogmatic views about the rest, all sure that their island is the best island and that all the others are just over-hyped sandbars.

Then again, perhaps this balkanisation was inevitable given our unholy conception. The entity we call South Africa, created in 1910 as a kind of divorce settlement between Britain and the Cape Colony, the Natal Colony, the Orange River Colony and the Transvaal Colony, was a creature of empire and therefore a Frankenstein's monster of a thing; an undead, unhappy lump forced into existence by grafting kingdoms onto republics, bolting fiefdoms onto autonomous collectives, and sewing languages and histories together and seeing if they would take. From the moment the colonial overlords and local politicians zapped its brain with a lightning bolt and cried, 'It's aliiiive!' this heaving, twitching, unfortunate mass was supposed to be a single thing with a single identity. Which is quite mad. Cut out a map of South Africa and hold it over other pages in your atlas and you will see that it covers an area roughly from Bucharest and the Black Sea coast of Bulgaria up to Kyiv in Ukraine, into Belarus, as far north as Moscow and east as Volgograd. Put it over the Great Lakes region of Africa, and it comfortably swallows Uganda, Kenya, Rwanda, Burundi and parts of Tanzania, South Sudan and Ethiopia. Turn to Western Europe and you'll see that the distance from Cape Town to Polokwane is the same as from Wales to Warsaw or from Greece to Switzerland. If you were to announce to the good people of Romania, Bulgaria and Ukraine that they were now bound by statehood to Russia, or told Ugandans, Kenyans, Rwandans and Burundians to choose one party to govern them all, you would either be laughed at or shot at. Is it any wonder that South Africans find it so difficult to forge a single, national identity?

In some respects this effort to find each other, or at least to talk about finding each other, is noble. But perhaps that question – what is South Africa? – remains so difficult to answer because many of us don't want an answer, perhaps because we won't like what we'll see: an abandoned mining operation, its riches exhausted, with a small, poor town teetering on its periphery, at the end of a disused railway.

This is hard to accept. Nobody wants to feel that they're a bit player in a Western, living in some one-horse town at the end of the line. We want to believe that we live in a place that is, if not central, at least within reach of the world's centre, a place formed by its own choices. Most of all, we want our home to be a place that has some inherent value, and not simply a chicken bone tossed aside by distant diners once they'd eaten all the meat. It's not surprising that, without a larger consoling myth, we keep our eyes fixed so firmly on the few nationalist symbols, institutions, personalities and scapegoats that serve as placeholders – flags, anthems, sports teams, politicians, immigrants – anything, in fact, so that we don't have to see the dystopian little settlement clinging to the edge of the still-bloody hole out of which foreign fortunes were ripped by the colonial project.

Consider, for example, our determination to see a legitimate, respectable national border around our northern boundary, rather than a scar carved across the continent by colonial prospectors and administrators. Consider our affection for our peculiarly utilitarian name, a name that, after 110 years, still sounds temporary. 'South Africa' isn't something you call your home; it's a set of directions you show to a steamboat captain. 'Africa bound, are we? Oh, *south* Africa. Right you are, I'll give you a shout after we've gone round west Africa.'

The hole, however, is immense and inescapable. Long after the Company had taken what it wanted and pulled out, the mine's new owners – locally born whites, tossed the pickings because they were the next caste down – kept digging until it was no longer profitable or possible to keep the workers in line with violence. Nominal ownership of the mine was transferred to black senior shop-stewards, with some conditions in place to protect existing fortunes, and work continued. But the gold, both metaphorical and literal was gone. In 1993, 619 million tons of gold were hauled up out of the hole; in 2018, just 120 million tons came up. Coal and platinum were making new fortunes, but the feeding frenzy was over: when multinational extraction companies are forced to broaden the scope of their plunder to include not just resources but tax rands in the treasury, as the Guptas tried to do, you know the hole is exhausted.

I told you it wasn't a nice story. In fact, as something to build a shared future on, the Story of Us So Far is about as uplifting as roadkill. Yes, we didn't all murder each in the 1980s or 1990s and, yes, we have an extraordinary constitution and a tough judiciary and relentless corps of investigative journalists; and yes, our very lovely landscapes and desperate little currency make us fairly popular with tourists. But I'm afraid as stories go, ours is basically: 'Once upon a time a tragic and violent place managed, thanks to surprisingly cool heads, the threat of mutually assured destruction and plenty of luck, to avoid a civil war and become substantially less tragic, at least politically, although not very much changed economically, especially for everyone who was still living in poverty, which was about half the population. The End.' It's not exactly *The Notebook*, is it?

But that's okay, because national myths that are powerful enough to shift societies, or at least bind them into a single identity, are never about who we are: they are always about who we'd like to be. A story is Clark Kent, being a charming but inept office drone, unable to pluck up the courage to ask Lois on a date. A myth is Superman.

Taking the story of who we have been, and turning it into the myth of what we might be, will be difficult. The world has become much more cynical and much less optimistic since the myth-makers of the British Empire or the US or the Soviet Union built their golden towers on bright clouds of credulity, hope and, sometimes, weapons-grade gaslighting. Even the creation of a symbol as wholesome as Superman would be impossible today. I think it speaks volumes about our collective demoralisation that the most popular (or at least the most lucrative) superheroes over the past decade have been Batman (a self-pitying billionaire endlessly obsessed with his alienation and rage), Iron Man (a snarky, narcissistic billionaire with daddy issues) and The Joker, an utterly failed human being who entertains us by murdering people and then blaming 'society' for it.

Our myth-makers will also have to be careful to keep their work safe from politicians who, being opportunists and megalomaniacs, will see it as a vehicle for their own ambitions. *PM Narendra Modi: Story of a Billion People* confirmed that there is no claim a politician (or a politician's fart-catchers) won't make. The title alone implied that Modi had transcended not only politics but mortal constraints too, and was now the living embodiment of an entire continent, less a politician than a god. To be fair, the film probably would have struggled to put bums on seats if it had been called *PM Narendra Modi: Story of a Guy Whose Party Won 37 per cent of the Vote in the 2019 General Election*. But the fact remains that if our myth-makers don't guard their project from the snake-oil salesmen in parliament, we might soon see cigarette smugglers turning into movie producers and welcoming us to the premier of *Saving Private Malema*, a noisy and violent epic about a brave young soldier crawling up a beach to liberate the treasury from the tyranny of auditors.

Then there will be the complex, delicate task of rewiring the divergent and often contradictory beliefs, expectations and assumptions of South Africa's society into one, single narrative. I know that any suggestion of creating a homogenous culture will alarm those who believe that diversity is strength. But I would argue that diversity is only strength if it is pulling in the same direction towards the same, idealised future. Indeed, without a shared, common purpose, diversity can sleepwalk into balkanisation, where a society becomes little more than a student digs full of diverse but uninvested housemates, each one ignoring appeals for it to do the dishes, or waiting for the right moment to stake a claim for the big bedroom or do a runner just before the rent is due.

Yes, it will be difficult to write a story that convinces us that we are more similar than we are different, and that our differences, where they occur, are the differences between a gear and a piston in the same supercharged engine. But if our best propagandists are given their way, it can be done, and I imagine it will go a bit like this.

The first step will be to draw out those admirable traits we already possess and to make them gleam. South Africans are resilient; we must be made to feel that we might be indomitable. We are sentimental; we must be made to feel big-hearted and kind. We are hospitable to international visitors; we must be taught to be equally welcoming to the people who live next door. We have the philosophy of *ubuntu*; it will have to be scraped off the soles of the politicians' pointy shoes and gently, kindly, nursed back to life. *Ubuntu* is a beautiful idea – I am because you are – but in modern South Africa it has been utterly perverted and turned into the mocking victory cry of the elite: 'I am rich because you are poor. Thanks, suckers.' This cannot stand.

Next, our less impressive tendencies must be gently nudged into more constructive directions. Our burning sense of exceptionalism, for example – that jingoistic prejudice that has convinced some South Africans that they are God's chosen people and others that this country is not in Africa – must be matured into an understanding that being exceptional is about what you do, not who you are or what you say you are. Our parochial tendency to lurch wildly from triumphant self-righteousness to gloomy self-loathing and then back again must be tempered with the perspective provided by education and contact with the outside world.

Which brings us to the propagandists' next task: cannibalising the best elements from other countries' national myths while carefully leaving the worst behind. This could mean, for example, embracing the Soviet (or at least socialist) trope of celebrating professionals who feed, educate, nurse and build the country, while politely declining other tropes such as terrified obedience to the state, the obliteration of personal enterprise and the odd mass murder. From the American Dream, likewise, we could borrow the belief (now abandoned) that immigrants are not invaders determined to take your job but rather an infusion of energy and expertise, without also borrowing the American fetishisation of gun violence, the poisonous smugness of Manifest Destiny, or the belief that the world is divided into 'winners' and 'losers' and that those deemed 'losers' therefore deserve everything coming their way. Traditional African and Arab hospitality; Canadian politeness; the Scandinavian aversion to displays of wealth . . . The world offers our myth-makers plenty to plagiarise.

And the good news is, we're doing it already so it won't feel like a shock. For millions of South Africans, life's highest purpose is to find fame in the United States. An American-inflected accent dropping American slang is a potent status symbol. American celebrities carry South Africans' projections and aspirations to an extent that no South African ever has or ever could. If the choice was dinner with Malema or Beyoncé, even the most revolutionary Economic Freedom Fighter would burst out of their red onesie like a little sweet potato out of its skin and rush straight for the Capitalism R Us Elitist Evening Wear Emporium. I don't have a problem with this, by the way. Wishing away the triumph of the American cultural empire is to be like a Gaulish elder in the first century, muttering gloomily about how all the youngsters in your village are worshipping Roman gods instead of the much more sensible trees and boulders. I simply mention it because it is proof that we might not know who we are but we definitely know what we like, and since we're already so good at helping ourselves to it and making it our own, let's have more of it.

Finding and amplifying the good in us, however, or enlarging it with the good from elsewhere, isn't enough. The most important and perhaps hardest task our progressive propagandists will face will be to start challenging the bad. Powerful taboos must be created around those traits that keep dragging us back into dysfunction and despair, such as our deep infatuation with clearly dishonest and incapable politicians, our crippling belief that someone else will do something if we complain long enough, the terrifying ease with which we resort to violence, and the casual bigotry, whether deep-rooted misogyny or racism, that threatens to keep us a small-minded people of little consequence. Like putting fluoride in the water or vaccinating babies, this must be an unembarrassed, unequivocal programme of social engineering, less brainwashing than brain scrubbing. The bigots will howl that any effort to eradicate white supremacy is 'reverse racism'. The patriarchs will grumble that teaching children that women should have the same rights as men is 'radical man-hating feminism run mad' or an 'attack on our traditions'. Poverty will make some of its ideals seem like a middle-class fairy tale. But that's what unifying myths often are.

The dirty politicians won't have it, of course. Which is why, to do any of this, we would first have to hose them out of parliament.

Martin Luther King suggested that the arc of the moral universe is long but that it bends towards justice. With respect to Dr King, it doesn't. The arc of the moral universe only bends towards justice if it is bent that way. If the story of South Africa is to transcend demoralised mediocrity and tragic waste, and become a shining history of dignity restored and justice delivered, then we will have to deal with the great hole that remains at the centre of our history and therefore at the centre of our society. Which means that, whichever way our myth goes, and whichever way it chooses to take us there, it must take us towards justice and towards an attempt to provide redress for victims of the immense economic crime that lingers in the darkness at the bottom of that hole.

For that to happen, the current calcified cabal of high priests who claim to be progressive democrats, and their coterie of corporate pirates who prattle about the free market even as they help themselves to the takings of state capture, must be replaced, at absolute least, by adequate leaders and moderately capable administrators who once saw an economics textbook. And I'm not just referring to the ANC and its cronies: both sides of the parliamentary aisle are haunted by a great many people who believe that they are there to represent a republic of one. And who could blame them? Thanks to the current system of proportional representation, MPs answer to nobody except their boss. Not one citizen of this democracy is directly represented by an MP who lives and works in their community. Which is why steam-cleaning parliament will only work if it is accompanied by electoral reform, perhaps instituting proposals made by people like Frederick Van Zyl Slabbert who advocated combining proportional representation (which counts every vote and therefore gives small parties a voice but which puts MPs out of the reach of voters) with direct representation, whereby MPs have to answer to you and me in the constituencies where we live.

Nothing will change, however, as long as South African voters remain trapped in their abusive relationship with South African politics, endlessly convincing themselves that economic illiteracy is proof of revolutionary zeal, that pushing and shouting signify authority, that evidence of criminality is evidence of virtue and martyrdom, that posturing is leadership and that contempt is a form of care. This relationship has turned struggling democracies into failed states, and is guaranteed to do the same in South Africa if we don't break free from it.

That, however, will require a tectonic shift not only in how voters see themselves but also in what we believe we are capable of, and in where we believe we will go once we leave; of who we are if we aren't part of the ANC, DA, EFF or any other party. This is why our new myth will be so important. 'Better the devil you know' is a powerful idea, but we are a fantastically suggestible species. For God's sake, some of us are taking pictures of products and posting them on Instagram *on purpose*. If we can be persuaded that providing free advertising for corporations makes us look attractive and sophisticated, it shouldn't be too great a stretch to convince all of us that lying is bad, that stealing is wrong, that convicted fraudsters probably shouldn't be in government, and, once we've got those baby steps worked out, the most important one of all: that politicians are service providers, to be hired and fired according to the job they actually do rather than the wild promises they make.

In the end, Google wasn't wrong.

South Africa can be a 'truly an amazing country'. Sometimes it feels as if it is 'falling apart' and 'burning'. It is still 'a democratic country'. But most of all, it is 'islands'. And mythology is full of islands.

In the great myths, islands are a transformative place, home to destructive mysteries but also to magic and wisdom. Islands change the people who wash up on their shores, and islands change themselves, altering their shape or hiding themselves entirely. In myths, islands don't have to remain isolated and jagged, lost in a distant southern sea. They can be reimagined as things that heave themselves from the seabed and float or walk; as things that slowly begin to find each other. We can write them coming together, becoming an archipelago bound together not by mere geography but by a shared fate. When we write the new myths, islands can become a country. They can become a home.

I hope we write ours well.

Chapter 15

The Frank-N-Furter Theory of Everything

I started this book with a frog in a pot. I want to finish it with a sweet transvestite from transsexual Transylvania.

When I was young and stupid, and deep in thrall to the weaponised snobbery of a certain kind of Oxbridge academia, I believed that the world was a pyramid. At the top of the pyramid were Great Things – whether books, plays, ideas, countries or people – followed by Good Things and Quite Good Things. Then came Bad Things and Terrible Things, which were, now that I think about it, pretty much everything that lay beyond the tiny academic bubble in which I floated. They say that academia can open your mind. Mine, already half-closed by the inexperience and anxious dogmatism of adolescence, got slammed very firmly shut: in the six years I spent studying literature and creative writing, the only time I heard the names of the world's most read writers was as the punch-line of snobbish jokes. Lord, how embarrassing to be Stephen King with all that money and all those millions of adoring readers! What a loser!

I am grateful for my time in that system because it introduced me to a few wonderful teachers who wanted to share their authentic, generous, unpretentious love of reading and writing with their students. I was also exposed to writers whose work remains a pleasure and a comfort to me. But in retrospect, I think I might have been saved a great deal of unhappiness, and the many years I subsequently spent unlearning my prejudices, if I had also been formally introduced at university to *The Rocky Horror Picture Show* and its star, the aforementioned Transylvanian, Dr Frank-N-Furter.

About halfway through that charming mess of a film, Frank-N-Furter has finally completed his masterpiece – a muscle-bound sex toy named Rocky – and proudly shows him off to his assembled guests. His acolytes gush, except for Columbia, who coolly says, 'He's okay.' Distinctly put out, Frank-N-Furter leads Rocky over to guests Brad and Janet, hoping for a more enthusiastic reaction. But Janet, mostly for the sake of her somewhat unathletic husband, demurely replies that she doesn't like men with too many muscles.

Frank-N-Furter is mortally offended and, baring a set of teeth that are almost prehensile, he snaps back at her:

'I didn't make him for *you*!'

It is the petulant, peevish response of a demented, egotistical, thin-skinned megalomaniac. But it's also such a great piece of wisdom that I've started wondering if I should emboss it on a rubber bracelet – WWFNFD? – and make it my mantra.

Because Frank-N-Furter was right. He might have been looking for affirmation from his audience but ultimately he didn't make Rocky for Janet, or Columbia, or anyone else. He made Rocky for himself. And if Rocky makes him quiver with antici . . . pation, then that's job done and to hell with the rest.

Learning to channel my inner Frank-N-Furter has helped me to start seeing the world not as a pyramid, carved in stone, with Good things at the top and Bad things at the bottom, but rather as a vast gothic castle on a rainy night, in which seven billion mad scientists each work away at creating their own Rocky. For some, that takes the form of a certain kind of life, or a way of having relationships, or a particular political outlook. For others, their Rocky is an expression of their creativity and their tastes. Most aren't interested in introducing their Rockys to strangers. But a few are. Which means that most days, most of us will be asked a few dozen times, 'Well? What do you think?', as birthing sarcophaguses are thrown open to reveal Rockys ranging from the newest K-pop album and Hollywood blockbuster to a particular political analysis to a finger-painting of something that might be a cat but might also be a whale, depending on which way up you hold the soggy paper. Inevitably, given the number of Rockys I'm shown every day, I find some of them unimpressive. But where once I would have condemned them as Bad, and even felt somewhat offended that their creators had assumed I would like them, I now focus on the only fact that matters: that they didn't make it for me.

I acknowledge that moving away from Good/Bad binaries has its own problems. Taking Hamlet's advice – that 'there is nothing either good or bad, but thinking makes it so' – can, at least in theory, take us down a relativistic rabbit hole in which genocide is only bad if you think it's bad, and where NASA decides that, instead of playing Bach, its next deep-space probe should blast Baby Shark at the cosmos. I'm also not suggesting that when someone says or does something highly objectionable that we shouldn't find it distasteful.

This book, however, has been about trying to resist the knee-jerk responses that professional manipulators want us to have, or finding the kind of perspective that make us less inclined to have those responses in the first place. And remembering that they didn't make it for you – that you are not the target audience – can, I think, provide some of that perspective.

A fairly extreme example of this is Julius Malema's statement in 2016, when he told supporters: 'We are not calling for the slaughtering of white people – at least for now.' Understandably, many white South Africans reacted with outrage and fear, feeling that Malema had made a barely disguised threat aimed directly at them. But I would suggest that it wasn't a real threat but a performance. Malema hadn't made it for them. He made it for his followers. The last thing a hedonistic capitalist like Malema wants is for this country to be wiped flat by a racial civil war. After all, how would he buy his pointy shoes if there was no parliament to pay him his enormous salary or functioning businesses to keep donating money to the EFF? No, if you are white, Malema didn't put on his poisonous little show for you, to frighten you or make you want to flee. He made it for his audience; to give his closest disciples a hard-on and to make his followers swoon. He made it for the journalists whose job it is to report the news. He made it for money. You were simply the stage across which he pranced as his audience got ready to roar to its feet and throw its underwear at him.

It is sensible to take note when a politician – even one representing only a tiny fraction of the electorate – implies that he might, in future, demand your murder. But whether taking note must be escalated into taking precautions or taking flight, well, that depends on how authentic you believe the politician is being. And in that case, there was no authenticity whatsoever. It was simply a belligerent gesture, a hand raised by a schoolyard bully when the teacher isn't looking, to feed his own insecurities and to impress his gang of hangers-on. It was barely even politics: it was self-soothing.

Yes, every day some Frank-N-Furter thrusts their Rocky towards us, to which we are either asked to react or, more often, imagine that we should. The internet can be especially fraught in this regard. Thanks to social media having persuaded the world that enforcing personal boundaries is an act of aggression rather than self-care, it has made billions of people believe that literally everything is their business and that any statement, no matter how inconsequential, requires their commentary.

This is how, almost every day, someone arrives on my Facebook page to tell me that they are not interested in that thing I wrote. Just that. Sometimes less than that. On a few occasions, the comment has simply read, 'Boring'. It's rude, but it's also bonkers, like someone walking into a butcher's shop and saying, 'Oh, I see you sell meat. Well, I'm a vegan.' In the real world, the butcher would make sure it wasn't a candid camera prank (because nobody could be that stupid or solipsistic, right?) and then say, 'With all due respect, this shop isn't for you.' On the internet, however, such a response would be met with surprised indignation. *Geez, diva, take a chill pill, it was just a comment! Oooh, someone's having a bad day! Also, why do you hate vegans?*

At its most extreme, this widespread belief that personal boundaries are a sign of aloof disregard (and therefore proof of moral failings) can lead to an absurd feeding frenzy of self-righteousness. I see it less now, but a few years ago it was quite common to see people demanding not only a reaction but a reaction to a reaction and then a reaction to a reaction to a reaction . . .

'Behold! Here is a very sad- or angry-making thing that has happened on the other side of the world! We should all care about it! To make sure we all do, let's see who has failed to react with enough sad or angry emojis . . . Aha! You there, just getting on with your day! Do you care about that thing that happened? Yes? Well, the absence of your commentary says different! Clearly you don't care enough and are a bad person! Yes! Taste the sting of our collective disapproval! Do you taste it? Not really? You *monster*! Why don't you care more about not caring enough? What kind of a callous psychopath are you, that you don't change your beliefs and emotional responses to align with people you don't know, will never meet, don't want to be friends with and whose only role in your life is to tell you off for thought crimes?!'

No, these days saying 'I didn't make him for you' about the Rockys we put into the world risks opening all sorts of cans of worms. Which is perhaps why it's also becoming increasingly difficult to pause when we encounter other people's Rockys and ask ourselves whether they were made for us.

But I think it's worth trying, because in South Africa the Rockys come thick and fast. Expropriation without compensation! National Health Insurance! Ramaphosa saying something different to what he said last year!

It feels like we need to react, to feel something, to say something. But nine times out of ten, they didn't make it for you. Expropriation without compensation and NHI sound like economic disasters that require urgent protest, but so far they are nothing but ideological sex toys, brandished by squealing ANC politicians whenever they dress up as revolutionaries and roll around on waterbeds full of champagne. Ramaphosa is vacillating and making you feel like he's taking you for a fool? Well, that's a fair response but he's not vacillating for *you*: he's tap-dancing for an audience inside the ANC, wooing a tough room with very divergent ideas about how best to wreck a country, trying to impress and convince them to let him keep dancing. Yes, the ANC exerts extraordinary dominance over our lives for a party that is supported by just 27 per cent of voting-age adults, but it wasn't made for you. Not even if you voted for them. Not even for the rest of the 27 per cent. In its modern form, the ANC was made for the people who own it and are using it as a licence to print money. You and I do not matter to the ANC and never will. So perhaps the trick, for our collective sanity, is to try to make it matter slightly less to us.

In *Ash Wednesday*, one of TS Eliot's more religious poems, the speaker prays: 'Teach us to care and not to care'. These are not separate things. We must remain engaged with ideas, with politics and with each other, but not become entangled with them. We must remain open to and excited by good information, without dabbling in bad. And we must distinguish between the people who are actually in our lives and those who are not. Of course empathy is admirable, but empathy without strong and clear boundaries, especially online, and without the ability to say, 'I didn't make this for you, and you clearly didn't make this for me', verges on enmeshment.

It's not just me. It really is getting hotter in here, isn't it? Still, I hope this book has reminded you that we are not frogs passively boiling to death in a pot, but rather people grappling to make sense of confusing, anxious, chaotic times in a country that is often absurd. I hope that you have found something in these pages to give you pause, respite, or perhaps even hope. I hope that you've found my Rocky relatively attractive. But if you haven't, perhaps because you don't like men with too many muscles, I hope that instead of telling everyone that the book is terrible you'll just shrug and say, 'I suppose he didn't make it for me.' If nothing else, I hope it has entertained you.

Most of all, however, I hope it has helped you to care and not to care; to start finding a new perspective on the received ideas and political dogma that saturate our tired brains in the country; to step off the carousel and, just for a moment, gaze in wonder at what a wild little ride it is.

Acknowledgements

I could not have written this book without the encouragement, insight and word-wrangling skill of Tanya Meeson, whose husband I have the great privilege of being. No writer could ask for a better reader.

I am also extremely grateful to Jean Dixon, who gave me a space in which to discover the writing process anew.

To my publisher, Gill Moodie, thank you not only for nudging me in the direction of this book but also for your supreme calm and patience as I started treating deadlines as abstract suggestions rather than facts. That your sternest admonition was a single devil emoji is testament to the serenity you brought to this project.

Thank you also to Alison Lowry, my first publisher, who offered her invaluable care and attention to this book as it reached its final stages.

Then, some more general thanks.

Firstly, to those unknown, unsung, prospective Cape Town smash-and-grabbers who almost certainly saw my laptop on the back seat of my car during that long December afternoon and decided to walk on by, my nerves (and those of my publisher) are eternally grateful.

Secondly, I feel it's only right that I thank South Africa's politicians and their coterie of hypocrites, fart-catchers, lickspittles, toadies, political doormats, bullies and fools for providing so much of the content of this book, and, indeed, for giving me a career.

And finally, without sarcasm and with much gratitude, I would like to thank you, the reader, for joining me on this wander through this peculiar place. Let's do it again some time.

About the Author

TOM EATON is a *Business Day* and Times Select columnist and the author of the bestselling *The De Villiers Code.* His other books include *Texas, The Wading, Twelve Rows Back: Some Mutterings from Tom Eaton* and *Touchlines and Deadlines* (with Luke Alfred).